The Sexual century

THIS IS A CARLTON BOOK

Design copyright © 1999 Carlton Books Limited
Text copyright © 1999 Tom Hickman

This edition published by Carlton Books Limited 1999
20 St Anne's Court
Wardour Street
London
W1V 3AW

A CIP catalogue for this book is available from the British Library

ISBN 1 85868 799 3

Executive Editor: Sarah Larter
Senior Art Editor: Diane Spender
Picture research: Alex Pepper/Catherine Costelloe
Production: Garry Lewis

Printed and bound in Italy

The Sexual century

T O M   H I C K M A N

CARLTON

CONTENTS

FOREWORD

There is truth in the view that, where sex is concerned, the twentieth century has only continued what the late-nineteenth century began. The first scientific attempts to dissect human sexuality, the fight by women to win universal suffrage, the vulcanization of rubber which allowed the production of reliable contraceptive barriers – and the struggle to spread contraceptive knowledge all originated before the turn of the century.

But the century in which we live lays claim to its title as *The Sexual Century* for other reasons, most of them to do with the leaps and bounds in medicine and technology. More fundamentally, the title belongs because of the manner in which the century has thrust sex into the mainstream as a cultural force – something that history had never previously seen.

The heroes – or villains, depending on your point of view – of this sea-change in human sexuality are the handful of sexual reformers who, like prophets, argued that sex, as the primary function of life, should be uncoupled from 2,000 years of Judaeo-Christian repression. By questioning the Victorians "exclusive commitment to adult, marital, heterosexual intercourse", they preferred an understanding that much behaviour considered deviant or wrong was merely variant – an insight for many into their own sexuality.

The emerging field of sexology was dominated by medical practitioners – some in the new discipline of psychology – who appropriated to science issues that previously had been the province of religion and the law. No form of behaviour – from masturbation and homosexuality to masochism, sadism and fetishism – escaped their professional scrutiny.

It must be said that the work of these pioneers in trying to identify and explain every aspect of sexual activity was frequently wrong-headed – there were dangers in applying to sex the methods applied to the study of human disease, which was, in fact, how sexuality was approached well into this century. But it was through their efforts that ignorance and prejudice were combatted and people were offered freedom from guilt and shame.

The Sexual Century is the sum of many other inter-related factors. Of them, the most important are the experience from two world wars, particularly the second, which gave unprecedented sexual licence not just to heterosexual men, but to homosexuals and to women; and the emergence of the second wave of feminism – underpinned by the availability of the Pill, giving women for the first time control of their bodies – which politicized the demand for equality between men and women – and that included sexual equality.

Sexual liberalization has not made people happier, but, then, how could it? The conflict between human identities and their less rational sexual drives remain ever present. It is a moot point as to whether the profound change in the general attitudes to virginity, marriage and abortion have benefited society. Liberalization has certainly created new conflicts: unrealistic sexual expectations, a decline in the steadfastness that once characterized relationships, a coarsening of everyday language. Sex may no longer be a matter of morality, but it may have been reduced mere mechanics. As the millennium nears, sex sells everything.

Willingly or unwillingly, society has allowed sex to assume a disproportionate importance.

The rich and complex story of *The Sexual Century*, which began with prophets unchaining sex from repression, ends with sex shackled to post-industrial profits. But the story itself has no ending. Human history is cyclical. Everything changes – and everything remains the same. "So we beat on," ends Scott Fitzgerald's *The Great Gatsby*, "boats against the current, borne back ceaselessly into the past."

S E X U A L
E X P L O R E R S

As the world leaves the twentieth century, sex has become the currency of the day. Sexual images bombard us from every quarter. Nudity and acts of intercourse are as common as car chases in mainstream cinema and penetration is widely available on video and the Internet. Ordinary men and women appear on television shows to discuss their sexuality and relationships in the frankest detail. Television, radio and magazines give platforms to experts who hand out helpful hints using a vocabulary once confined to medical manuals.

Sexologists send patients to sex surrogates to resolve their difficulties. The media picks over the peccadilloes of the famous in unblinking detail. Even the President of the United States' liking for fellatio, peppermint or chocolate-cherry flavoured, delivered at the point of power in the Oval Office, is a fit subject for everyday discussion. The last decade of the twentieth century is obsessed by sex or has made it so routine that there is no longer any mystery. No-one questions that women's sexuality is as much a driving force as that of a men. The modern consensus view is that intercourse does not have to be sanctioned by marriage vows. Masturbation and oral sex are normal expressions of intimacy. Everyone who is sexually active and does not want children practises safe birth control. Homosexuality is not a deviancy but merely another form of sexuality.

At the other end of the twentieth century all of this would have been truly shocking.

Throughout history, sex in the Eastern cultures of China, India and Japan was regarded as a sacred duty; the path to holiness was through the bedchamber. In the West the path to holiness was through celibacy. In the fourth century, St Augustine – who as a young man did his share of whoring while praying to God, "Give me chastity – but not yet" – followed a line of Christian thinkers in decreeing that the act of intercourse was fundamentally disgusting. "I know of nothing," he wrote, "which brings the manly mind down from the heights more than a woman's caresses and that joining of bodies." He believed that the sin of Adam and Eve was passed down

The depiction of sexual acts in Japanese art, frequently involving exaggerated genitalia, is common. But there is never nudity — a matter of aesthetics, not morals.

from generation to generation through the sexual act and was an explanation for the perverse independence of the sex organs. Coitus was for procreation and was otherwise a sin. It followed that the only sanctioned contraception was abstinence. Some eras — notably the Renaissance and the eighteenth century — threw off the shackles of the Church and indulged in erotic pleasure. For the rest, Western history remained a tale of Christian repression and Christian guilt, which culminated with the Victorians, who all but suffocated in an air that was as thick with degeneracy and hypocrisy as it was with soot.

An oddity of Victorian morality stemmed from the period's love affair with all things mediaeval and the Romantic movement's revival of a kind of courtly love. The troubadours of the Middle Ages sang of women worshipped from afar, while love remained unconsummated. The Victorians somehow translated this into a belief that virtuous women did not or should not enjoy sex ("the full force of sexual desire is seldom known to a virtuous woman"). Deep in the psyche of the period was the view, expressed by Thomas Aquinas in the thirteenth century, that man's superiority to woman embraced intercourse as it did all else. Man's role was active and therefore nobler; woman's passive and submissive. Writing *The Women of England*, published in 1842, Mrs Sarah Ellis was in deadly earnest when she exhorted women to recognize "the superiority of your husband simply as a man." A similar idealized view manifested itself in America where "the little woman" was put on a pedestal. In the late 1880s, when the British Prime Minister Gladstone (known for prowling the London streets at night to save fallen women) refused women the vote, it was on the grounds that he had too much respect "to trespass upon the delicacy, the purity, the refinement, the elevation … to involve them in the vulgarities of political life." The image of the chaste woman above enjoyment of the exchange of body fluids persisted into the middle of the twentieth century. Writing *Lady Chatterley's Lover* in the late 1920s, D.H. Lawrence was to have Parson Trownson tell Clifford Chatterley that "women's natures are quite different from ours; indeed it is a kind of profanity to think that it could be otherwise … My good man, you don't suppose for one moment that women have animal passions like ours …"

The burgeoning Victorian middle-classes could afford to indulge their sexual idealism. The poor could not. The factories of the Industrial Revolution gave one stratum of society great prosperity, but those below it, who had helped create that prosperity by toiling in the new factories, lived in over-crowded squalor and abject poverty. For many women life was also a perpetual round of pregnancy and abortion. Others were forced into prostitution – which Augustine condoned because, like the sewers, it carried off the filth of the day. The trade offered more female employment than either industry or domestic service. Indeed, prostitution was almost a service industry, relieving middle-class men from imposing their animal passions on their wives too often. The by-product was an epidemic of venereal disease.

All of this, following history's continuous game of pass-the-parcel, was what the twentieth century would soon inherit from the nineteenth.

As the Edwardian era dawned there were 80,000 whores working the streets of London; 20,000 in the much smaller city of New York. At some time or another, according to the British Suffragette movement, 80 per cent of men had been infected with gonorrhoea and "a considerable percentage" with the deadlier syphilis. The authorities said the claim was inflated, but a survey in New York which produced findings of 75 per cent and 5-18 per cent suggested otherwise. The topics of prostitution and venereal disease filled the newspapers. What no-one discussed was the incidence of VD among women who were not prostitutes, although in 1904 Dr Prince Morrow, founder of the American Society of Social and Moral Prophylaxis, suggested in his book *Social Disease and Marriage*, that there was "more venereal disease among virtuous wives than among prostitutes."

There was, however, a good deal of hand-wringing. Both Britain and America had tried to regulate prostitution, like the practical French and

St Augustine:
**"Give me chastity –
but not yet."**

Sex for sale at the turn of the century: a madam lines up her girls for a rake's consideration.

Germans, in the previous century. Britain's Contagious Diseases Acts of the 1860s had compelled prostitutes and suspected prostitutes in dockyard and garrison towns to register for medical examination. The whores, and the brothel-keepers, thought the measure was beneficial. The Suffragettes regarded it as "a dirty and demeaning business" which infringed the rights of prostitutes as women and after twenty years the Acts were repealed. American attempts at similar legislation in the 1870s foundered on the same rocks. Failure engendered caution. Governments preferred to leave sin and morality to find their own uneasy equilibrium. The Suffragettes on both sides of the Atlantic, as well as a motley assortment of social reformers and purity movements, were not like-minded. Writing in *The Suffragette*, Emmeline Pankhurst's solicitor daughter Christabel castigated men who

crave for intercourse with women whom they feel no obligation to respect. They want to resort to practices which a wife would not tolerate … Marriage does not "satisfy" them. They fly to women who will not resent foul words and acts and will even permit unnatural abuse of the sex function.

She had the answer to society's problems: "Votes for Women and Chastity for Men".

For some social reformers, contraception for the poor was a more pressing issue. Sponges and douches were available but were impractical in the living conditions of an underclass

Early twentieth-century spermicidal pessaries, ointments and jellies.

largely ignorant of the benefits. Condoms – "sheaths" to the educated, "French letters" to the masses, "Malthusian devices" to older policemen – had been mass-produced since the 1870s and the days when manufacturers could be prosecuted for sending leaflets about them through the mail and pharmacists sent to prison for displaying them in their windows, had gone, at least in Britain. Condoms, however, were viewed with distaste by many who could not bring themselves to buy them on grounds of decency or morality. And they were far beyond the pocket of the working man. The poor tried the prolonged nursing of one child in the hope that it would prevent another, which sometimes was effective. Most practised withdrawal. Heterosexual anal intercourse as a contraceptive method was as prevalent as it had been down the ages. The commonest method of all was abstinence; the commonest method of sexual relief, masturbation.

Masturbation was a nineteenth-century obsession that spilled over into the next century, a cause, it was believed, of insanity, imbecility and feeble-mindedness. It was a disease – a vice – and, because it was carried out solely for pleasure and usually in secret, a particularly dreadful sin. Pamphlets with such titles as "What a Young Boy Ought to Know" were Edwardian diatribes against "self-pollution", a graver sin, in the eyes of Thomas Aquinas, than fornication. "Words are scarcely capable of describing the dreadful consequences which are suffered by those who persist in this practice," said one. "Boys often have to be put in a straight-jacket or their hands tied to the bedposts or to rings in the wall."

Books such as *Manhood* (1919) by Charles Thompson argued that purity and good health were bed companions. As editor of *Health and Efficiency* magazine Thompson wrote to the thousands who sought his advice that they should read the poets and ensure that "the gas-clouds of suggestiveness" did not penetrate "the mask of purity." Generally, young men were advised to buy dumb-bells and a chest-developer. Lord Baden-Powell, founder of the scouting movement, warned in *Rovering to Success* (1922) that masturbation "cheats semen of getting its full chance of making up the strong *manly* man you would otherwise be. You are throwing away the seed that has been handed down to you as a trust, instead of keeping it and ripening it to bring a son to you later on." Unbelievable as it may seem there were books of sex instruction which followed the same line right up into the Seventies.

For those whose willpower was weak, there were devices to stop sexual desire at source. The "Timely Warning", patented in America in 1905, was a ring with a serrated inside edge that fastened to the penis and was advertised as "Preventing night emissions by arousing the wearer" – an erection brought the teeth into play. A higher

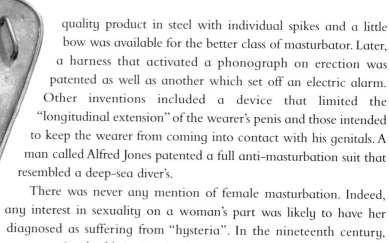

quality product in steel with individual spikes and a little bow was available for the better class of masturbator. Later, a harness that activated a phonograph on erection was patented as well as another which set off an electric alarm. Other inventions included a device that limited the "longitudinal extension" of the wearer's penis and those intended to keep the wearer from coming into contact with his genitals. A man called Alfred Jones patented a full anti-masturbation suit that resembled a deep-sea diver's.

There was never any mention of female masturbation. Indeed, any interest in sexuality on a woman's part was likely to have her diagnosed as suffering from "hysteria". In the nineteenth century, treatment involved bringing the disease to a crisis by manual massage of the vulva; by the turn of the century electric vibrators were being used. In America, "The Chattanooga", available in 1904, sold for $200 — to doctors only. Trade was as brisk as it had been in the previous century when treatments for hysteria comprised as much as three-quarters of a physician's income. Publicly, the medical profession did not admit female sexuality, but in the privacy of their consulting rooms they were making the connection. So were a lot of women. By the outbreak of World War One, the *Sears Catalogue* was offering home vibrators ("Very useful and satisfactory for home service") at $5.95.

A device guaranteed to prevent a night-time erection.

Generally speaking, women had no idea of their own biology, never mind the male organ or how intercourse worked. That was hardly surprising when information manuals used phrases like "Nature has made the man's sex organ to fit exactly into that of the woman in the most marvellous and beautiful way." *Talk with Girls* by E.B. Kirt, published in 1905, was directed firstly to parents who could vet it by tearing out the few perforated pages that contained what passed for real information. If they had not visited a prostitute or had no knowledge of pornography, many men coming to their marriage bed were as ignorant as their wives. Indeed, doctors were known to advise young men to visit a prostitute on the night before their wedding.

In the wake of Darwin, who told the world that the sex drive was the fundamental life force in humans as in animals, the nineteenth century pioneers in sexology had begun their work, although most viewed their subject in terms of "perversion" and "mental degenerations". The major exception was the Berlin physician Albert Moll, who was the first to compare normal and abnormal sexuality and who studied the sex life of the child. Probably the most important pre-Freudian was the Viennese psychiatrist Richard von Krafft-Ebing, whose *Psychopathia Sexualis* dealt with homosexuality, fetishism, sadism and masochism, and masturbation. Reviewing it, the *British Medical Journal* found it "nauseous" and suggested the book was fit only to be "put to the most ignominious use to which paper can be applied."

A more influential figure was the English doctor Havelock Ellis. Straddling the nineteenth and twentieth centuries, Ellis was the first modern sexologist, and the first to say that sex could be separated from reproduction. "Reproduction," he wrote, "is so primitive and fundamental a function of vital organs that the mechanism by which it is assured is highly complex and not yet clearly understood. It is not necessarily connected with sex, nor is sex necessarily connected with reproduction."

Ellis believed that all individuals were sexual beings with sexual impulses. He wrote: "Sex penetrates the whole person; a man's sexual constitution is a part of his general constitution … a man's sexual constitution is all-pervading, deep-rooted, permanent, in large measure congenital." He did not consider sexuality to be black or white, right or wrong – and importantly stressed the sliding scale of sexuality between "normal" (by which he meant common) and "abnormal" (uncommon). Love in marriage, he passionately believed, ideally combined the erotic and the parental. He was contemptuous of the physiologists and physicians of his time who tried to decide what the frequency of intercourse should be:

It seems quite unnecessary to lay down any general rules regarding the frequency of coitus. Individual desire and individual aptitude, even within the limits of health, vary enormously. Moreover, if we recognize that the restraint of desire is sometimes desirable, and often necessary for prolonged periods, it is as well to refrain from any appearance of asserting the necessity of sexual intercourse at frequent and regular intervals.

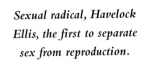

Sexual radical, Havelock Ellis, the first to separate sex from reproduction.

To which Ellis added:

Sexual needs are the needs of the two persons, of the husband and of the wife. It is not enough to ascertain the needs of the husband; it is also necessary to ascertain the needs of the wife... The art of love is based on the fundamental natural fact of courtship; and courtship is the effort of the male to make himself acceptable to the female.

Ellis considered Christian morality "profoundly antagonistic to the art of love" and "denied altogether that [the theologian] is competent to deal … with sexual matters." He

2000 1990 1980 1970 1960 1950 1940 1930 1920 1910 1900

mocked the wives who had never looked at their own nakedness let alone a man's, and the husbands who, even after twenty years, had never seen their wives entirely naked. And he gave short shrift to the idea of conjugal rights:

> The husband had the right and the duty to perform sexual intercourse with his wife, whatever her wishes may be, while the wife had the duty and the right (the duty in her case being usually put first) to submit to such intercourse, which she was frequently taught to regard as something low and merely physical, an unpleasant and almost degrading necessity which she would do well to put out of her thoughts as speedily as possible. It is not surprising that such an attitude towards marriage has been highly favourable to conjugal unhappiness, more especially that of the wife, and it has tended to promote adultery and divorce. We might have been surprised if it had been otherwise.

But Ellis went much further. He showed that masturbation, an element of "auto-eroticism" (his own term), along with day-dreaming, fantasies, erotic dreams and nocturnal emissions, was perfectly natural: "Among animals in isolation, and sometimes in freedom – though this is less often observed – it is well known that various forms of spontaneous solitary sexual excitement occur." He called for the decriminalization of sexual practices that harmed no-one, such as homosexuality and prostitution. In analyzing prostitution as a social outcome of society's indifferent treatment of so many women, he commented: "It is merely a situation of degree whether [a woman] sells herself to one man, in one marriage, or to many men … Marriage is, indeed… merely a more fashionable form of prostitution." He went furthest of all in suggesting that a loving relationship was permissible between two unmarried people – and it did not matter what the sex of the two people was. So long as theirs was a partnership of "mutual help and consolation" they should be free to practice sex in whatever way they desired.

Ellis's master work, *Studies in the Psychology of Sex*, was written over a thirty-year period, the seventh volume appearing in 1928. Only the first – on homosexuality – was published in England and was quickly banned, a judge describing it as "a pretence and a sham." Thereafter, Ellis, by then notoriously famous, was forced to publish in America where medical works were less frequently prosecuted. An enormously sincere and humane man, a utopian, a dreamer, Ellis thought he could change the world by changing attitudes to sex. His own sexual interest stemmed from an almost Damascene revelation when he was sixteen, living in Scone, north of Sydney in Australia, and adolescently in love:

> I determined that I would make it the main business of my life to get to the real natural facts about sex, apart from all would-be moralistic or sentimental notions, and to spare the youth of future generations the trouble and perplexity which this ignorance caused me.

It cannot be said that Ellis's personal sex life was a model for future generations. His marriage to Edith Lees was passionate but may not have involved intercourse (she had strong lesbian tendencies). He did have public affairs with some powerful women, including the South African feminist Olive Schreiner and the founder of the American birth-control movement, Margaret

Sanger – indeed, when Lees died Ellis married one of her lovers. He also invited women who sent him naked photographs of themselves to meet him. But all his relationships were possibly devoid of full intimacy and later he was impotent. His main sexual gratification would have been a perversion in most people's eyes and perhaps still would be: he was a undinist. At the age of twelve he had seen his mother lift her skirt in the grounds of London Zoo to urinate. From that day on, he preferred watching women relieve themselves to any other sexual activity.

Ellis wrote freely about his fetish – and the obsessions of others. From a prostitute who worked the Strand he found out about the young man who had orgasms when she and a friend wrung the necks of pigeons while naked; of another who paid her a guinea for licking her boots; of yet another who liked her to urinate on him. Other Ellis case histories included a lecturer who ejaculated when he burnt himself with hot wires and a butler who found coitus impossible unless he was caressing a shoe. In the late 1940s Kinsey would expose almost all of the dark side of sexuality; but Ellis began the task, just as surely as he cleared some of the ground to allow Sigmund Freud to develop his theory of the unconscious where repression, seeking to control the sex instinct, created guilt. From the moment his *Three Essays on the Theory of Sexuality* was published in 1905, Freud became more important than Ellis or anybody else in the province of psycho-sexuality. Hardly anybody read him – they would have struggled to understand him if they had. But they read articles about him, understood that

Sigmund Freud, who said that repression, seeking to control the sex instinct, creates guilt.

sex underpinned everything and tried to lose their inhibitions.

The Lithuanian-born American anarchist, Emma Goldman, heard Freud speak on his only visit to the States in 1909 and took to heart his message that repression was destructive: it strengthened her belief that Ellis was right in saying marriage was not necessary for sex. A highly sexual woman, Goldman had been jailed for incitement to riot in New York and she used a code when writing to her long-time lover in case her letters were opened by the authorities. Candice Falk's *Love, Anarchy and Emma Goldman*, gives a sample of the code, showing what a progressive woman was doing – and what most women were missing:

Her treasure box longed for his Willie, and she longed to have his face between her joy mountains - Mount Blanc and Mount Jura. She wanted to suck the head of his fountain of life which stood over her like a mighty specter. Both lovers revelled in an orally focused sex that particularly emphasized clitoral-area stimulation. On one occasion she wrote, "I press you to my body close with my hot burning legs. I embrace your precious head... But one condition I must make: No whiskers – no, the t-b cannot stand for that.

Emma Goldman, anarchist and supporter of contraception.

Because she wanted to free women from the trap of biology, Goldman began to campaign for contraception in her anarchist monthly, *Mother Earth*. Meeting Goldman – who gave her Ellis to read – drew Margaret Sanger to the cause.

Born into an Irish working-class family, Sanger witnessed the slow death of her mother, worn out after eighteen pregnancies and eleven live births. While working as a nurse and midwife in the poorest neighbourhoods of New York, she saw women deprived of their health and unable to care for their children, much less have any interest in sexual fulfilment. In 1912 she attended a poor patient who was recovering from trying to abort yet another pregnancy and she listened to the woman plead with a doctor for information on how to prevent another mishap. She was to write:

"Oh, ho," laughed the doctor, "you want your cake while you eat it, too, do you? Well, it can't be done. I'll tell you the only sure thing to do. Tell Jake to sleep on the roof."

Three months later the woman died from a botched abortion she had carried out on herself. Sanger got there ten minutes too late. It was on that night, she said, that she vowed to fight abortion – and given the times she lived in, that could only be done by controlling conception. Soon she was in the radical environment of Greenwich Village proclaiming not only the beauties of sex and orgasm in marriage, but that contraception was the only basis for happiness.

Contraceptive information in America was so suppressed that it was a criminal offence to send it through the mail. Yet the educated and wealthy had access to such information and could use subterfuge to buy "French" products (condoms) and "feminine hygiene" products (spermicides). It was this injustice that inspired Sanger to write a series of articles called 'What Every Girl Should Know', which was published in a Village newsletter, the *Call*. When the final instalment was advertised as being about venereal disease, the Post Office threatened to revoke the *Call*'s mailing permit. Sanger replaced the article with three lines:

> What Every Girl Should Know –
> Nothing.
> By order of the Post Office.

She also got her photograph in the papers, having a gag tied around her mouth. The following year she raised the money to start a newsletter of her own, *The Woman Rebel*; the fourth edition was suppressed for obscenity. Intending to leave the country rather than go to jail, she wrote a pamphlet entitled *Family Limitation*, outlining all she knew about birth control, arranged for 100,000 copies to be printed for sale at 25 cents, and took a train to Canada. Then she travelled to England on a false passport where she met the middle-aged Ellis. Their affair might seem poor reward for Sanger's husband William, who went to prison for thirty days in her stead, but his wife, a mother of three, had already begun to experiment with the free-love theory of her friends – "as a service for the women of your time," William wrote in a sad letter to her. He refused to take mistresses of his own as she suggested:

I will let my name be associated with no other woman. I would be amiss to all the fine emotion that surges within me if I fell from grace. It cannot be, that's all.

In 1916, when Sanger

Birth-control pioneer Margaret Sanger after a court appearance, with some of her supporters.

A range of twentieth-century cervical caps.

returned to the States, the charges against her were dismissed – the publicity she attracted was by now an acute embarrassment to the authorities. She went on to open America's first birth-control clinic, in Brooklyn – a "crime" for which she received a sentence of thirty days in the work-house, even as hundreds of women lined up outside her clinic. A limousine was waiting for her when she came out: she was now a national figure, soon an international one.

Family Limitation was not entirely accurate (failure to give a woman an orgasm, Sanger wrote, might lead to a "disease of her generative organs") but it sold ten million copies and went on to be translated into thirteen languages. More importantly, Sanger persisted until she forced a change in the law. A New York court declared it legal to dispense birth control information to women whose health required it: the door was opened. Soon Sanger was extending her neighbourhood clinics, dispensing a "woman-controlled" form of birth control – the diaphragm – and starting sex counselling. In two months the clinic she opened on Fifth Avenue saw nearly 3,000 women and handed out 1,000 diaphragms. Until an American company began to produce them in the late Twenties, Sanger got her hands on supplies wherever she could. While birth control was illegal she had them smuggled in from Holland in liquor bottles; her second husband, J.Noah Slee, brought in others from Canada, hidden in trainloads of 3-in-1 Oil.

In the Thirties, novelist and historian H.G. Wells, who advocated "free love" and was genuine in his support of equal rights for women, wrote that the crusade to legalize birth control "will grow to be, a hundred years from now, the most influential of all time." He was given to exaggeration and his liking for sex extended into his social principles; nonetheless his admiration for Sanger was unstinted: "When the history of our civilization is written, it will be a biological history, and Margaret Sanger will be its heroine."

In time, expediency made Sanger distance herself from her radical past and soften her language; eventually she was talking about "family planning" rather than "birth control". The long game required compromise – and Sanger was going to be around a long time.

THE CAMPAIGN IN BRITAIN

Compromise was never a word in the vocabulary of Sanger's English counterpart Marie Stopes who, unlike Sanger, did not believe that sex was primarily for having children but was for enjoyment in its own right. Pre-marital sex was certainly not on her agenda and she abhorred "perversion", particularly homosexuality (although, because of her interest in poetry, she became friends with Lord Alfred Douglas, who wrote brilliant sonnets but is rather better known for his association with Oscar Wilde). Ellis's books, she said, were "like breathing a bag of soot." But she did agree with him that women should have some fun in the marital bed. Something else linked her to Ellis: impotency. When Ellis succumbed to the condition, he did not see it as a problem; Stopes saw her first husband's condition as the all-consuming one.

Stopes, a paeleobotanist was intellectually brilliant: a degree from University College, London and a PhD from Munich made her the first female science lecturer at Manchester, where she specialized in fossil plants and coalmining. But "an explosive sexual being unaware of the depth of her sensuality," according to her biographer June Rose, Stopes "wanted a lover who was a mixture of Tarzan and Einstein." The Canadian geneticist Reginald Ruggles Gates, whom she married quickly at the age of thirty-one after an unsatisfactory romance while lecturing in Japan, fell sadly short of the mark. Four years later she demanded an annulment because her marriage had not been consummated. In the 1990s, the era of the "born-again" virgin thanks to micro-surgery, a doctor's certificate might not be substantive proof. But in 1911 it was, confirming that "there had not been penetration by a normal male organ." When Stopes stepped into the divorce court witness box, she was quite prepared for the questions she was asked. "With regard to your husband's parts, did they ever get rigid at all?" "I only remember three occasions on which it was partially rigid, and then it was never effectively rigid."

Determined that other women should be spared from a marriage as bad as hers, Stopes met Margaret Sanger and signed up for women's liberation. In the British Library she bullied her way into the locked section which houses literature to inflammatory for the open shelves, read Ellis and every other author represented there in English, French and German, and

For the Victorian poor, life was a round of childbirth and abortion.

2000 | 1990 | 1980 | 1970 | 1960 | 1950 | 1940 | 1930 | 1920 | 1910 | 1900

Marie Stopes: determined that married women should enjoy sex, she took on the Church and the medical profession.

produced *Married Love* – "out of pure frustration," Rose thinks.

Stopes had great difficulty in finding a publisher willing to take the book on, which led to her meeting the man who became her second husband, the aircraft manufacturer Humphrey Roe. At the time he had a webbing factory in Manchester where, because his female staff were frequently away through problems associated with having large and often sickly families, he had offered a considerable sum of money to various local hospitals in the hope, unrealized, that one of them would establish a specialist birth-control department. Once they were introduced Roe and Stopes quickly found out they were made for each other. Roe, without whose business sense Stopes might not have been able to set up her clinics, got *Married Love* into print in 1918.

In an era when priest and doctor fought birth control tooth and nail, it is interesting that the first edition carried a preface contributed by a Jesuit – interesting that he was prepared to contribute to it, equally interesting that Stopes thought it expedient to give her book a patina of respectability:

> You write primarily as a scientist, though a very human scientist. I, on the other hand, writing as a Catholic, regard our earthly life as essentially and inseparably connected with an eternal existence which reaches out beyond the grave. Let me take an illustration of my meaning, the case you give of the worn-out mother of twelve. The Catholic belief is that the loss of health on her part for a few years of life and the diminished vitality on the part of her later children, would be a very small price indeed to pay for an endless happiness on the part of all.

"So the quality of life, the death of the woman or of the children, is of no consequence," reflects Harry Stopes-Roe, Marie Stopes' son. "That was one of the atmospheres that my mother was having to fight." By the end of the year, *Married Love* had gone through five editions and 17,000 copies and went on to sell more than half a million by the mid-Twenties (by which time Stopes had turned out another dozen books, a play and a paper on the classification of coal, still regularly quoted in its field today). Women read it in their drawing rooms in brown paper covers and kept it tucked under the seats. Working women read it in queues, sharing copies. Even men read it. In 1935 American academics listed *Married Love* with Hitler's *Mein Kampf* and Karl Marx's *Das Capital* as the world's most influential books. It proved so popular it was even made into a movie, *Masie's Marriage* – with Stopes herself playing a cameo role.

Married Love was fresh and explicit and used words and ideas never before mentioned in a popular book. For example, a pregnant women who felt she could not allow her husband "to enter the portals of her body will readily find some means of giving him that physical relief which his nature needs." (But how many women did not realize that meant masturbation?) This was the clinical side of Stopes. The opening sentence of *Married Love* – "Every heart seeks a mate" – was the romantic in her. Like Sanger, she was not always accurate. She talked of women's "rhythms" and "sex tides" which came and went every fortnight, leading her to advise four days of "repeated unions" to be followed by ten days of abstinence; and she was convinced that women absorbed "the highly stimulating secretions which accompany a man's semen," which was why she was against condoms – she favoured a small rubber cap

A mother seeks contraceptive help from Marie Stopes, whose book sold half-a-million copies.

which she called a "check pessary". The semen theory was not Stopes' alone: it had other supporters. A pharmacist in Chicago was selling tablets containing secretions before 1918 and in the Twenties a Harley Street doctor in London was subscribing "male secretion" treatment for deprived wives whose husbands, presumably, used condoms.

Stopes' "practical sequel" to *Married Love*, *Wise Parenthood*, which set out the argument for birth control, faced hostilities that had not greeted the earlier book. The First World War had ended: nations that had lost millions of men were waking up to the need to rebuild. In this climate those who opposed birth control again found some public sympathy in saying that it was morally repugnant. Stopes stuck to her guns. Unlike Sanger in the States she was not prosecuted. But that the authorities were against her was clear when, in 1921, she opened Britain's first birth-control clinic, in London's Marlborough Road. A doctor recklessly said in print that she was taking advantage of the poor and subjecting them to harmful experiments. She sued him for libel, lost, and lost again on appeal to the House of Lords.

Despite Stopes' dislike of the condom, sales, no longer restricted to "marrieds" only (as if, in all truth, they ever had been, whatever the law), began to increase dramatically. Couples who announced their engagement in the newspapers were sent free samples. By the mid-Thirties over 120 million condoms a year were being sold in the UK and over 300 million in the US. Condoms were even available from barber shop vending machines that were left out all night and from slot machines that were going into some public houses, a development the

2000 1990 1980 1970 1960 1950 1940 1930 1920 1910 1900

House of Lords tried to stop. "The poor man's club," fumed Lord Darcy de Knath, was being converted "into premises for retailing the accessories of the brothel."

At the turn of the century the birth-rate was 2.8 per cent; by the mid-Thirties it was 1.5 per cent and falling. Contraception, always available to the professional classes – which kept its birth-rate a quarter of the average – had now extended downwards to the clerks and shopkeepers of the lower middle class.

Marie Stopes' first clinic, which was in London. "Mothers" meant married women only.

Sanger and Stopes were neither the first nor the last of the century's pioneering women who brought sexual knowledge to the masses. Earlier in the century there had been Ida Craddock, whose campaigning cost her life; later there was Mary Ware Dennett, through whose courage contraceptive literature was removed from the list of what was considered obscene.

Craddock was not completely sane. A spinster who believed herself to be the wife of a divine spirit, she had for years belonged to the US Free Love movement and had written pamphlets with such titles as *The Wedding Night* and *Helps to Happy Wedlock*. In a longer work, *Right Marital Living*, the first modern married manual written by a woman, she told women graphically:

> Bear in mind that it is part of your wifely duty to perform pelvic movements during the embrace, riding your husband's organ gently and, at times, passionately, with various movements up and down, sideways and with a semi-rotary movement, resembling the movement of the thread of a screw upon a screw.

She also encouraged women to "go right through the orgasm, allowing the vagina to close upon the male organ." There were references to praying to God during intercourse and being one with Nature at the moment, which signalled Craddock's religious motivation, but that did not save her from being arrested for sending "obscene literature" through the mail. The man responsible was Anthony Comstock.

Comstock was virtually the national censor – self-appointed. He had begun his crusade as long ago as the 1870s; in 1908 he formed the National Board of Review which searched for anything unwholesome in books, pictures, magazines, calendars, saloon paintings, advertisements, even sheet music. Anything that he declared obscene could result in arrests.

Comstock also formed a vigilante group, the Committee for the Suppression of Vice (which later became incorporated as the New York Society for the Suppression of Vice), and took a suitcase of pornography to Washington, persuading Congress to pass a bill intensifying the punishment of those using the mail to send obscene materials; in the process he was appointed special agent of the Post Office. The problem for Craddock and those who came after her was that the legislation, commonly known as the Comstock Act, added "contraceptives, abortfacients and things intended for immoral use" to the list of what was considered obscene.

The method which Comstock used to snare Craddock was dubious. Posing as Miss Frankie Streeter, who was "past 17 years", and giving a box number in Summit, New Jersey, he wrote to her asking if young girls were admitted to her lectures and enclosing 50 cents for a copy of *Wedding Night*. Craddock wrote back:

> My chief reason for not admitting minors to my lectures is that there are those who believe that people should be kept as ignorant as possible of all that pertains to the marriage relation. It is thought by many people that it would somehow render young people impure if they were told previous to marriage anything of details ... It does not matter how delicately and chastely the teacher may instruct that young girl or young boy; that she should instruct them at all is expatiated on as an effort to corrupt the morals of innocent youth ... For this reason, much to my regret, I could not even consent to give you ...the desired instruction. ... nor do I care to send you *The Wedding Night* for a similar reason; and I return you your 50 cents herewith.

Comstock arrested her for sending the desired instruction to others and she received a three-month suspended sentence. Almost immediately she was rearrested on what was probably a trumped-up charge (Comstock told the judge that he had seen Craddock give a copy of *Wedding Night* to the daughter of the janitress of the building in which she had her office, although the building did not have a janitress); the jury found her guilty without leaving their seats. On the day the sentence was to be passed, Craddock put her head in the oven. Her suicide note read:

Happy Games, *a saucy painting by Chabal, whose September Morn *was *considered pornographic by Anthony Comstock.*

I am taking my life because a judge … has declared me guilty of a crime I did not commit – the circulation of obscene literature. Perhaps it may be that in my death, more than in my life, the American people may be shocked into investigating the dreadful state of affairs which permits that unctuous sexual hypocrite Anthony Comstock to wax fat and arrogant and to trample upon the liberties of the people, invading, in my own case, both my right to freedom of religion and to freedom of the press.

It is unlikely that the burly, bull-necked Comstock turned a hair; a sinner had merely compounded her sin with the sin that could not be repented. Comstock believed he had been chosen by God to protect the moral purity of children; as God's representative he strode the streets of New York seeking whatever would cause him offence. It could certainly be argued in the context of the times that some kind of restraint on what was openly for sale was needed. But Comstock did not know where to draw the line. He viewed art as Satan's work. He arrested a young woman from the Art Student's League for sending him a catalogue of nude studies; and when a copy of a highly discreet painting of a nude by Paul Chabas entitled *September Morn* – which had been awarded a medal of honour in the Paris Spring Salon – was exhibited in a bookshop window and drew a crowd, he ordered its removal. There was nothing more sacred than the form of a woman, he said "but it must not be denuded." He added that everyone would agree with him. They did not. Prints of *September Morn* sold in millions and became the symbol of the new freedom. When Comstock banned George Bernard Shaw's *Mrs Warren's Profession* because the play dealt with prostitution, Shaw coined the term "comstockery". By the end of his career Comstock was the butt of jokes and satirical cartoons.

Over forty years Comstock arrested more than 3,600 people – enough, he would say, to fill a passenger train of 61 coaches. As the century opened, his catch was 2,385 – at which time he had destroyed 73,608 pounds of books, 877,412 "obscene" pictures, 8,495 negatives for making "obscene" photos, 98,563 articles for "immoral" use of rubber, 6,436 "indecent" playing cards and 8,502 boxes of pills and powders used by abortionists. A newsreel in the first decade of the twentieth century showed a haul of 25,000 books going into a police furnace – "half a million dollars-worth at current prices for such filth. Hot stuff getting hotter … enough to keep police headquarters warm for two days, saving six tons of coal." In the course of his office he drove some fifteen people to their deaths; and countless hundreds felt his wrath, including Emma Goldman and Margaret Sanger both of whom he hounded out of the country. It was Comstock who went after William Sanger when his wife had fled to England, and got him jailed. There were many who smiled when Comstock died of pneumonia – from a chill caught during the trial.

A decade after Sanger, Mary Ware Dennett, founder of the Voluntary Parenthood League, was a victim of the same law that trapped Craddock. When, however, she was charged for distributing 30,000 copies of a pamphlet, *The Sex Side of Life*, by post, something deemed "obscene, lewd, lascivious and filthy, vile and indecent, against the peace and dignity of the US", she fought back. And, in March 1930, she won a landmark victory. Reversing an earlier court decision, Justice August Hand said:

The defendant's discussion of the phenomenon of sex is written with sincerity of feeling and with an idealization of the marriage relations and sex emotion. We think it tends to rationalize and dignify such emotions rather than to arouse lust. We hold that an accurate exposition of the relevant facts of the sex side of life in decent language and in manifesting serious and disinterested spirit cannot ordinarily be regarded as obscene.

A sex-publishing industry developed during the Twenties and Thirties, with works of sexual advice by the serious and the seedy: doctors, psychologists, clergymen, quacks, pornographers. One book which became as famous as *Married Love* was written by a Dutchman, Theodoor Van de Velde, whose *Ideal Marriage: Its Physiology and Technique* was the first sex manual in the modern sense. Van de Velde stressed the importance of foreplay, including attention to the nipples, penis and vagina. On the other side of the Atlantic Dr W.F. Robie swiftly followed with *Rational Sex Ethics* and *The Art of Love*, which was Van de Velde without the earnestness. He told men to stimulate the clitoris and woman to "follow her inclinations as to the force, distance or rapidity of the in-and-out motion" and tried to get couples to add a little variety to the "husband above and astride" position. Stopes took something of Robie to heart, in one of her later books, giving approval to his injunction "to kiss a wife's lips, tongue and neck and, as Shakespeare says, 'If these founts be dry, stray

Marie Stopes dressed as Isadora Duncan. The romantic in Stopes identified with the controversial American dancer.

2000 1990 1980 1970 1960 1950 1940 1930 1920 1910 1900

lower where the pleasant fountains lie.'" She had nothing to say about women returning the favour. In *Why We Misbehave* Samuel Schmalhausen coined a phrase still popular today when he noted that in the sexual revolution "the center of gravity has shifted from procreation to recreation." The sex manuals of the Thirties shifted the emphasis from masturbation to a new danger: petting. Roy Dickenson was typical when, in writing *So Youth May Know: New Viewpoints on Sex and Love*, he asked whether any decent young man would want "secondhand goods or a woman who has been freely pawed over for a sweetheart, wife and mother or his children." Oh yes: Dickenson also claimed that kissing transmitted syphilis.

But no book made the impact of Stopes' *Married Love*. Women from all over the world wrote to her in their tens of thousands, opening their hearts, asking about simultaneous orgasm, the size of the male member on the wedding night, the indelicacy of condoms, the longevity of sperm. Forty per cent of her correspondence was from men. One man thanked her for defining what an orgasm was – he thought his wife was having some kind of fit. In *Male Sexuality 1900–1950*, Lesley A. Hall studied the letters men wrote to Stopes and did not find husbands secure in their superiority as men; they were as uncertain of themselves as their wives and no more knowledgeable.

You emphasize ... the importance of conjugal intercourse being a joint act, ie, the gratification of the discharge should not be confined to the male but should be shared by the female... But the difficulty must often be that the discharges do not coincide in time. If that of the woman is late, it is difficult to see what ought to be done, as to prolong coition would be for the man a serious strain.

I have noticed that if in love-making I touch my wife near the entrance, she is much more "lively" and satisfaction comes much more readily ... having done this once or twice I notice the difference. Can you tell me whether men and women usually experience these unions unencumbered with clothes... or whether it is customary for women and men to retain some of their night garments because of the instinct of modesty.

I have been engaged for over a year...Lately I have felt a sexual longing when sitting on the couch with my fiancée. I often get this feeling. It is as if, although both are fully dressed, I long to get near her ... Am I normal and natural to feel this sexual longing or am I abnormal? I suppose I should try and smother my sexual feelings?

I am over 70 and have never had any connection with women, my brain being set on other matters ... Would you kindly tell me if a man over 70 is likely to have heirs? ... can you guide or give advice as to the Mode to proceed by to have sons?

It was virtually impossible for Stopes to deal with the deluge of correspondence, even with a staff of secretaries – one series of articles in *John Bull* magazine brought 20,000 inquiries. But she tried. And she fought the same kind of bigots that Sanger fought, those clergy who saw contraception in terms of fire-and-damnation, an often arrogant medical profession (which hated this woman for drawing their august calling into the same orbit as the squalid abortionists) and a frequently hostile press. She even had to contend with feminists who, as Paul Ferris wrote in *Sex and the British*, "might have been expected to welcome contraception, [but] were more inclined to see it as another male trick to allow them easier access to women's bodies."

If Stopes was a public celebrity, privately she was as clinical and ruthless as she was romantic and idealistic. It seems she "castrated" the men she married or took as lovers (although the word "lovers" should be in quotation marks: Stopes was always ambivalent about whether she did or she did not). June Rose believes poor Gates, Stopes' first husband, was "absolutely petrified" in bed and out. When she married Roe she wrote to a literary figure who had been a suitor to tell him that at last she had had sex – "I think she tormented that man," Rose says. Stopes lost all interest in Roe when her son Harry was born and he finally left home at the outbreak of World War Two. Poor Roe could only visit when she did not have literary friends in the house and even when he begged to come home, promising to do the washing up and make the breakfast, she refused. At sixty-five he cut a pathetic figure. Later, when Stopes' son married against her wishes, she cut off all contact with him; the relationship was patched up but remained strained until her death.

Stopes was well aware of the contradictions in her life and of the charge that, ultimately, she did not practice what she preached. To that Stopes-Roe says: "I think her basic belief about the necessity of fulfilment and happiness in marriage was something she practised so far as she could with my father, very much so. But when difficulties came ... she tended to look upon herself as an exception."

Stopes' problem, Rose adds, is that she did not find a man who was her intellectual equal and "always chose weak men because she knew instinctively that a strong man wouldn't allow her to be the self she needed to be." Her tragedy was that, while she showed hundreds of thousands of men and women how fulfilling the married relationship could ideally be, she was unable to achieve it for herself. What Stopes needed, Rose reflects, "was a very sensual working-class stud. Even one-night stands might have helped her." She thinks it hard "not to think of Marie as a monster," but adds, "she was a superwoman, unique ... Really, there's only been one Marie Stopes and it's difficult to think of anybody who could equal her."

Homosexuals and lesbians found freedom in Twenties' Berlin.

Impossible woman that she was, Stopes was unable to work with other people – she even quarrelled with Margaret Sanger – and gradually was edged out of the birth-control movement. She eventually became a little dotty, writing to the Lambeth Conference to deliver a message on God's behalf that husbands and wives were to "use the means which God now sends through science to raise the race." Desperate to live up to her self-image as a great woman, she decided to become a literary lioness, and turned to poetry. In August 1939, when English critics ridiculed a book of her poems, she sent a copy to Adolph Hitler:

> Dear Herr Hitler,
> Love is the greatest thing in the world. So will you accept from me these love songs for young lovers, that you may allow the young people of your nation to have them. The Young must learn love from the particular till they're wise enough for the universal.

Herr Hitler did not respond.

A NEW SEXUAL POLITICS

If the German dictator disappointed Stopes, he devastated Magnus Hirschfeld who in 1919 had opened an Institute of Sexual Science in Berlin. Containing the world's largest library on sex (20,000 volumes, 35,000 drawings and photographs) the institute, which provided a marriage counselling service as well as advice on contraception and sex problems, and which paid special attention to transvestites, was famous worldwide. A doctor and a homosexual, Hirschfeld had devoted himself to the subject of sex after one of his patients, a young army officer who was also homosexual, killed himself on the eve of his marriage, tormented by his double life. Hirschfeld campaigned for the acceptance of homosexuality as a "third sex" which should be protected by law rather than prosecuted. It was a brave stance to maintain as Germany came under the Nazis. Homosexuals were regarded as dangerous, belonging to secret cabals like the Freemasons, and sneered at in the street as "175-ers" (after paragraph 175 of the penal code). A Jew, Hirschfeld was beaten up in the street and his public meetings were broken up.

In 1933 Hitler destroyed Hirschfeld's institute as he did the Reichstag.

Hirschfeld had already left the country when the Gestapo visited the institute to remove papers, then sent lorry-loads of students, accompanied by a brass band, to wreck the place. All Hirschfeld's books were burnt in front of the Opera House. Hirschfeld found out what had happened from a cinema newsreel, in Paris. For him, watching his work go up in smoke was a vision of hell. For Hitler and the Nazis it was a dramatic way of showing that sex was the stuff of the devil. Quickly Hitler declared homosexuality and sexual excess to be diseases, a canker of pathological foreign elements infecting Germany that had to be rooted out. Henceforth, German sex was to be pure, the very apotheosis of the German spirit; and women were not to be objects of desire but, rather, breeders of good Germans; Party members were to have a minimum of four children. Birth-control was banned along with contraceptives. For a moment in time, Hitler achieved something which had never been done on such a scale.

He hijacked human sexuality for political purposes. There were those in Britain and America who approved of some of Hitler's actions against permissiveness. Even a curb on nudism which he imposed got approval in some quarters. The movement, which was German, had spread to America and Britain and was not widely favoured – the founder of one British club had been fined for using "insulting words" when he advocated nudity from a soapbox at Speakers' Corner.

The psychology of the Nazi state fascinated one of the strangest and most brilliant of the sexual explorers, Wilhelm Reich, a former disciple of Freud who, like Hirschfeld, had left his native Austria, for Scandinavia. Reich, who was convinced of the necessity of regular orgasms for the mental health of men and women, wrote *The Mass Psychology of Fascism* in which he argued that Hitler succeeded precisely because he did not try to appeal to the intellect of the German people: he appealed to their emotions. More specifically, said Reich, the rallies Hitler so brilliantly stage-managed with swelling music, aroused crowds and phallic architecture let loose Germany's sexual energy; even the swastika was a simple line drawing of the sex act. Without sexual liberation, Reich concluded, there could be no political liberation. His views got him expelled from the Communist Party and the International Psychoanalytic Organization – but would make him a cult figure during the sexual revolution of the 1960s.

Meanwhile, the countdown to war had begun. And sex was ready to go to war.

German students march behind a swastika before beginning the destruction
of Magnus Hirschfield's sexual institute.

THE GOOD, THE BAD AND THE NAUGHTY

MANKIND'S SEXUALITY HAS DEMANDED SEXUAL IMAGERY FROM THE BEGINNING OF TIME, BUT THAT DEMAND LURCHED FORWARD IN PARIS DURING THE SECOND HALF OF THE NINETEENTH CENTURY. PAINTINGS OF NUDES, UNTIL THEN USUALLY DISCREET AND STYLIZED, BECAME INCREASINGLY REALISTIC AND FRANK. FIN-DE-SIÈCLE PARIS WAS A PLACE WHERE 14,000 ARTISTS — THE LIKES OF RENOIR, DEGAS AND LAUTREC AMONG THEM — CROWDED INTO MONTMARTRE AND PICKED UP POOR YOUNG WOMEN IN PIGALLE TO USE AS MODELS AND MISTRESSES. THE CREATIVE IMPULSE WAS MALE; WOMEN WERE THE OBJECTS THEY TRANSFORMED INTO ART.

Paris was also where the new art of photography had begun to be used in the creation of sexual imagery that was a long way from the Reverend Dodgson's studies of little Alice. In the first age of cheap printing such images were sold on the street corners of the capital cities; even more explicit material could be had from catalogues which addressed themselves "to you, young man, whose tool stands up" and offered "postures". Looked at almost a hundred years later from an age which now sees the explicit as virtually the norm, such postcards reveal the participants' sense of novelty in posing for the camera, even a curious kind of innocence – a view that would have had America's "Mr Vice", Anthony Comstock, reaching for his carbine.

From the very moment that films were first made, four years before the twentieth century began, film-makers knew that people wanted sex. The recently invented mutoscope, which housed sequences of photographs that became animated when a handle was turned offered numerous subjects; but the saucy nudes, the artists models and the women who dressed and undressed were by far the most popular. When film came, first in peepshow machines which invited the potential viewer to watch *How Girls Go to Bed* and *How Girls Undress*, no-one can have been surprised that the pattern did not change. One historian recounts a meeting of the board of directors of the British Biograph Motion Picture Company which, in discussing the daily take from one of its arcades, found that *Rip's Sleep* took twice as much money as *Battleship at Sea*; *Ballet Dancers* took four times as much; and *Girl Climbing Apple Tree*, fourteen times. The decision was made to have more subjects of the girl climbing tree variety — henceforward market forces and sex were joined at the hip. The following year, *How Bridget Served the Salad Undressed*, at ninety seconds a full half-minute shorter than *Girl Climbing Apple Tree*, was an even bigger money-spinner.

The first kiss in cinema history — described by moralists as a "wall-sized monster".

The first box-office hit in the new-fangled cinema where film was projected was *The Kiss*, transferred from a Broadway play. "For the first time in the history of the world it is possible to see what a kiss looks like," commented the *New York Evening World*. "Scientists say kisses are dangerous, but … the idea has unlimited possibilities." *The Kiss* caused a scandal ("Sex Ten Feet Square!"), though the couple involved were middle-aged and somewhat unattractive. A Mr Herbert Stone was moved to write in protest: "The prolonged pasturing on each other's lips was hard to bear. Magnified to Gargantuan proportions and repeated three times over it is absolutely disgusting." So disgusting, in fact, that by the end of the first decade of the twentieth century, the nickel palaces in America and the penny arcades in Britain had been overtaken by the cinema.

The moralists in both America and Britain were quickly alive to the double danger. The darkness in which films were viewed was a direct invitation to sin; and the behaviour of the flesh-and-blood characters on the screen was likely to give the audience "ideas". The first act of censorship concerned a film of a Coney Island belly dancer. An earlier version of her performance had been seen without protest or interference in the peepshows, but once transferred to the big screen someone thought fit to superimpose white stripes on her gyrating parts. Early audiences in Britain congregated at the foot of the screen, peering up in the hope of seeing behind the stripes. Pressure was brought to bear to lighten the darkness and prevent the sexual exploration that may have been happening in the auditorium. Some showmen tried putting their screen in a darkened alcove and illuminating the room, but found that did not pay and abandoned the experiment. "The public prefer it," said one showman flatly, "especially the young couples, who like to see the pictures and have a canoodle at the same time." And why not? "Take your girlie to the movies," ran a song of 1913, "if you can't make love at home."

For the bright young entrepreneurs – many of them Jews from Eastern Europe – who pioneered the movies, sex was the essence of their emerging industry. And again, why not? In the outside world sex was everywhere, scandals in the newspapers as well as anxiety about the white slave trade, which reached hysteria in America. "Slavers Kidnap 60,000 Women Each Year" was a headline that the reformers turned into a placard: "Danger! Mothers beware! 60,000 innocent girls wanted to take the place of 60,000 white slave who will die this year in the US!" It was quite simple: sex sold. The 1913 film *Traffic in Souls* which dealt with the subject played simultaneously in 28 New York City theatres and grossed $450,000.

The American belief in the white slave trade, despite any evidence, resulted in the Mann Act of 1910, which forbade the transportation of "any woman or girl for the purposes of prostitution or debauchery" over state boundaries. The intention was to stop criminal trafficking in innocent women. What it did was catch well-to-do yahoos off for a bit of debauchery with their mistresses. Sometimes it caught the prominent or the famous, such as Charlie Chaplin in the 1940s. Notoriously, soon after the Mann Act was passed, it caught Jack Johnson, the first black heavyweight champion of the world. The most hated man in America because he had

Black heavyweight boxing champion Jack Johnson, a victim of America's hysterical belief in the white-slave trade.

beaten a white man, Johnson was seen as "an uppity nigger" for another reason: he had married a white woman and kept several white mistresses in various parts of the country. "Transporting" one of them across a state line got him a year in jail, the governor of South Carolina commenting: "The black brute who lays his hands upon a white woman ought not to have any trial." One might speculate how much Johnson's fate was to do with a fear of black sexuality as it was of miscegenation.

HOORAY FOR HOLLYWOOD

Hollywood soon established itself as the world's back lot. But the world's first sex star, Theda Bara, was created at a studio in Long Island. "Created" is the word. Her publicity promoted her as the love child of a foreign actress and her Italian lover; born in the shadow of the Sphinx, "foreign, voluptuous and fatal"; she had been suckled by crocodiles; her lovers died of a poison from mysterious amulets. Perhaps the world was then credulous enough to believe this stuff. In reality, Bara was Theodosia Goodman, a tailor's daughter from Cincinnati. But that did not matter. The film in which she starred, *A Fool There Was*, captured the popular imagination. And it gave the language the word "vamp" (a contraction of vampire) which Bara used to describe her part as a sexual predator who watched two married lovers die in front of her – and laughed. Bara, one critic commented, "had a maternal figure and looked remarkably like a suburban housewife," but she went on to play Cleopatra, Madame du Barry and Salome, all women who destroyed men. Her entire career was implausible but, as Larry May observed in *Screening Out the Past*, "The vamp thus embodies the most ominous warning of the vice crusaders: Sex could destroy the social order."

The movie business made a lot of people very rich in the early decades of the century. A lot of them, according to Kenneth Anger – one-time boy actor, maker of homoerotic underground films, best known for exposing *Hollywood Babylon* – had neither class nor breeding and no idea of social behaviour. In 1922 an English woman taught them. Her name was Elinor Glyn.

When she was young, Glyn had married a much older man who hired a small Brighton indoor swimming pool for two days so that, as she was to write in her memoirs, she could swim naked, "allowing him to appreciate the beauty of the mermaid he had married." The marriage had not lasted (Clayton Glyn's gambling bankrupted him) but during its course, unhappy and emotionally starved, Elinor Glyn published *Three Weeks*, a tale of adulterous love, an innocent young Englishman, a predatory older woman from eastern Europe, and a love scene on a tiger-skin rug. *Three Weeks* contained nothing that would make any headmistress today remove it from her school library shelves. But in the early twentieth century it was risqué enough to be banned, here and there, in England and America. When Glyn tried to protect her book rights in the courts she was told by the presiding judge,

That's why the lady is a vamp: Theda Bara, the first – and perhaps most unlikely – sex star.

"Copyright cannot exist in a work so grossly immoral as this." The book sold splendidly on the back of that judgement and, perhaps, even better because these lines had been penned by some anonymous wit:

Would you like to sin with Elinor Glyn on a tiger-skin?
Or would you prefer to err on some other fur?

It was only a matter of time before Hollywood wanted to make *Three Weeks* a "property".

The Glyn who arrived there with several novels more and a stint as a war correspondent in France behind her, was not the long-haired mermaid of her honeymoon. She was edging towards sixty and, according to Anger, "wore a red wig, had false teeth" and was so stout "she could hardly eat, her corsets were so tight." But she knew what she was doing. Having got *Three Weeks* on screen, she made a niche in the brash community by promoting herself as the source of all knowledge on matters of sex and romance. There was an irony in this which, it has to be said, Glyn would not have recognized. As is clear from her memoirs, she rather considered sex as something to be endured, not enjoyed:

No-one can possibly imagine the unpleasantness of a honeymoon until they have tried it ... As for the thought of a second honeymoon – unbearable, terrible, impossible. Better, much better, to die and have done with it!

Hollywood's English advisor on romance and manners: Elinor Glyn.

Undoubtedly the bosses found her ridiculous, but it seems they believed her when she said "American men of those days simply could not make love. Not even the leading screen actors had any idea how to do it." She showed them, drawing, one presumes, on her imagination. She also taught British etiquette to many of the stars: that certain knives and forks were to be used for certain dishes, that a man should stand up when a woman entered the room, that a woman should smoke from a long cigarette holder and never light her own cigarette. Many of the small social graces of the age which Glyn passed on to the former "manicure girls and garage mechanics who didn't have a clue, even though they were earning millions" – Anger's words – found their way on to the screen. It was Glyn who taught Valentino, or so she claimed, to kiss the palm of a hand rather than the fingertips, a gesture that sent mothers as well as daughters swooning. "He was always willing to acknowledge that I had taught him a great deal about the art of making love before a camera," the memoirs inform. One doubts that Rodolpho Alfonzo Raffaele Pierre Filibert Gugliemi de Valentina d'Antonguolla required any such instruction.

Valentino was a star – the first international male star – from the moment he appeared in *Four Horsemen of the Apocalypse*, a cigarillo clenched between his teeth and blowing smoke down his flaring nostrils. The film grossed $4.5 million and the tango he performed made the dance all the rage. *The Sheik* established him as the sex symbol of the decade. Women adored him and Anger knows why: "It may seem like a hoot now, but men then weren't supposed to

Valentino in the **Son of the Sheik,** *his last film. The orgasmic look on his face when he
seduces Vilma Banky caused trouble with the censor.*

2000

1990

1980

1970

1960

1950

1940

1930

1920

1910

be sexual, they were just bread-winners. Valentino looked at women, not just the women on the screen but all those invisible women who were spellbound in the darkness, and everything about him said, 'Hey, I want you, I want your body.' And he was very gentle with women. Watch his hands in a love scene, they creep across the back, each finger caresses. He seduced through touch, not looks."

American men called themselves "sheiks" and kissed the palms of the girlfriends they called "shebas". But men were threatened by Valentino. Anger puts the reason simply: "They didn't like taking their wives and girlfriends to the movies because they'd try a little embrace and get pushed away. Women didn't want advances during the love scenes with Valentino because it just reminded them that they weren't sitting next to Valentino." Rumours circulated that he was homosexual after both his wives (who were self-confessed lesbians) denied in their divorce proceedings that their marriages had ever been consummated. In fact, as David Bret's recent biography, *Valentino: A Dream of Desire*, makes clear, the star was rampantly bisexual. Two weeks before he died in a New York hospital, aged thirty-one, as the result of a perforated ulcer, the *Chicago Tribune* published an article called "Pink Powder Puffs", accusing Valentino of making the American male effeminate. That did not stop several women from committing suicide or a crowd of 30,000 from attending his funeral. Hollywood found the spectacle such good box-office that they shipped his casket across the country to California and did it all over again.

As many as 9,000 people an hour, ten hours a day for three days, filed past Valentino's lying-in-state in New York. The crowd was so dense the windows of the funeral parlour shattered.

Elinor Glyn had a hand in the projection of another sex star, Clara Bow, the year after Valentino's death. Bow appeared in a comedy called *It*, which Glyn had written from another of her novels, which she produced and in which she took a part – as herself. "It" was sex appeal and was indefinable, Glyn wrote, "the fortunate possessor having a strange magnetism … there must be physical attraction, but beauty is unnecessary." Bow was known as the "It Girl" or the "Jazz Baby" (how many Americans knew that jazz was not only black music but a euphemism for intercourse?) until talkies revealed her Brooklyn accent and ended her career, probably to the relief of those assigned to keeping her off-screen escapades out of the papers. Bow may have looked like a fresh-faced dairy maid but had the mouth of a fishwife (she had referred to Glyn as "a shithead") and the morals of an alleycat, on one occasion taking on the entire University of Southern California football team, which included a hulking tackle named Marion Morrison – John Wayne.

"It Girl" Clara Bow: the mouth of a fishwife and the morals of an alleycat.

Kenneth Anger called his exposé of Hollywood, *Hollywood Babylon* with good reason. Hollywood was a place crazed by sex. Hundreds of girls set out for California in search of fame and fortune in the new movie business and there were powerful men waiting to exploit them. The mandatory screen test frequently involved a wannabe taking off her clothes to ascertain whether or not the camera loved her, as they say. One surviving piece of film shows an unknown sitting naked in a bath being asked to react to the sudden appearance of a rat. Most of the rats in Hollywood were sitting behind large executive desks. The theatre impresario Florenz Ziegfeld in the days before the movies arrived initiated every girl who joined his Follies on top of his desk; they were all teenagers and he was old enough to be their grandfather. The tradition was carried on in Hollywood by such producers as Mack Sennett (who really did have a casting couch in his office) and D.W. Griffith, and by such moguls as Darryl Zanuck, Harry Cohn and Louis Mayer. Zanuck had a hidden room at the back of his office. Budding actresses were conducted there every afternoon and were known as "the four o'clock specials". Cohn had a private corridor built between the studio and his office.

America's favourite fat man, Roscoe Arcbukle – until he was accused of the rape and murder of starlet Virginia Rappe (below). Arbuckle was acquitted but his career was ruined.

Comments Anger: "The men in power had feudal rights; we're talking Dark Ages here."

A lot of what was happening remained hidden. A lot also got into the papers, making one American senator decry "the Jews, Dagos and Gypsies at the root of a vile conspiracy to debauch America." But the wheels started to come off in September 1921 when a wild three-day party at the Saint Francis Hotel in San Francisco ended in tragedy. Roscoe "Fatty" Arbuckle, the slapstick star, was implicated in the rape and subsequent death of a starlet named Virginia Rappe, who had attracted some attention when she appeared on the cover of the sheet music of *Let Me Call You Sweetheart*. The details of what happened on that Labor Day weekend in San Francisco were confused and unedifying, with a large number of people drinking a great deal of prohibition hooch and indulging in a great deal of sex. The incident involving Arbuckle may, or may not, have concerned penetration with a champagne bottle. After three trials on a charge of involuntary manslaughter Arbuckle was acquitted on evidence of a ruptured bladder and a botched abortion, the foreman of the jury saying: "Acquittal is not enough for Roscoe Arbuckle. We feel a grave injustice has been done him and there was not the slightest proof to connect him in any way with the commission of any crime."

Asked to comment on this sad tale which had all the elements of sex in the Twenties – procuring and attempted blackmail included – that arbiter of taste and decency, Elinor Glyn, said: "It was beastly and disgusting and things like that should be stamped out. If

Hollywood stars are flagrantly immoral, hang them; do not show their pictures, suppress them. But do not make us all suffer for a few. As for drink and dope parties, I have never seen any sign of them. If there are any, they are very small."

While Arbuckle sweltered through his second trial, a second scandal broke: director William Desmond Taylor was shot twice through the heart with a .38. In the ensuing investigation, which ultimately went nowhere, there was sensational evidence of comings and goings on the fateful night, revelations about indiscreet love letters, a horde of pornography and a collection of lingerie tagged with initials and dates. The careers of Mack Sennett's leading lady Mabel Normand and the virginal Mary Miles Minter were destroyed.

The newspapers depicted Hollywood as a sink of depravity. Almost 40 separate state bills called for film censorship

Censorship of the movies was already an administrative problem. In the early years, Comstock's National Board of Review had been industrious in trying to monitor film output – according to one account, in one year more than 100 female volunteers had viewed films non-stop, examining 571 and eliminating "75 scenes, ten reels and three entire movies". But America's national censor had been unable to keep down "the rising tide of filth". By now hundreds of local censorship boards in different states and cities were applying different rules. Chicago would have nothing to do with police violence or bribery, but were not particularly worried about sex, whereas in Pennsylvania a mother could not be shown making clothes for an unborn child because "thousands of children believe that babies are brought by the stork, and it would be criminal to disillusion them."

But the Arbuckle and Taylor episodes had taken the problem beyond the administrative to the ethical. Hollywood realized it needed to set up its own censorship machinery before congress forced something on them. And so, in 1922, came Will Hays to be president of the hastily formed Motion Picture Producers and Distributors of America. According to Anger, a "small, bat-eared guy with bad teeth," Hays had previously served as Postmaster General in the Cabinet of Warren Harding, the first US president to be caught in flagrente in the Oval Office. Hays was as devious and corrupt as any in an administration now regarded as one of the most corrupt in the history of Washington but, a darling of the purity movement because of his opposition to "obscene materials" in the mail, he was able to tell the American people what they expected to hear: "The potentialities of motion pictures for moral influence and education are limitless. Therefore its integrity should be protected … Above all, our duty is to youth. We must have toward that sacred thing, the mind of a child, toward that clean and virgin thing, that unmarked slate …" The conclusion could be drawn more quickly that Hays' sentence of politician-speak: the movies were to enter an

Bat-eared Will Hay,
"czar of all the rushes".

age of purity. Within days of Arbuckle's acquittal Hays announced that the actor would not work in Hollywood again. America's favourite fat man died of drink and despair.

Dubbed "the czar of all the rushes", Hays began by demanding that moral clauses be put into every contract: actors would "conduct themselves with due regard to public conventions and morals and will not do anything tending to degrade him or her in society, or bring him or her into public hatred, contempt, scorn or ridicule, or tending to shock, insult or offend the community or outrage public morals or decency, or tending to prejudice the company or the motion picture industry." This "morality clause" stipulated the immediate suspension of anyone involved in a scandal.

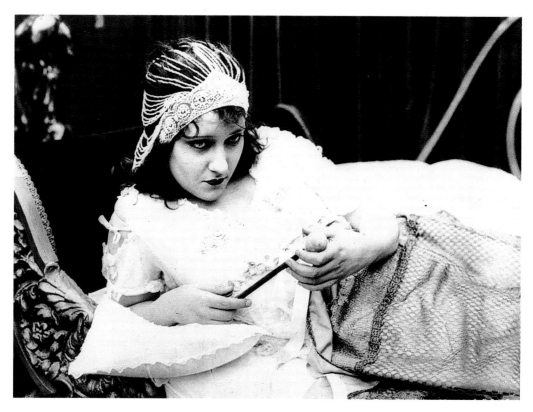

Former Mack Sennett Bathing Beauty Gloria Swanson brought a more realistic sexuality than Theda Bara's to the silent screen.

By 1924 the Hays Office had completed the draft of its Production Code, commonly referred to as the "Do's, Don'ts and Be Carefuls". Studios read them, agreed that actors would play bedroom scenes with one foot on the floor – and largely ignored the rest, adopting, in effect, the formula used by D. W. Griffith in the making of films like *Intolerance* and *Birth of a Nation* a decade earlier – "six reels of sin, one of retribution". Like Griffith, Cecil B. De Mille got away with bare breasts in his biblical epics (as did Fred Niblo in Ben Hur) and Erich von Stroheim with an orgy in *The Merry Widow*, a rape in *The Wedding March* and a flagellation in *Queen Kelly*, although he was eventually shunned, partly for his on-set decadence (excessive even by the lowest Hollywood standards – starlets were said to emerge bruised and bleeding from behind his locked studio doors) but mostly because of the huge budgets he demanded. Also, as the decade progressed, actresses arrived on screen – Bow, Gloria Swanson, Pola Negri, Greta Garbo – who displayed a more realistic sexuality than Bara's femme fatale. A lot of censored footage wound up on the cutting-room floor, but barriers continued to be pushed back. And when the talkies arrived, a new dimension of sexuality opened up. Once on-screen cards of stilted

Joan Crawford as a prostitute led astray in **Rain** *– one of the more explicit productions of the Thirties when the studios fought for survival.*

dialogue vanished, audiences found a thrilling intimacy that had not existed before. Now they could be seduced by actors' voices – and by the sounds of passion.

By this time, however, the Catholic hierarchy in America had decided that Hays was a failure in his job. Cardinal Mundelein of Chicago got together a group of clergy and lay figures in his archdiocese to draft the "Cardinal's Code" – a document which pulled Hays' guidelines into a strict code of production. Faced with the Depression precipitated by the Wall Street Crash, and the threat of losing that third of the audience which was Catholic, Hollywood agreed to adopt it. From now on, scenes that made adultery or illicit sex seem attractive were forbidden. There was to be no gratuitous passion, excessive or lustful kissing, lustful embraces or suggestive postures. Seduction or rape should be never more than suggested. And there was to be no sexual perversion, no white slavery (America could not rid itself of the notion of white slavery), no scenes of childbirth (the birth-control issue was still being bitterly fought, especially by Catholics) and no sexual relations between whites and blacks.

The recession began to bite. Audiences fell from 90 million to 60 million in two years. Finding themselves in deep trouble, the studios fought each other for survival – and the Production Code gradually fell by the wayside. Films became more explicit, pushing the envelope with gritty subjects: Joan Crawford, a prostitute led astray by a preacher in *Rain*; Barbara Stanwyck in *Baby Face* and Jean Harlow in *Red-Headed Woman* both using sex as a passport to success – Harlow's gold-digger not only not hitting the buffers of retribution but ending the film making love to a sugar-daddy on the Riviera – and his chauffeur. But what price sin? The Hays Office demanded cuts in almost everything it saw, but there was a limit to what could be done and still leave a releasable film. *Red Dust* with Harlow and Clark Gable, a tale of two illicit loves set on a plantation in Indo-China, was cut to ribbons but still had

enough pulsating sex to be a sensation. Some films were refused release but came out anyway, albeit with a limited circulation – some producers using the slogan "Banned by the Hays Office" in their publicity. Even musicals gave the Code the finger, with Busby Berkeley creating erotic kaleidoscopes from women's scantily attired bodies in a veritable riot of suggestive postures.

The cynical, wisecracking heroine who flaunts her body and takes the consequences was the creation of the Thirties. The epitome was Harlow, the "blonde bombshell", who thrust out a hip like a streetwalker and made her nipples stand up by applying ice cubes. Men swallowed hard when they heard her say, in *Hell's Angels*: "Excuse me while I slip into something more comfortable." Could there be something flimsier than what she was already wearing? In *Dinner at Eight* she told an older woman: "I was reading a book the other day – a nutty kind of book. Do you know that machines are going to take the place of every profession?" "My dear," came the reply, "that's something you need never worry about."

The woman who made the strongest connection between female sexual desire and its gratification was Mae West. She was already thirty-nine when she got to Hollywood. Five years earlier she went to jail for eight days when the New York City authorities closed down *Sex,* a play she both wrote and starred in – this after 375 performances. On her release she wrote, *Diamond Lil,* a play equally raucous and successful; and Paramount wanted to film it. While the studio was getting the production together, it gave West a small part in a George Raft movie, *Night After Night*. She inserted her own lines and stole the picture, right from her very first scene. "Goodness, what beautiful diamonds," exclaims a hat-check girl. "Goodness has nothing to do with it, dearie," West replies. "The best entrance of a woman in Hollywood history," says Kenneth Anger and the exchange set the tone for all her roles.

Diamond Lil was released as *She Done Him Wrong,* beat all box office records and rescued Paramount from the verge of bankruptcy. The public loved West – her earthy mix of wit and vulgarity, her self-mockery, her acknowledgement that there was a comic side to sex, her sheer over-the-topness. Forty-six million Americans saw the two films she made with Cary Grant. Her sexual puns and single entendres were knowing, true, but never prurient. "It isn't what I say but how I say it," she said. But that was never the whole story:

> "Marriage is a great institution. But I'm not ready for an institution."
> "Between two evils, I always pick the one I've never tried."
> "Give a man a free hand and he'll try to put it all over you."
> "When women go wrong, men go right after them."
> "I used to be Snow White but I drifted."
> "It's not the men in your life that counts, it's the life in your men."
> "A hard man is good to find."
> "How tall are you son?"
>   "Ma'am, I'm six feet seven inches."
> "Let's forget the six feet and talk about the seven inches."

Even Busby Berkley's kaleidoscopic girlie numbers ignored the production code.

2000

1990

1980

1970

1960

1950

1940

1930

1920

1910

1900

Mae West: the actress who made the strongest connection between female desire and gratification – and did it with humour.

"Is that a gun in your pocket or are you just pleased to see me?"

One can only speculate how men and women sitting in darkened cinemas more than sixty years ago reacted to West's deadpan throwaways. But we *do* know how the Catholic Church reacted: Cardinal Mundelein urged Catholic youth to boycott West's "obnoxious pictures". There was a lot of "obnoxiousness" about. De Mille's *The Sign of the Cross* flouted every rule in the book, featuring sex, orgies, nudity and perversion, not to mention mass murder. And Marlene Dietrich, an international star as a result of *The Blue Angel*, arrived from Berlin to appear in *Morocco* wearing a man's tuxedo – never before seen in modern America and regarded as daring, shocking, though not so shocking as the kiss she planted on the lips of another woman. The outer edges of sexuality was already being explored by continental film-makers, although their messages had not got through to audiences in America and Britain – the censor's scissors had rendered them incomprehensible. However, Dietrich's performance, orchestrated by her Svengali, Joseph von Sternberg (who had all her molars extracted before *Morocco* to give more shadow to her cheeks) was a first step in Hollywood's

2000

1990

1980

1970

1960

1950

1940

1930

1920

1910

1900

The nudity of Hedwig Kiseler (later Hedy Lamarr) was cut from **Ecstasy**, *but a close-up of her face in orgasm still got the film confiscated.*

recognition of the many-sided nature of human sexuality. For those convinced that the movies were making the world slide into the pit, a Czech film, *Ecstasy*, was in the theatres, introducing a young actress named Hedwig Kiseler (who later in Hollywood became Hedy Lamarr); under the Hays Code a nude scene had been cut although, oddly, a close-up of her face in orgasm remained untouched. The film was on the circuit for a while before the US Treasury Department confiscated it, citing it as an inflammatory "celebration of sexual intercourse".

The Catholic Church decided to give Hollywood another bible bashing. The newly appointed apostolic delegate from Rome endorsed a crusade and the Catholic Legion of Decency was formed. Between seven and nine million Catholics took a pledge against impurity in the movies (M = immorality, O = obscenity, V = vulgarity, I = immorality, E = exposure, S = sex). Viewing such impurity was declared a mortal sin, carrying the prospect of eternal damnation. Seventy thousand students in Chicago marched with placards: "An admission to an indecent movie is an admission ticket to hell".

The upshot was that Joseph Breen, an amiable but bigoted Irish-American Catholic who had helped draw up the "Cardinal's Code", came into the Hays Office as the administrator. He had new weapons at his disposal: the power to vet scripts and the Purity Seal, without which a film could not be exhibited. Breen could also impose a $25,000 fine on any producer who went around him. What he felt about the people he was taking on is clear enough from this letter:

They are simply a rotten bunch of vile people with no respect for anything beyond the making of money. Here in Hollywood we have paganism rampant and in its most virulent form. Drunkenness and

Tarzan's Jane lost her clothing as she jumped into a pool. The film lost the scene.

debauchery are commonplace. Sexual perversion is rampant. Any number of our directors and stars are perverts. These Jews seem to think of nothing but moneymaking and sexual indulgence. The vilest kind of sin is a common indulgence hereabout and the men and women who engage in this sort of business are the men and women who decide what the film fare of the nation is to be. They and they alone make the decision. Ninety-five percent of these folks are Jews of an Eastern European lineage. They are probably the scum of the earth.

Breen meant business and Hollywood pulled in its horns; the letter of the Code was observed. In one three-year period Breen sent down almost 30,000 directives. The average length of a screen kiss dropped from seventy-two inches of film (four seconds) to eighteen (one-and-a-half seconds); references to breast-feeding, pregnancy, childbirth and abortion were censored. Some decisions were whimsical, to say the least. In Johnny Weissmuller's first appearance as Tarzan, Jane (Maureen O'Sullivan) lost what little she wore on a branch as she jumped into a pool and swam in the altogether. There was to be none of that in future, Breen decreed, cutting the scene. The loveable *King Kong* was withdrawn from cinemas so that the scene in which he playfully plucks off a few shreds of Fay Wray's clothing could be removed. The brilliantly photographed aerial finale of the Astaire-Rogers musical *Flying Down to Rio* which featured chorus girls on the wings of aeroplanes was chopped because Breen objected to them losing their skirts in the slipstream, revealing one-piece bathing suits. In six *Thin Man* movies which ran until the mid-1940s, Dashiell Hammett's detective Nick Carter (William Powell) and his wife Nora (Myrna Loy) slept in twin beds – in the world according to Breen, there *were* no doubles. But, then, in *his* cinematic world no bathroom had a toilet.

Breen further tightened the screws on the studios through the powerful National Legion of Decency by giving C ratings

Fay Wray lost a some clothing to King Kong's fingers. The film also lost the scene.

(condemned) to films which passed the Production Code but of which he still disapproved. And he gunned for Mae West. One wonders why West so put the fear of God into Breen and the Catholic hierarchy: perhaps suggestiveness was more dangerous than physical carnality. Says Anger: "When she says 'Come up and see me sometime', that 'sometime' doesn't mean next week, it means 'maybe tonight'. Her 'sometime' is 'I'm hot, I want it'. That was her code." And, Anger adds, West was a threat to men: "It was never Cary Grant saying, 'Hey, babe, let's have a roll in the hay'. She was the aggressor. She was actually playing the male part." When West's last film, *It Ain't No Sin*, was in production, Breen stationed a minder on the set to ensure she added nothing to the agreed script. It was not any of Breen's doing that when posters for the film went up on Broadway, priests from the Legion paraded in front of them with signs reading "It IS". The title was changed to *Belle of the Nineties*.

But if Anger is to be believed, Breen did conspire with the newspaper magnate William Randolph Hearst to see the back of West. In *Hollywood Babylon*, Anger notes that from 1936 Hearst's papers denounced West as "a monster of lubricity" and "a menace to the Sacred Institution of the American Family". The real reason for the sustained attack, he says, was because Hearst was enraged by a crack West made about his lover, a mediocre actress named Marion Davies. Whether true or not, West's studio, Paramount, felt under so many pressures that, with abject cowardice, it did not renew her contract. West left with a smile, just as she arrived, though she might have been tempted to use a line she had used on screen in reply to a magistrates question. "Are you showing contempt for this court?" "No, I'm doing my best to hide it." On another occasion West said: "Men are all alike, married or single. It's their game. I happen to be smart enough to play it their way." In the end, that was not true. Sexual equality was a long way down the line.

The Thirties were the golden age of Hollywood. That, said Hays, was because there was less sex. But Hays and his henchman Breen failed to strap a chastity belt on to the movies. The sex certainly became less overt, but producers developed their own codes – ways of showing one thing and meaning another. The censors could cut lines of dialogue, even scenes. What they could not censor was what the Production Code could not express in rules: the suggestiveness of a look, a gesture, the sexual electricity between two people. And they could do nothing about sheer animal magnetism.

The British Board of Film Censors – like the Motion Pictures Makers and distributors of America a self-regulating body able to release or refuse to release any film, but unable to prevent local authorities from making their own decisions – was less happy than Hays. It had begun with only two rules: no portrayal of Christ and no nudity. Griffith's *Intolerance* featured both, but seems to have caused no particular anxiety; neither did the early De Mille biblical epics. But the Board's 1925 annual report protested against gratuitous displays of flesh and

the growing habit with actors of both sexes to divest themselves of their clothing on slight or no provocation. For instance, in what is a common scene when the heroine is assaulted by the villain, she almost invariable contrives to pull her dress well off the shoulders and this is done even by the leading actresses.

In 1926 the British censors removed twenty-three minutes from the released version of *Flesh and the Devil*, Garbo's most erotic silent film. More footage of Jean Harlow wound up on the cutting-room floor than anybody else: thirty-five minutes from *Hell's Angels*, her entire performance from Chaplin's *City Lights*. *Red-Headed Woman* was banned outright.

One might suppose that social issues should have been rather up Britain's street, but they caused the British censors considerable anxiety – they did not see such matters as being part of entertainment, which was how cinema was viewed by the establishment. Social propaganda, they thought, was better suited to being seen in educational institutions and church halls. They refused a certificate to *White Slave Traffic* and *Damaged Goods*, a morality tale of a married man who contracts syphilis after a night with a prostitute and passes the disease to his wife. The film was shown in some places, but cut to the point that it came close to being a series of subtitles. In Belfast, it was allowed to be screened to a segregated audience, with men on one side of the aisle and women on the other. Instances continued to occured – one film lost a scene in which a man take up a streetwalker's offer because it was "so repugnant to the English conscience" – until

British censors chopped **Red Dust** *even after extensive cuts in the United States.*

If Harlow had not died aged 26, Joe Breen would have ruined her film career as he did Mae West's.

the Board clashed with Marie Stopes. When she turned her book *Married Love* into a script, the Board insisted on changing the title to *Masie's Marriage* in an attempt to divorce the film from any association with her. Stopes lived with that but ensured that the film's title card make the association perfectly clear:

G.B. Samuelson presents
MASIE'S MARRIAGE
A Story specially written
for the Screen
by DR MARIE STOPES DSc PhD
in collaboration with
Captain Walter Sommers

In an ensuing row, the Home Office became involved. It was only when Stopes threatened to sue that objections were dropped and British censors accepted that social propaganda and entertainment might be intertwined. It did not mean that they were always prepared to give "propaganda" the green light.

The world turned, regardless of the movies. The relationship between men and women evolved and nothing changed more dramatically than the mating game. The century had arrived when a man and a woman could get acquainted only if introduced. A relationship advanced only if the man, seen as a potential suitor, formally called. If there was to be any courting it would be in the woman's home, under the eye of her parents. Now there were creatures who had not existed before – boyfriends and girlfriends. Boyfriends called, but only to collect girlfriends and take them out heaven knows where. Edison had said that electricity speeded up the world. It speeded up sex, too. "Do you believe in love at first sight?" Mae West was asked on screen. "I dunno," she replied, "but it sure saves an awful lot of time." In 1913 the American *Current Opinion* magazine concluded: "A wave of sex hysteria and sex discussion seems to have invaded this century. Our former reticence on matters of sex is giving way to a frankness that would startle even Paris." It was, said *Current Opinion*, "sex o'clock in America." And the clock was also ticking in Britain, even if it was an hour or two slow.

The Twenties roared, at least for the rich: most people were picking up the pieces of their lives after the Great War. In the age of jazz (that word) and dance crazes, their antics got them into the papers and, in America, into the novels of F. Scott Fitzgerald. When they were bored, the beautiful people from Belgravia and Long Island travelled – the Riviera, Venice, Paris, Berlin, New York to London, London to New York. On both sides of the Atlantic "petting

parties" were said to be all the rage ("Pet and die young," said the YMCA), pyjama parties, carefree drinking made cool by Prohibition in America and by the American example in Britain. Casual sex was seen to be sophisticated and, among the well-to-do, a lot of it was going on. As Dorothy Parker quipped: "If all the girls at Yale were laid end to end – I wouldn't be surprised." In *The Long Party*, a history of high society in the Twenties and Thirties, Stella Margetson wrote:

> Moreover, the young women of the Twenties no longer had the Edwardian sword of Damocles poised above their heads ready to drop on their necks if they were foolish enough to be caught in a compromising situation. A "reputation" lost, which had meant ostracism in high society and a quick withdrawal abroad to recover, had ceased to be a cardinal sin and divorce … could be gone into without too much fear of the social consequences.

Dance crazes and songs of love sold sheet music in the millions in the Twenties and Thirties.

Fashions also changed. At the end of the nineteenth century a woman's public attire weighed thirty-seven pounds – a mere seventeen pounds around the house. At the start of the twentieth century the figure fell to seven pounds and a decade later it seemed to be a few ounces. Wearing the new brassieres under skimpy dresses or evening gowns with no brassieres at all, or skirts short enough to show her powdered knees, the flapper sheared her hair, plucked her eyebrows, and painted her face as only the demi-mondaine had done before the war.

Wall Street crashed. US brothel owners thought that business would die. In fact there were more customers than they could handle, initially at least: men made bankrupt and in despair turned to sex, sometimes as a final act before committing suicide. One brothel owner noted that men "behaved like satyrs", another that the atmosphere was "more that an insane asylum than a bordello." The Thirties arrived, with an edge of dissipation, and cynicism – the frivolity of the Twenties a thing of the past. Irrespective of the Depression, the many public facets of sex continued increase. Now there were film fanzines, magazines of spicy fiction, romance, gossip; magazines which presented nudity in the name of art and which were done, as the late English comedian Kenny Everett used to say with sarcastic humour, "in the best possible taste." Material continued to be seized for obscenity. Books by serious writers like Dreisler, Hemingway, Lawrence and Joyce, which took on "the lying gospel that sexuality is somehow degrading," were banned from time to time, along with lesser writers. At the Federal Bureau of Investigation J. Edgar Hoover fumed about the "hot pillow trade" in the new motels and tourist lodges and the "passion pits" of the new drive-in movies. But the *American Nation* suggested that the time had come for "permitting grown-ups to decide for themselves what books they shall buy, what plays they shall see and even what pictures of undressed females they shall look upon," and John

Marlene Dietrich sings "Falling in Love Again", in **The Blue Angel.**

Sumner, who succeeded Comstock at the New York Society for the Suppression of Vice, quietly indicated a withdrawal from censorship, intimating that his predecessor had been "something of a religious fanatic who also loved notoriety."

Britain began to catch up in the shift from chastity. The well-to-do had always taken extra-marital weekends in Brighton; the middle-classes were now following suit. The working classes went to Blackpool for the blue comedians at the end of the piers, the rows of mutoscopes still cranking out what the butler saw, the naughty postcards – and a bit of sex on the sand when the sun went down. The women's magazines began to offer advice on sexual problems; the newspapers started to copy them at the end of the decade. Only a small proportion of the correspondence was explicit. Kissing was a constant topic – the amount of it going on in public places was what now outraged the moralists. The advice regarding it was that a girl should have regard to what MIGHT LIE BEYOND IT and not to let things GO TOO FAR. The capital letters were possibly less effective than lyrics that said "Your lips may say no, no, but there's yes, yes, yes in your eyes."

All of this and more informed the cinema, where reality was turned into fantasy which in turn became the new reality. Sometimes, what purported to be reality on-screen became reality off-screen – Hollywood's ban on the double bed actually created the twin singles, a standard of the American way of life. Cinema did not create sex. Society created sex. Newspapers, magazines, radio, popular music – all of these shaped people's attitudes to the issues of sex, to all the kinds of sexual venality, to the joys and dangers, to the etiquette. So did the cinema – it was the great synthesizer. But the cinema did more. It made sexual imagery take its place beside the sex act itself as part of human experience; and it took sexual activity, in all its aspects, from the private to the public domain, creating fantasies that were shared by millions who were given a common grammar in the language of love. What the stars did on-screen affected peoples lives. Harlow shifted the erotic centre of men's gaze from the leg to the breast, where it has remained. The likes of Harlow and West virtually created the peroxide production-line, as Dietrich's tuxedo created an entire industry – women had not worn slacks before Dietrich. And the on-screen image of so many beautiful bodies helped create the beauty business and the female quest, which still continues, for something approaching physical perfection, or something akin to it. What the stars did off screen undoubtedly affected people's lives, too. When Mary Pickford and Douglas Fairbanks divorced their respective partners to marry in 1920, there was genuine dismay among ordinary people – divorce was not something that happened – but the pair returned to their old popularity, indicating, at some level, that divorce was now seen as something that could be forgivable. Chaplin's first two divorces in the formative years of cinema are unlikely to have affected sexual mores, though if one wants to take a sociological view they did raise questions about paedophilia – and the second made public a word if not a deed with which, until then, neither America nor Britain was familiar: fellatio.

At the 1939 New York World Fair, a vision of "World of Tomorrow" was offered. Sixty nations were represented, with Germany notably absent. In the one area one exhibitor presented magazine covers for an imagined *Romantic Life* magazine dated ten years into the future. All were of topless women. Nearby, Salvador Dali created a "Dream of Venus" in which women naked to the waist swam in water tanks filled with giant rubber telephones and melting watches. A local minister complained and officials ordered "mandatory bras and net coverings"; outside, the city mayor Fiorello La Guardia convened a court to try and sentence three men who were attempting to hold a Miss Nude 1939 beauty pageant. What was clear was that, whatever the future held, the tussle between sex and morality would sure as hell be part of it.

2000
1990
1980
1970
1960
1950
1940
1930
1920
1910
1900

WAR, LUST & MARRIAGE

WAR IS AN APHRODISIAC, A HEADY MIX OF PATRIOTISM AND EXCITEMENT, AND OF FEAR. FEAR THAT A MAN GOING OFF TO FIGHT MAY NOT RETURN — FEAR, EVEN, THAT THERE MAY BE NO TOMORROW. IN THE CENTURY'S TWO WORLD WARS, IN WHICH SUCH FEELINGS CHURNED, IN WHICH THE SOCIAL ORDER BECAME SUSPENDED AND MORALITY WAS STOOD ON ITS HEAD, WOMEN FACED THE DILEMMA: WHY HOLD BACK ON WHAT THEY HAD TO GIVE?

Some, in both wars, rushed into marriage, a wedding-ring giving legality to their sexual desires. Others simply did not hold back. Some held back and regretted it.

> Some months ago my boyfriend asked me to do wrong, but I would not. He then said he was only testing me to see if I was worth fighting for. Now I have bad news that he is missing and I am heartbroken because I think that I would like to have given him what he wanted.

This letter appeared in *Woman's Own* in June 1944. There is nothing particular about it — hundreds like it appeared in magazines during both conflicts; its pain and sexual confusion could just as easily have been expressed thirty years earlier when Kitchener's call to arms brought young men pouring into the recruiting offices all over Britain and sent them marching off to war, their girls lining the streets to wave goodbye. The scenes of passion on railway stations and at ports of embarkation were too frank for the eyes of many of those who had grown up in the reigns of Victoria and Edward. There were complaints about lack of propriety and, worse, "looseness".

Almost from the beginning of the First World War the newspapers carried stories about "khaki fever". Promiscuity was reported all over Europe — in France women were said to be giving themselves to the departing troops "in a patriotic fever." There were tales of teenage girls flooding to military training camps and meeting soldiers in the woods. In the south of England older woman, too, were said to swarm to the big depots. The inevitable moral backlash closed the dancehalls in some towns, in the belief that in unnatural times they were a focus of sin. There were

The Women's Police Volunteers on railway station duty during the First World War.

other, peculiarly British, attempts to restrain sinfulness. A Miss Damer Dawson, "a mountaineer who drove a car", sent forth the Women Police Volunteers to garrison towns where they were empowered by the army to enter any building within a six mile radius and eject girls and soldiers from their beds; their successes were in the hundreds. In response to a rallying cry from a bishop's wife, the Women's Patrols were formed from the ranks of middle-class women of mature years, who worked in pairs to flush fornicators from dark alleys and parks with lanterns and, in London – where the Home Secretary, Herbert Samuel, saw the cinemas as places of particular danger – to put a stop to any inappropriate behaviour that was occurring in the flickering dark. The patrols also set up laundries near military establishments to discourage the camp followers whose excuse for being where they were was that they were washerwomen. By late 1915 a war baby crisis loomed and with it a public row, because the

A young couple cuddle in a yard undisturbed by the Women's Police Volunteers.

broad-minded wanted to make social provision for "the children of our dead heroes."

The mood of the country darkened as the war worsened. The casualties, "steady and appalling", the zeppelin raids, anxieties about shipping and food supplies, and strikes, led to public hysteria and a further slackening of sexual behaviour. Following the slaughter on the Somme in 1916 and the introduction of conscription which eventually took every available man up to the age of fifty, "a kind of madness" gripped Britain. On New Year's Eve the streets of London were thronged with soldiers and women shouting "To hell with 1916" and indulging in "open acts of congress". Sexual matters – prostitution (which the Government was nervous about tackling in a volatile atmosphere, for fear of enraging the Suffragettes), the white slave trade, venereal disease and women's "foolish sensibilities" – filled the papers in an unprecedented way, the very publicity, as sane voices pointed out, escalating the problem. The romantic novelist Marie Corelli tried to get women to concentrate on the war effort: "Men want the women but not for pleasure – but for work!"

There was a lot more for women to contribute to the war effort than the metal strips from their corsets which they had already contributed. As more and more men went to the front, more and more women took their place on the land and in the factories; for the final two years of the conflict they were in uniform, attached to the army, navy and airforce. Once America was drawn out of its isolationism and into the fight in 1917, women there followed suit. And on both sides of the Atlantic women sacrificed their crowning glory to the war effort: nurses tending men in trenches and makeshift field hospitals had neither time nor facilities to tend long hair, while women in munitions factories found it could be dangerous near machinery – and it attracted gunpowder dust. The cropped style that became such a part of the

Poster for a 1930 film harking back to the Great War and the eternal theme.

2000

1990

1980

1970

1960

1950

1940

1930

1920

1910

1900

Hamburg in 1949: in a licensed street of prostitutes, clients barter through the windows.

flapper's image in the Twenties was a product of First World War necessity.

The very fact that women were now in masculine environments attracted the ire of traditionally minded men, moralists and those motivated by hate or envy who were not necessarily either. Rumours of women using their new-found freedom for immoral purposes circulated. But women who had escaped from the home before the war had already been subjected to that charge. In 1913, B.S. Steadwell, president of the World Purity Federation, had written:

> During the past 50 years, girls and women have taken their places beside boys and men in schools, colleges, stores, offices, factories and shops, and have in constantly increasing numbers entered commercial life. This close association has brought opportunities for sexual gratification of which full advantage has been taken.

America's entry into the war succeeded in achieving what the anti-vice crusade waged since the nineteenth century had failed to do: it shut down the brothels. Within months, all the brothels within five miles of naval bases were closed – including Storyville.

Brothels existed in America from the Atlantic to the Pacific. Entire neighbourhoods of cities like New York, San Francisco and Chicago were given over to prostitution. But there was nothing like Storyville. Over thirty years it had grown to occupy a thirty-eight-block square in New Orleans, that city of liberal French attitudes. Storyville was a city within a city, a place where a man arriving by train or boat could purchase a "what's on" guide to the saloons and bordellos, where more than 2,000 whores, licensed and regularly checked for disease in the continental way, plied their trade. Storyville, it was said, was where jazz was weaned. Storyville was unique. But Storyville shut down. Every important red-light district in the country soon followed, including New York's Tenderloin. The following year, prostitution itself – which gave employment, it was estimated, to 600,000 whores and a million "clandestines" – was declared illegal. The moralists were triumphant, although all that happened was that a system of sex for sale which was at least open, was driven underground.

Legal or illegal, men joining up for Uncle Sam scurried to the cat-houses, wherever they were. The owner of one later wrote:

> Every man and boy wanted to have one last fling of screwing before the real war got him. Every farm boy wanted to have one big fuck in a real house before he went off and maybe was killed … It wasn't really pleasure at times but a kind of nervous breakdown that could be treated only with a girl between him and the mattress.

Millions of men experienced what was virtually a collective nervous breakdown once they reached the front in the First World War. War is hell, but no war has been the unrelieved hell of this war, where armies dug in facing each other across a few hundred yards, kept up a constant bombardment of each other's positions and periodically lost countless thousands of men in gaining a piece of ground on one day that would be lost the next. Men entered the war thinking of sex, remembered those at home to whom they might not return – and indulged in sex whenever the opportunity offered. In a static conflict there was leave, sometimes; or a lucky wound which might get a man to a hospital behind the lines. And there were women to accommodate the troops, wherever they went. The English poet Robert Graves once saw 150 men queuing for the services of three resident whores at a house in Bethune in northern France. If a man got to Paris he found the city thronged with thousands of prostitutes – and women seeking a good time, thrilled by danger. London, it was estimated, had 60,000 prostitutes, two-thirds of them refugees from France and Belgium. Even in the field there was sex to be had occasionally, when some enterprising pimp brought up a girl and a wagon, the only privacy a tarpaulin thrown over it.

As the war settled into stalemate, the Germans set up military brothels in cities behind the lines. In his history of the war, Magnus Hirschfeld noted that the soldiers were given treatment before and after intercourse and that details of each man's partner were taken. It was hard work for the girls: between 4pm and 9pm they averaged ten customers, but during a rush period that could be reduced to ten minutes a man, timed by the duty sergeant.

The French set up brothels, too, and supervised them medically. The American and British commands would have done so had their hands not been tied by fears of reaction on the home front, but they did allow their troops to make use of the French facilities – until the Association for Moral and Social Hygiene published an article in 1917 describing a brothel at Cayeux-sur-mer where fifteen women serviced 360 men a day. As a result, the British government demanded that all brothels be put out of bounds. The British commander, Haig, was infuriated: not only did the order take 400 military police away from other duties to enforce, it meant that his men would go elsewhere and probably "catch the clap". He protested at the "clamouring of religious sentimentalists," but the order remained in force until peace came. And, without doubt, some of Haig troops duly reported with a dose.

Throughout history, venereal disease has been all but packed in a soldier's knapsack. Armies in the nineteenth century were ravaged by VD. During the Boer War, 500 out of every 1,000 men admitted to army hospitals had VD. The incidence of venereal disease during the First World War was appalling. At one time or another, a quarter of all the armies engaged in the conflict were taken off active duty for treatment which, besides being prolonged, was painful. In the first three years, more than 100,000 British soldiers were admitted, or re-admitted to hospitals in the UK, and a quarter of a million to British hospitals in France. The Americans were in the fight for half its duration, but venereal disease still cost them seven million days in manpower – and this despite their troops in training being shown graphic examples of the hideous consequences of untreated syphilis

German bacteriologist, Paul Ehrlich (1854–1915), discoverer of Salvarsan, a compound that could cure syphilis.

and then issued with condoms once they got overseas. "Men must live straight if they would shoot straight," exhorted the American Secretary of the Navy. Leaflets given to those going on leave urged them not to "sow wild oats," adding: "If you associate with prostitutes or contract a venereal disease, you are guilty of a moral crime … You must go home clean."

British troops were issued with the warnings. Far better, they were told, that they were "pumping lead into the Hun than lying in hospital having Salvarsan pumped into them." They also got army chaplains trying to make them to sign "pledge cards" promising chastity. But they did not get the condoms. There is some record of British officers using "preventatives", which carries an irony: because British condom production was small (the

London Rubber Company was set up only in 1915) almost all those available in Britain and therefore available to British officers in France, came from Germany. Condoms or no, a quarter of British officers returned with VD.

Military police take some of Naples' 50,000 prostitutes to hospital for treatment of venereal disease.

The British army could never make up its mind on the question of how to deal with venereal disease during the First World War. It would have preferred to make condoms available; it did not because of reluctance to run counter to the moral climate in Britain where faith in abstinence as the only prophylactic – however unrealistic – remained strong. Somewhat feebly the army set up venereal abolition rooms equipped with tubs of calomel cream and buckets of permanganate of potash which did have some medical benefit if applied soon after intercourse; but it is doubtful that the troops made any use of them. They obeyed their sexual urges and took the consequences. Tragically, those consequences came home when the men came home.

In 1916 a Royal Commission into venereal disease in Britain reported that "The number of persons who have been infected with syphilis cannot fall below 10% of the population in the large cities," and estimated the incidence of gonorrhoea at about three times that level – a finding that translated into figures of three and nine million. Those figures would halve in the next fifteen years as a result of free treatment introduced on the Commission's recommendation. But venereal disease would kill until something better than Salvarsan was found. Some idea of the virulence of syphilis can be shown from the statistics of death in 1924 which show

Armistice Day 1918: a day when in European capital cities "strangers copulate in doorways and alleys".

that, compared with 50,389 from cancer and 41,103 from tuberculosis, 473,235 were from syphilis – many as the result of exposure during the war. America's record was no better; a lot of GIs did not go home clean.

Venereal disease was a spectre at the feast on Armistice Day, but no-one was aware of that. In London, soldiers, sailors and airmen linked arms with civilians and, wrote Stella Margetson in *The Long Party*:

> danced and sang in the streets with a hectic, wild sense of relief, a clownish gaiety very close to the deliberate suppression of pain … Women danced with their skirts thrown over their heads and, according to one very young Guardsman, Sacheverel Sitwell, were rolled along the platform at Waterloo Station like so many barrels of beer.

In *Sex and the British*, Paul Ferris followed the revelry when darkness fell and "It became famous as the night when strangers copulated in doorways and alleys."

WOMEN AT WAR

War is an aphrodisiac – so in the second conflict as in the first. The Second World War was a different kind of war, bigger, on the move, fought in the air as much as on land and sea. It engendered the same heady mix of feelings: patriotism, excitement, fear – fear intensified in Britain by the danger of heavy bombing, which put civilians in the front line. And it resulted, once again, in intensified sexuality. What was different from twenty years earlier was that it no longer seemed scandalous.

Men from other countries poured into Britain. First, with the retreat of the British Expeditionary Force from Dunkirk, came the Free French, Czechs and Poles. Later came the Canadians and, following Pearl Harbor, the Americans. By 1944 there were one-and-a-half million North Americans based in Britain, with sexy accents just like in the movies and sharp uniforms (their British equivalents looked as if they had been badly cut from horse blankets). These were men with money, cigarettes, chocolates and access to nylons – temptation indeed for women forced by shortages to draw lines down the back of their bare legs with eyebrow pencils. British servicemen were resentful of their brothers-in-arms for being "overpaid, oversexed and over here".

Some Americans were resentful of other Americans. The US Army segregated its black and white troops and fights frequently broke out in British pubs where white GIs tried to enforce a colour bar to prevent black soldiers from fraternising with white women. It was suggested that Britain should co-operate fully with the US Army's policy but that, the Cabinet thought, was going too far: instead it issued instructions that black and white servicemen should not be invited to social gatherings at the same time – and stressed that British women should avoid black GIs. Women in the ATS were ordered not to talk to black GIs unless another person was present. In some areas police

White GIs in Britain tried to prevent their black countrymen from mixing with white women.

GIs meet the AFS in London. Rumours of promiscuity among British women in uniform proved baseless.

arrested white women for keeping black company. In fact, the British public generally found black Americans to be better behaved than their white countrymen and most British troops. Public unease about sexual relationships between British women and black GIs increased as the war wore on, but the blame was put on the women involved.

Women experienced a sexual freedom during the war that was unprecedented. Teenage girls hung around army camps; single women flocked to dancehalls – dancing, now, unlike in the First World War, was almost a patriotic duty. So did many married women whose husbands were elsewhere, frequently removing

their wedding ring and saying, or at least implying, that they were unattached – when a lost wedding ring was found at one dancehall and an announcement made, a significant number of women were suddenly seen to be looking in their handbags. In the shifts and drifts of war, many women found themselves not only separated from their husbands but also, because they moved to another part of the country to do war work, from their families and neighbours. Some mothers were also separated from their children who were evacuated to areas less exposed to bombing. The war created the kind of social upheaval where normal restraints were removed and the threads of conventional morality snapped.

The public viewed much of what was happening as "moral delinquency". Towns across the country complained about "the growing number of enthusiastic amateur prostitutes" and of "girls lying in wait for soldiers on all sides" – and the used condoms in the streets. There were calls for more women police, a curfew for all young women

and a ban on the sale of alcohol to them. One government response was to send women under twenty-three to borstal for sexual immorality.

In a letter to the *New Statesman* in November 1943, a Land Girl wondered whether "the value of all the tons of corn and potatoes brought in by the girls" were worth having at the price of "the really disgusting way" many of her colleagues lived:

> I read with great interest your remarks on "War Factory". I am ... living in an isolated hostel and I find the same, shall I say, moral decline among our girls here which was noted of women working in factories away from towns. The problem of the land girl strikes me as more

War is forgotten when romance is in the air ... a young couple sit this dance out.

important still, as here the girls are younger and less firm in character, away from home for the first time in their lives, doing work which is either very hard and dirty or else deadly monotonous, and they certainly find it hard to interest themselves in it. So all their interests are turned towards their spare time in the evenings. But again, like the factory workers, they care little about mental activities ... and, looking for any kind of entertainment, they find their satisfaction in pub crawling or flirting with soldiers. The girls in my hostel are mostly under twenty and know very well what they are doing, they confess they had never been drunk before they joined up and that their parents would be very upset could they know of all this "fun".

Fun, immorality: war blurred the distinctions. Maureen Riscoe was one British girl who had a wilder war than most. Daughter of a North Country comedian, she got her first West End show

Dancing was almost a patriotic duty – but how many of these women had husbands fighting overseas?

2000
1990
1980
1970
1960
1950
1940
1930
1920
1910
1900

in the chorus ten days before war was declared and all the theatres were closed. Soon she was in ENSA, entertaining the troops, first in England and then in North Africa, Malta, Sicily and Italy. "War released people's inhibitions because death was just round the corner, wasn't it?" she says now. "I mean, we literally didn't know, any of us, if tomorrow would ever come." She had, she says, "masses of boyfriends." Sex came into it, "but only very gently – men were gentlemen in those days. I don't really know who I went all the way with first." In England she "never got involved with the Americans, I was too busy dating the English and getting pregnant. I knew nothing about contraception, none of us were told anything about it. We thought men knew everything, only they talked about these ghastly 'French letters', 'johnnies', and 'I can't feel you, darling, if I wear one of these things'. 'That's all right, I used to say, it's much nicer without'. I enjoyed myself, I enjoyed sex, I don't mind admitting it – but I did get pregnant quite a bit, about six times I think in all." She was forced to visit back-street abortionists, "once literally between shows with one of the other girls holding my hand," until "a certain actress told me I

British Tommies meet the chorus at the Drury Lane Theatre, after a show to entertain the troops.

was being a bit silly not to take any precaution at all and showed me this vast thing. I said, 'I couldn't get that in me,' and she said, 'Well, you could go and see your doctor and get fitted up.' I was a bit more fortunate from then on."

The British were ambivalent in their attitude to women in uniform. There were widespread rumours about service women's promiscuity and a high rate of illegitimate pregnancy, which reached a point where recruitment was affected. In 1942 the government set up an inquiry which, in concluding that the rumours were baseless, noted:

Equality: a French woman fills shells in a First World War munitions factory.

> the innocent and the experienced, girls from good and girls from bad homes, are all thrown together. If a woman has learnt loose habits in civilian life, she brings those habits with her into the Services ... Allegations of general immorality in a camp, when investigated, have in our experience resolved themselves into one or two cases which, in the course of gossip, have been multiplied times over.

Donning uniform gave women a problem with servicemen, too. They were seen to have crossed a gender barrier which entitled men to approach them more openly than civilian women. An angry memo from Admiral P. Somerville, Commander in Chief, Eastern Fleet, fired off in 1944, said:

> It must be admitted that a considerable percentage of Wren ratings, who are daughters of officers, or of a different social status to men of the Lower Deck, find it most embarrassing to be continually addressed by sailors and even more embarrassing to disengage themselves ...

Women struck a massive blow for equality during this war. Within four years over two-and-a-half million women in Britain were in the auxiliary forces, in Civil Defence and the Land Army, in the munitions, aircraft and tank factories. They kept the buses, the railways and the postal services going. They took over jobs previously considered "unfeminine" – everything from bricklaying to steeplejacking. But men's attitude to working women were possibly worse in 1939–45 than in 1914–18, perhaps because there were so many more of them. On one hand. men appreciated women for standing shoulder to shoulder. But they

Women assemble the tail fuselage of a B-17 "Flying Fortress" bomber at the Douglas Aircraft Company in Long Beach, California.

resented them, too. The trade union movements believed that a man's skills were belittled if women could aquire them; women never received more than two-thirds of the money for the same job. Women were patronized ("Joan's doing a real job!", "No woman will ever have peace in her heart unless she helps this man!"). And snubbed: those who served in the anti-aircraft batteries, for example, were not allowed to wear the badges of their male comrades until Churchill happened to find out and got that changed – he said it was wounding, and he was right. In the BBC, a bastion of old-fashioned values, women were recruited as engineers, did exactly the same heavy work on the transmitters and took the same responsibilities in the studios and recording rooms, but were never called engineers; they were merely "operators". For the time being, women did their bit, putting in ten- and twelve-hour shifts, played hard if the opportunity arose and the fancy took them – and stored up ammunition for a battle of the sexes that was yet to come.

Women in the US also went to work in the war effort – 18 million by the end of 1945, a

The film of a book that showed sexual attitudes during World War Two.

third of the workforce. "Rosie the Riveter" became a national emblem. Women's experience there was much the same as in Britain, with one difference: there was jealousy between those who went into the factories and those who stayed at home. Accusations of "men stealing" on the production line made some factories impose a ban on make-up and tight sweaters, it was said that men virtually vanished from the streets of America – *They're Either Too Young or Too Old* became a popular song. On one college campus the ratio of women to men reversed from one to five to eight to one – colleges held seminars on how women could attract whatever men were available. On the big bases, however, there were men aplenty. In his history of the Second World War, James Jones, author of *From Here to Eternity*, gave this eye-witness account in Memphis:

> At just about any time of day or night there were always between half a dozen and a dozen wide-open drinking parties going in the rooms and suites...Money was not much of a problem. Nor were women. There was always plenty of booze from somebody and there were also unattached women at the hotel floor parties. You could always go up to the Starlight Roof and find yourself a nice girl and dance with her awhile and bring her down. Everybody screwed. Sometimes it did not even matter if there were other people in the room.

Unlike in the First World War, the British army was issued with condoms in the Second, in

2000
1990
1980
1970
1960
1950
1940
1930
1920
1910
1900

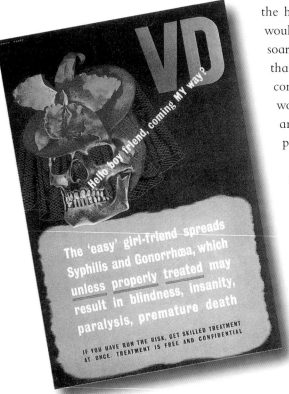

the hope, if not the expectation, that venereal disease would be controlled. In fact, during the first two years, it soared 70 per cent; by then the US army was finding out that 60,000 of the first million men drafted were contagious. Once US troops were in Britain, the figures worsened and the military said very little of it had anything to do with prostitutes. The Canadians pressed the War Office on the matter:

> For many months past the Canadian Corps Commander and this Headquarters have watched the increase in Venereal Disease among Canadian Troops with the greatest anxiety... Whenever possible we have endeavoured to identify and trace the source of infection, and in many cases it has been determined that one woman has been the cause of a multiplicity of cases.

Despite the films about VD and the sex instruction, the level of understanding among some soldiers in both armies was

Graphic posters warned against VD – but were largely ignored.

almost non-existent. They thought that VD could only be caught from prostitutes: or that and cured by having intercourse with a virgin: or that it could be got rid of by "passing it on".

VD was an epidemic in the First World War. It was not in the Second – but it was more than a nuisance. It might not have been even that if, during the Thirties – when the sulphonomides were developed – Britain and America had been less coy about tackling the disease. As American Surgeon General Thomas Parran wrote in *Reader's Digest*:

> We might virtually stamp out this disease were we

The enemy remains constant, whoever is fighting. This poster is from the Spanish Civil War.

not hampered by the widespread belief that nice people don't have syphilis, and that nice people shouldn't do anything about those who do have syphilis.

Early into the war, the British Ministry of Health approached the matter with long-handled tongs, producing a discreet leaflet that spoke of "the fineness and the lasting happiness of the right kind of sexual relationships"; self-control, it maintained, was the only reliable way to avoid catching venereal disease. Advertisements were placed in newspapers – a futile exercise because the Ministry allowed itself to be persuaded that some of the terminology was too explicit. What therefore appeared informed readers that the first indication of syphilis was an ulcer: the explanatory phrase "on or near the sex organs" had been excised.

It was, as Richard Davenport-Hine wrote in *Sex, Death and Punishment*, only the arrival of hundreds of thousands of Americans in 1942 – who helped send the incidence of VD soaring – "that the British Government became energetic." A series of direct notices appeared in all the women's magazines, warning of the hazards of casual sex; several hundred thousand posters were printed as part of the biggest public health campaign every mounted in the country until that time. Even the British Board of Film Control, which for a year had refused to allow an American drama-documentary, *No Greater Sin*, to be released because it fell foul of the "propaganda" argument, was forced to change its mind. The campaign, it was claimed, kept 15,000 men free of VD – the equivalent of an infantry division.

In war, when men are not fighting, they are thinking about sex – as the comedian Lenny Bruce was to say, if men were alone on a desert island they would do it to the mud. In every theatre of war in the six-year conflict, there were women prepared to offer sex, even when money did not change hands. Men always thought that other men elsewhere were getting sex. Sailors, probably, had fewer opportunities than other servicemen, but even in the Pacific there were some.

What is true is that men overseas were universally jealous of those at home. When Frank Sinatra, who was starting to make the bobbysoxers swoon in the early Forties, flew out to sing for the troops on a USO tour, he was booed. Ol' Blue Eyes, Young Blue Eyes then, was a symbol of a perceived threat. Men have always had a capacity for separating sex from love: it is a characteristic which, until this final decade of the twentieth century begins to show some signs of changing, has been a significant difference between most men and most women. During the Second World War for servicemen the world over, sex was sex. But, sometimes, there was love, poignant and almost certainly doomed. That is how it was for Nigel Davidson, a young Scots Guard commissioned straight from Oxford University, who had an intense affair with an educated Egyptian in Cairo. Because she had private means and was able to fly to join him as the war moved him around the Middle East, the affair was protracted. But the final goodbye came when he was posted to Italy. "I think that at one time Amina would have been terribly upset if she had thought that it wasn't going to be a life-long thing," he says, half a life-time later. "But war is war."

US servicemen overseas resented the men back at home – including new heartthrob Frank Sinatra.

Davidson learnt early in his army career that men in wartime will do anything for sex. Before leaving England he had been sent to Birkenhead to look after 2,300 French sailors who had been dispossessed of their ships in Portsmouth after the quisling Vichy government signed an armistice with Germany. One sailor tried to get through the perimeter wire, not to escape but "because hundreds of young women were outside ogling the men." It got him shot. Davidson shrugs: "A French sailor is a French sailor." And a British Tommy is a British Tommy. Davidson remembers how, in Cairo, British troops persisted in going to the brothel area and the ways in which the army tried to prevent them: "There was a kind of hall with photographs of men and women with the effects of venereal disease on them.

Guardsmen were made to march through and see these ghastly photographs of people in the last state of decay … sexual organs and other organs eaten away. They were very explicit and made tough guardsmen sick." But that did not stop them returning to the brothels. Patrols had "to remove men from beds" and continued doing so "until we moved into the Western Desert and there was no temptation for 400 miles."

The Americans were more aggressive in their approach to containing VD, but they were no more successful. Somewhere, in every theatre of war, the same posters looked down: "SHE MAY BE CLEAN – BUT". *Yank* magazine carried warning articles. Every six months, GIs were made to sit through more medical films. Every month they picked up their entitlement of eight condoms – 50 million in total, before the war ended. And promptly they went out to put themselves at risk. By the time the Americans got to Italy, the VD rate was 150 per 1,000 and the military authorities were hauling infected men off to the stockade where "VD" was painted in red on their uniforms; if they had been fraternizing with a German women they also got a $65-dollar fine. But none of that made any difference, either. Naples had 50,000 prostitutes; they infected one man in ten.

Five months before the war in Europe ended, news that a cure for the clap – penicillin – reached the front. The VD rate went off the scale. If apprehension about contracting venereal disease had held some men back, it did not do so now. Why should it when all a man had to do was to present his rump to a medic's needle for "the magic bullet?"

And what about prophylaxes and the enlisted woman? When an American report showed that 60 percent of enlisted women were sexually active, a decision was taken in 1943 to issue contraceptives to them. The story was leaked to the press. The decision was withdrawn. One could say that at least the Americans gave it some thought: it never entered British heads. Nonetheless, the reversal was a small-minded discrimination which indicated that, somehow, women were not as important as men. It was short-sighted, too: given the circumstances of war, the proximity in which serving men and women worked, it was most probable that, if they were having sex, it was with each other.

WAR WIVES

Across the two world wars, thousands of couples got married before men were conscripted or before they were posted overseas. Many were already engaged: war simply hurried things along. Others married hastily before or during war, ceremonies conducted on weekend passes, frequently between people who hardly knew each other. War made many unsuitable bedfellows in moments of rash romanticism. In the two years following the sinking of the *Lusitania* in 1915 during which Woodrow Wilson mobilized American public opinion, some men got married because they thought it was a way to dodge the draft. Stateside, in the Second, weddings rose 50 per cent after Pearl Harbor – only now men wanted someone to come back to. As war dragged on in both conflicts, the average age of brides fell.

In 1944 Daphne was sixteen. She lived in a village seven miles from Tunbridge Wells in Kent where, although under age, she worked as a live-in barmaid in a pub. She fell in love

One of 500 British GI brides, with 190 babies, leave London in 1946, prior to sailing to America to join their husbands.

*A group of British GI brides attend a meeting in Caxton Hall in 1945 to
protest about delays in their going to America.*

with an eighteen-year-old Canadian serviceman named Bill Smith and became pregnant. "It
was happening all over the country," Bill says, looking back. Daphne's mother wanted her to
"have the baby taken" but her father, home on leave from the RAF, "just put his arms round
me and cried and said, 'Do what you want to do.'" Daphne wore a borrowed dress when she
and Bill were married by special licence. Almost immediately he went away: D-Day had
come. He did not see his daughter until she was eleven months old.

   War begets babies: "farewell" babies, "welcome-home" babies. Sadly it also begets
unwanted babies. In the First World War the illegitimacy rate in Britain rose from 40,000 per
million to 60,000; in the Second, the year's figure of 26,000 at the beginning, in a birthrate of
650,000, became 63,000 in a slightly higher total at the end. Before the war, three-quarters of
premarital conceptions resulted in marriage before the child was born. The call-up took some
males away before this could happen, but it accounted for only a small percentage. The
greatest number of illegitimate births was not among teenagers but in the thirty to thirty-five

age group. A Home Intelligence report in 1944 deplored the "predatoriness" of some women "said to be duping as many as three or four US soldiers to provide for their coming child".

Among working people, unmarried motherhood became less of a stigma, but further up the social scale it engendered the same hostility as had been usual during the First World War – when it came down to it, whatever the relaxation of morality, a wedding ring was still the seal of respectability when it came to motherhood. During the 1914–18 conflict, many younger unmarried mothers found themselves taken into harsh Church homes and other institutions which "washed the mud of sin" from them and often sent their infants for adoption against their will. At least that did not happen so frequently thirty years on. Nor did the incumbent Archbishop of Canterbury fulminate against the army for paying allowances to common-law wives as had his predecessor in 1915. But women who had a child outside a legitimized union still had a difficult time, none more than those who found themselves pregnant while their husbands were overseas. Abortion was illegal (although many resorted to it) and it was impossible to have a child adopted without a husband's consent, even if he was not the father. Those in the worst predicament were those who lived in small communities where everyone knew everyone else and, one way or another, absent husbands were sure to be informed. There was, of course, subterfuge – if a woman could get away with it. In the post-war film *Stalag 17*, an American interned in a German POW camp reads a letter, and repeats over and over: "I believe it." "What do you believe?" another POW asks him:

My wife. She says "Darling, you won't believe it, but I found the most adorable baby on our doorstep. And I've decided to keep it for our very own. Now you won't believe it, but it's got exactly my eyes and nose." Why does she keep saying that I won't believe it? I believe it … I believe it … I believe it.

Perhaps. Most women in such a situation could only tell their husbands the truth and ask for forgiveness, if they wanted to save their marriage. A lot of men did forgive, but only on condition that the child be put up for adoption. Some men, however, were prepared to accept a child as their own. "I know of several in my own area," says Bill Smith, who settled here. "I admired the men who did that."

Letters kept relationships alive during both wars. Those from servicemen overseas were censored of anything that might be useful to the enemy, but the words that mattered peered through the inking-out, often expressing, however haltingly, what might not have been possible in spoken words. Every letter was a link, making chains that bound hearts to one another. The services urged men to write home; governments urged women at home to write to their men: a man who had someone to fight for, would fight. During the Second World War the Americans, with their flair for slogans, put more energy into organizing the traffic that streamed in both directions. "V-Mail is speed mail". "You write. He'll fight". "Be with him at every mail call". "Can you pass a mail-box with a clear conscience?" Men on active duty had less opportunity to write than those at home, yet what they wrote arrived more regularly – war moved men to where the fighting took them and the letters had to catch up. Sometimes men would receive no letters for lengthy periods, then get three or four together.

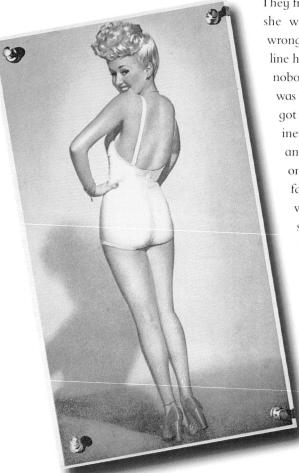

The most popular pin-up of the war: Betty Grable.

They fretted when there was nothing. Why the delay? Had she written? Had she not bothered? Was something wrong? It worked the other way, too, but men in the front line had a better excuse; if at times they did not, there was nobody to tell. At either end of the chain, a letter received was a declaration of love renewed. The back-up services got requests to buy gifts for wives and sweethearts – inevitably black lace underwear and negligees. Men and women planned what they would do together once the war was over. Letters fed dreams. And created fantasies. Distance lent women greater beauty, warmth and understanding; men, better looks, strength and character. When the war *was* over, the realities turned into disappointment for some.

During the Second World War the Americans created a collective fantasy so potent that the British adopted it as well: the pin-up. The word was not known before the war. Soon, the pin-up was everywhere, on barrack-room walls, on the inside of tanks and planes. Alberto Vargas's Girls in *Esquire* were as prized as the Hollywood stars – Lana Turner in her sweater, Rita Hayward, Marie MacDonald. Betty Grable in her bathing suit, her back to the camera, smiling provocatively over her shoulder, was the most popular of all. Those legs: a million dollars. American aircrews painted women on the noses of their B17s; the first to complete twenty-five missions was adorned by the Memphis Belle.

It would not be fanciful to say that, in both pin-up and aerial art, men were using female sexuality as a kind of shield, a talisman. But the woman who wrote to Monsignor William Arnold, the US Forces' Chief of Chaplains, to complain about the naked images painted on bombers she had seen in a newsreel, would not have been interested in the point of view. She considered the paintings "barbarous" and went on to say of the young men who were responsible: "They have left wives and little babies at home. It can be very little comfort to their suffering wives to see their husbands represented as wild pagans with no thought for decency." The Chief of Chaplains who – when he was not cataloguing complaints about profanity, dirty magazines and indecent advertisements that offered "wares for the prurient-minded" was busy trying to persuade comics like Bob Hope not to tell "unfit" jokes in front of mixed services audiences – drafted an order seeking efforts to stamp out "the transgressions of normal bounds of decency." No-one took any notice. In the roar of war the voice of the moralist was drowned out.

POST-WAR MORALITY

As the Second World War was entering its end-game in 1945, the US military compiled a report which it did not make public; indeed it thought it expedient to keep it classified for nearly forty years. It showed that half the married men stationed overseas for longer than two years had sex – as had eight out of every ten men. Whatever their own sexual behaviour, husbands' expectation concerning the virtuousness of their wives was little different in the Forties from that of their Victorian forebears. To find out otherwise was devastating. To receive a "Dear John" letter was, as *Playboy* put it, "like a bullet in the heart."

Bomber art: to some it was "barbarous", to the men who flew it was good luck.

> I have taken up with another man and am due to be laid up with his baby in May. It has been heartbreaking without you and I have tried but we were tempted and fell, nobody is infallible. I shall be living with this man. I would have waited until you came home to tell you but the baby is coming and I cannot wait.

This was written in 1916. Given a phrase or two, it could have been written thirty years later. Thousands were. Some men came home thinking everything was fine to find that their wives, either because of cowardice or decency, had waited to tell them there was someone else. Typically, some men reacted with violence. In *Britain in the Second World War*, Harold L. Smith wrote:

> Although it was accepted that husbands in the armed forces would engage in sexual activity, marital conflict often resulted when wives did so while their husbands were away. Judges upheld the right of husbands to punish their wives physically, even to the point of death.

Those men who took their spouses' lives did not face the death penalty. No man in Britain was sentenced to more than five years and some were set free without penalty. That there was a double standard in sexual relations was undeniable and some women, like Dorothy Wilson who wrote to *Wife and Citizen* in August 1945, were indignant:

There can be few of us who have not felt considerably irritated by the one-sided outlook portrayed in the spate of heartbreak articles which

Rita Hayworth (opposite): wartime pin-up – and icon of a new sexual frankness.

have appeared lately on the unhappy plight of servicemen returning home to discover their wives have been sexually unfaithful. Whether mere physical satisfaction, sought while a loved partner is forced to be absent for years … should be called unfaithfulness is a debatable subject. In the past it was a debatable point whether there should be licence in sexual matters. THIS IS NO LONGER SO! The War Office, in allowing the free issue of contraceptives to men serving abroad, whether married or single, has adopted the principle that married men must be free in these matters. We civilians have acquiesced in the adoption of this principle in that we have not raised our voices against it. We have not even insisted that the issue of contraceptives should only be made to men whose wives are agreeable. There has been no suggestion of issuing contraceptives to wives who have had to adjust themselves to living without their service husbands for four or five years or longer. WHY THIS DIFFERENCE? The sudden cessation of their sex life has been as unendurable a privation to these women as their partners. These women, in facing the hardships of life on the Home Front, have been warriors no less courageous than their men serving abroad. Not only have men and women failed to admit and recognize that a woman's sexual needs are as urgent as a man's, but the pendulum has swung as sharply as ever in the opposite direction, giving the male partner in marriage greater freedom and at the same time attempting to tie the woman more closely … Are we to slip back to the principles of the so-called Dark Ages or shall we go forward?

The end of in both world conflicts sent the divorce rate rocketing – in Britain, in 1918, to an unprecedented 1,000, in 1947 to another unprecedented total of 60,000. Between 1940 and

1946 in America the rate doubled and reached a million by the end of the decade. In the vast majority of cases, men cited their spouses for adultery. Yet neither country stopped believing that love and marriage were horse and carriage or that, when society's strictures were reimposed, it was morally unacceptable to have one without the other. After World War Two, marriage boomed on both sides of the Atlantic – rising to 16.4 per 1,000 in the US,, a quarter more than in 1942; 50,000 British brides went to America along with

Journey's end for GI brides as a transport ship docks in New York. For some, however, wartime romance would turn to disappointment in the reality of peace.

2000
1990
1980
1970
1960
1950
1940
1930
1920
1910
1900

German, French and Italian. The transition was not necessarily easy. Cultures clashed; expectations were sometimes too high. And, divested of their sharp uniforms, less glamorous in routine jobs, some men may now have seemed less of a catch. As one marriage counsellor was to remark: "For too long American men have been using chewing gum and chocolates instead of conversation."

Hollywood – which turned out 1,700 films during 1942–45, 500 of them with war themes – picked up the sexual tensions which the war engendered and reflected the changing sexual climate. The comedy *The Miracle of Morgan's Creek* – in which small-town girl Betty Hutton gets drunk at an army party, marries a soldier whose name she cannot remember, has trouble getting someone else to marry her without admitting she is pregnant, and finally becomes a heroine by presenting the nation with sextuplets – was an outrageously accurate comment on the morals of war. More influentially there was film noir – including such movies as *The Maltese Falcon, Double Indemnity, The Postman Always Rings Twice, Dead Reckoning, Gilda* among others – which juggled the idealization of women that became part of servicemen's fantasies, with their paranoia that, in their absence, women might be behaving like whores. Film noir also showed that women had become more sexually open – and no longer necessarily saw marriage as the only pathway to expression of their sexual desires, or children as the only fulfilment. Men no longer necessarily ruled the sexual roost simply because they were men. Women were no longer passive and were as capable of betrayal as men. As Alan Ladd's unfaithful wife Veronica Lake told him in *The Blue Dahlia*: "I go where I want with anybody I want. I just happen to be that kind of girl." And women were as capable of revenge as men, if betrayed – Jane Greer in *Out of the Past* emptying a revolver into Robert Mitchum's groin.

With the changing sexual mores, the Production Code gradually gave way. At one time, anything that appeared to undermine the sanctity of marriage would have had the Hays Office hopping. By 1944 the *Miracle of Morgan's Creek* was passed without any cuts. The sexual act was still forbidden, but film-makers were now masters of the metaphor. In *Gilda*, Rita Hayworth only removed a long evening glove – but the illusion was that she stripped naked; when she danced erotically in *Miss Sadie Thompson*, as Gerard Lenne wrote in *Sex on the Screen*, "the overflowing froth on the sailors' beer mugs [was] an obvious allusion to ejaculation."

Since Harlow, breasts had given the censors problems. In 1941 the billionaire eccentric Howard Hughes almost gave Code enforcer Joe Breen apoplexy. After viewing his film *The Outlaw*, which starred Jane Russell, Breen wrote to Hughes:

> In my more than ten years of critical examination of motion pictures, I have never seen anything quite so unacceptable as the shots of the breasts of the character of Rio … Throughout almost half the picture the girl's breasts, which are quite large and prominent, are shockingly emphasized and in almost every instance are very substantially uncovered.

Breen ordered thirty-seven breast-shot cuts. Hughes refused. Two years later he booked the finished film – "*The Outlaw* conclusively proves that sex has not yet been rationed" – without a seal of approval, into a San Francisco theatre for a sell-out showing, then mysteriously took

The dates along the right margin: 2000 1990 1980 1970 1960 1950 1940 1930 1920 1910 1900

The Outlaw *was a fanciful tale of an encounter between Billy the Kid and Doc Holliday, but was really about Jane Russell's cleavage.*

it out of circulation for three years. Re-released, still without the Hays imprimatur, *The Outlaw* became a sensation. A judge, upholding the ban on the film, declared that Russell's breasts "hung over the picture like a thunderstorm over a landscape."

Breasts – Margaret Lockwood's – made *The Wicked Lady* the first British film to be censored by the Hays Office. Throughout the war years, British films were long on stiff upper lips and short of carnality. But Lockwood and her leering co-star James Mason gave *The Wicked Lady* a sexual jolt. But the British had side-stepped the issues of sexuality raised in the current climate: the film was period stuff. Still, as Tom Dewe Mathews wrote in *Censored*, the way in which the couple "mauled, punched, scratched, slapped and whipped each other in a frenzy of subliminal sex" wowed the box-office. British contemporary convention demanded that the pair pay for their hedonism with their lives, "but film-goers were quick to forget the moral message as they revelled in the unholy couple's exhilarating ride to damnation."

The Wicked Lady, *starring Margaret Lockwood, brought sexuality to British film-making.*
It was the first British film to be cut by Hollywood censors.

And yet, as the war ended, it was another British film which was a portent of the immediate post-war future. *Brief Encounter* gave the cinema two middle-class, middle-aged lovers, Trevor Howard and Celia Johnson, married to other partners, who gave up their wartime affair, to the strains of Rachmaninov, to do what was right. "Doing what was right" was what millions of women did: they gave up their war-time jobs to the returning men – and went back to the kitchen.

Women had tasted a degree of equality, and economic freedom, during the First World War when they contributed to the war effort. What they did even won them the vote – "a symbol," as Reay Tannahill wrote in *Sex in History*, "representing the end, at long last, of 5,000 years of masculine supremacy." But they ceded to the masculine order at war's end. As Tannahill further commented about the vote: "It would take almost forty years for women in Britain and America to realize that it *was* only a symbol. Another revolution was needed." The pattern was repeated at the end of the Second World War: women moved over to allow men back into their jobs. Of course, they had no choice, but they did so with little fuss – something that the feminists of the Sixties would contemplate with perplexity.

There were reasons: relief that the war was over, happiness that the men were back, desire for stability. The post-war period was not a time for sexual revolution. In a devastated Britain that faced the long process of rebuilding, where shortages and rationing were to stretch into the next decade; in America, untouched by the destruction of war, where an immediate boom brought new homes filled with new consumer goods, women were offered a future that simply appeared too enticing. And both sexes, whether or not they had secrets they would not tell, wanted to delude themselves that "everything could be the same," whatever that meant, and that the shifts in the balance of power between the sexes could be ignored.

But twenty of the forty years that Tannahill talked about had elapsed. The countdown continued. Women would not always accept the status quo. As British Home Secretary Herbert Morrison, a keen advocate of women doing war work, remarked: "You can't help thinking they're going to be a little hoity-toity after the War."

Women were offered an enticing post-war world but found it less than enticing.

"THE DECADENCE OF THE ROMAN EMPIRE"

WHAT WAS THE STATE OF SEXUAL RELATIONS IN THE POST-WAR YEARS WHEN THE SOCIAL FRAMEWORK WAS BOLTED BACK TOGETHER ON BOTH SIDES OF THE ATLANTIC? THE VENEER WAS CERTAINLY POLISHED BRIGHT. THE BABY BOOM RAISED THE BIRTH-RATE IN AMERICA, WHERE THE DEPRESSION HAD LOWERED IT TO 18.4 PER 1,000, TO 25.3 PER 1,000. FAMILIES WITH THREE CHILDREN DOUBLED, THOSE WITH FOUR, TRIPLED. THE US POPULATION INCREASED BY 28 MILLION IN TEN YEARS AT A RATE FASTER THAN INDIA'S AND THERE APPEARED TO BE AS MANY COPIES OF THE WORKS OF DR BENJAMIN SPOCK AS THERE WERE BIBLES. IN BRITAIN THE BIRTH-RATE DID NOT BEGIN TO RISE UNTIL THE FIFTIES, WHEN THE COUNTRY FINALLY CRAWLED OUT FROM UNDERNEATH THE BOMB-DAMAGE. BRIDES GOT YOUNGER: HALF OF THOSE IN AMERICA WERE TWENTY, HALF OF THOSE IN BRITAIN UNDER TWENTY-FIVE.

Hosts of government committees and programmes in the US and the UK bolstered marriage and the family as the bedrock of society – a bulwark against the global fear of the new Cold War. Stateside, national prosperity ensured that most newlyweds could move into new homes that mushroomed around the big cities. "For the first time in our history," said *McCalls* magazine, "the majority of men and women own their own homes and millions of these people gain their deepest satisfaction from making them their very own." Britain had to wait before it could afford to start similar developments; in the meantime, most young couples started married life living with the in-laws, usually hers.

The 1957 film version of Grace Metalious's **Peyton Place** *started a fashion for small-town sex exposés.* **Peyton Place** *later became a long-running television series.*

But all was not sexual sweetness and familial light. Beneath the veneer there were tensions. Some men missed the excitement of their war and the sexual freedoms that went with it, and could not settle into the bland routine of everyday respectability. American women, with none of the day-to-day hardships faced by women in Britain, had time to resent the replacement of the masculine status quo and the loss of their wartime freedoms. Some fantasized about living in a small town like *Peyton Place* where the sex was rampant; more simply popped tranquillizers and, as the teenage phenomenon took hold of the culture, worried what their daughters were doing with whom. On both sides of the Atlantic, women felt locked in – even by fashion, which put them into buttressed bras and panty-girdles that sculpted them into almost Victorian shapes, appeared to remove their nipples and made their flesh inert. Even the sexuality of the film noir blonde was disarmed, or humoured, or made virginal again, reincarnated as Doris Day. Screen womanhood could be carnal, but only if it was child and cartoon at the same time: Jayne Mansfield and Marilyn Monroe could have come to life from the nose of a B17.

"A sex symbol becomes a thing,"said Marilyn Monroe (opposite). "I hate being a thing."

2000

1990

1980

1970

1960

1950

1940

1930

1920

1910

1900

In Britain, apparent male supremacy reinstated itself so firmly that a 1950s guide on *How To Be The Perfect Wife* could advise:

> Be a little gay ... catering for his comfort will provide you with immense personal satisfaction ... show sincerity in your desire to please ... speak in a low, soothing and pleasant voice ... remember he is the master and as such will always exercise his will with fairness and truthfulness ... you have no right to question him ... a good wife always knows her place.

But what was that place? The missionary position, on demand or, at least, request? Was there any sexual equality? Was there nothing more to human sexuality that profunctuary procreative intercourse passionlessly conducted behind the bedroom door? Perhaps sex did not happen – that was certainly an inference to be drawn from the situation comedies on the new medium of television which blanketed America and then Britain. In television's never-never land even pregnancies (known as "expectancies") appeared to happen by divine intervention. Of course sex was happening. But what did people *do*? What did they think? What did they think others thought, or did? The early post-war years may have raised such questions but did not ask them. That was before Dr Alfred Charles Kinsey provided the answers without being asked, in statistical detail, exposing the chasm that existed between what America supposed – or at least was prepared to admit — and what the story really was.

THE KINSEY REVOLUTION

Alfred Kinsey was a biologist from Indiana University, Bloomington, who had spent 18 years studying the gall wasp. In 1938, when the university began a marriage course, he was one of the professors from different faculties who began teaching it. Questions his students asked led him to start taking down their sexual histories. Right from the very beginning he created controversy by asking male and female students about the frequency of their orgasms and female students about the length of their clitorises. There were complaints from local clergy and from other academic staff who thought he should at least say that premarital sex was wrong. Nevertheless, two years later, with the university's backing and funding from the Rockefeller Foundation, Kinsey founded the Institute of Sex Research.

Kinsey, who had collected four million gall wasps in his career and personally taken 700,000 separate measurements of them,

Father of the Sexual Revolution, Alfred Kinsey, who set himself the staggering goal of collecting 100,000 sexual histories.

believed in sampling. Before him, no sexologist had based findings on more than a few hundred case histories. Kinsey the entomologist regarded that as "puny". He admired Freud as a theoretician, but was critical of the small database on which his theoretical edifice was constructed. Above all, he admired Havelock Ellis, but was equally unimpressed by his research (Ellis presented only thirty-three homosexual and six lesbian case histories in *Sexual Perversion*, the first volume of *Studies in the Psychology of Sex*). Having looked at the work of those who proceeded him, Kinsey remarked: "You know, there isn't much science here." He set himself the astounding goal of amassing 100,000 case histories and mapped out his projects for the next twenty years: *Sexual Behavior in the Human Male; Sexual Behavior in the Human Female; Sexual Outlet in the Negro; Sex Offenses and Sex Offenders; Sex Factors in Marital Adjustment; The Heterosexual-Homosexual Balance; Sexual Adjustment in Penal Institutions; Sex Education;* and *Prostitutes, Male and Female.*

Sexual Behavior in the Human Male, the distillation of 1,800 interviews, thumped on to the bookstands in January 1948. It was 804 pages long and weighed three pounds. From its thicket of prose, charts and diagrams, America learnt that:

- two-thirds of men with higher education, and virtually all of those with lower education, had intercourse before they married – an average of 85%.

Time magazine described Kinsey – here with wife Cora, son (behind) and two daughters with their husbands – as an "almost monotonously normal human being". But Kinsey had dark secrets.

2000

1990

1980

1970

1960

1950

1940

1930

1920

1910

1900

Only four people had access to Kinsey's case histories. One was his associate, Wardell Pomeroy, seen conducting an interview – which typically took two to four hours.

- 40% of married men were unfaithful.
- 69% had some experience of prostitutes.
- 92% masturbated, often in middle and old age.
- only 62% over the age of 55 found sexual release through intercourse with their wives, 19% achieving orgasm (Kinsey preferred the word "outlets") from "the dream world which accompanies masturbation or nocturnal emissions."
- 37% had reached orgasm at least once through homosexual contact and for 10% contact was more than casual.

As for oral sex, Kinsey noted: "Mouth-genital contacts of some sort, with the subject as either the active or the passive member in the relationship, occur at some time in the histories of nearly 60 per cent of all males."

Kinsey went on to emphasize that neither human male nor female was "inherently" monogamous. Furthermore, he said, everyone was "pan-sexual", an individual mix of overlapping heterosexual and homosexual impulses (as Ellis and others maintained). He put forward a seven-point scale on which exclusive heterosexuality registered zero and exclusive homosexuality a seven – and most people were somewhere in between. Among his interviewees, he pointed out, were those whose only homosexual contacts had been during pre-adolescent sex play; those whose homosexual experience had been limited to one partner on a single occasion; those whose homosexual behaviour was prodigious, involving as many as 20,000 contacts; and those who maintained a bisexual balance throughout their lives. "There is no American pattern of sexual behaviour but scores of patterns," Kinsey wrote, "each of which is confined to a particular segment of our society." Like Ellis, he separated sexuality from morality: "This is first of all a report on what people do, which raises no question of what they should do."

In an America where adultery remained an offence in almost all states (at least on paper), fornication in three-quarters, and the dissemination of information on birth control and venereal disease in some, Professor Kinsey – "Prok" to his friends – became a folk hero almost overnight. Journalists told America bout the man they dubbed "Doctor Sex". The middle-aged father of three came from a Methodist background, loved classical music, flowers and was an expert on ornithology. Kinsey could not have been more "Middle America" – a fact that helped to endorse his objectivity as a scientist. Indeed, *Time* magazine, making some fun of his crew cut and his penchant for bow ties, described him as "an almost monotonously normal human being." Kinsey was asked to endorse everything from bras to Simone de Beauvoir's soon-to-be-celebrated feminist book, *The Second Sex*. Politicians wanted to be seen to endorse him – at a Republican convention in Philadelphia delegates wore "We want Kinsey, the people's choice" badges. Mae West asked to meet him. When he gave a talk in a basketball stadium, 9,000 people crammed in – 2,000 more than the record attendance at a game there. "Hotter than Kinsey" became a national figure of speech and comedians had a field day – there was irresistible material in all the recesses of *The Kinsey Report*: the average American man had 1,523 orgasms before marriage, compared with a woman's 223; compared with the 2.88 orgasms a week experienced by the average man between adolescence and the age of thirty, one of Kinsey's case histories averaged thirty a week for more than thirty years; 75 per cent of men ejaculated within two minutes of beginning intercourse. Kinsey even made sex a matter of geometry: the angle of erection in most men was slightly above the horizontal, but forty-five degrees in 15–20 per cent of men. And gave a new twist to Hamlet's "country matters": one in six farm boys experimented with zoophilia.

If the mainstream media was overwhelmingly favourable to Kinsey, some publications were not. A number of papers refused to carry any details. The *Reader's Digest* asked: "Have our conventions and modesty … been outmoded by the findings of modern science?" Predictably, men of the cloth were outraged. The Right Reverend Monsignor Maurice Sheeny of Washington's Catholic Union of America declared *Sexual Behavior in the Human Male* to be "the most anti-religious book of our times." That judgement was of no concern to Kinsey who regarded religion as the fount of repression and human misery. But an attack by the distinguished cultural anthropologist Margaret Mead did wound him. She criticized him "for upsetting the balance between ignorance and knowledge upon which social restraint depends." Mead also attacked his "flagrant puritanism": "Nowhere have I been able to find a single suggestion that sex is any fun, not anywhere in the book, not a suggestion." To Kinsey, Mead suggested, sex was sex and there was little for a man to choose "between a woman and a sheep." There were more balanced assessments. Perhaps the most considered came from the lawyer Morris Ernst (successful defender of James Joyce's *Ulysses* against the US Customs and advocate of freely available birth-control literature) who in 1949 told a gathering of scientists:

Our laws have attempted to abolish all sexual outlets except marital intercourse, nocturnal emissions and to some extent solitary masturbation. The first Kinsey Report says that 85 per cent of all younger males are criminals, since they make use of other sexual outlets. Forty-four states have laws against adultery. There have been only a handful of prosecutions. Yet the Kinsey Report may well, in its final national overall figures, show that one-third of all husbands should be in jail if fact and law were the same.

Ernst poked fun at some anomalies:

For example, is there more fornication in Louisiana, where it is not a crime, than in Arkansas, where a first offense is appraised as worth $20? What about the amount of sodomy in Georgia, where the punishment is life, compared with New Hampshire, where it is not covered by a special statute? And if you have seduction in your heart, or wherever it resides, I suggest you pick Vermont or Utah rather than Georgia. It may spell a difference of twenty years of freedom to you.

In Britain, *The Lancet* gave the Kinsey Report a small review, recommending it to those interested in sexual deviation; the *British Medical Journal* merely listed it among "Books Received". The popular press, in the main, treated the report with mild ribaldry, although the *Sunday Pictorial* did commission a modest survey from Mass-Observation, a social research organization which in somewhat haphazard fashion had tried since the Thirties to keep track of the nation's sexual trends. Working within the restrictions of a tight budget and the pressures imposed by a panel of assessors made up of clergymen, doctors and marriage councillors – who saw to it that certain details did not get through into the five articles the *Sunday Pictorial* published – Mass-Observation's "Little Kinsey" as it was quickly labelled carried echoes of

Rock 'n' roll, an expression of youthful rebellion arrived in London in 1956.

its big parent: 58 per cent of men and 34 per cent of women had sex before marriage (usually with the person they later married); 25 per cent of men and 20 per cent of women committed adultery; 80 per cent of men masturbated; 12 per cent had some homosexual experience.

The statistics were almost certainly underestimates – in A *Secret World of Sex*, historian Steve Humphreys put the pre-marital sex percentages closer to 75 (male) and 50 (female). Even if they had been accurate, however, the national consciousness was not yet ready to accept their significance. A country in which many people confused austerity with moral rectitude was not ready to have a nest of sexual gall wasps stirred.

That was not the case in some circles, as jazz singer, writer and columnist George Melly can tell. "People imagine the 1950s were a very puritanical time. There was a general level of hypocrisy – authority still managed to present itself as respectable, very stiff and steady. But it was a pretty wild world

There was plenty of sex in austere Britain, if you were young and knew where to look, says jazz singer, George Melly, who fondly remembers "warm-hearted, promiscuous girls" all over England.

if you were young. The prostitutes thronged Soho, it was a sort of flower garden of them. If you wanted one you just went outside the door. But I beg to differ that other women had to be heavily seduced to have sex. There were women who made it perfectly obvious they were extremely keen on screwing. I remember finding myself on the floor having sex with a female journalist while others were playing darts at the other end of the room and one of them, irritated that I was screwing someone who was vaguely his girlfriend, threw a dart which landed quivering in my leg, turning me into a sort of prentice St Sebastian. Another beautiful girl came to bed in my dusty flat wearing black stockings and pearls. I thought, 'Well, this is really living, isn't it, this is what sophisticated London life is about.' There was plenty of sex if you wanted it and knew where to look for it."

2000

1990

1980

1970

1960

1950

1940

1930

1920

1910

1900

Melly had gone into art-dealing after the war but had left to join a jazz band. Britain, he remembers, as being "rather grim … as if we'd been occupied and were still occupied – but we did what we could to enliven it was drink and jazz and sex." On tour in the years of the jazz revival, he discovered "warm-hearted, promiscuous girls" all over England. "Preston across to Stoke-on-Trent, Liverpool, Leeds, Manchester – we called it the scrubber belt. These warm-hearted girls really liked sleeping with jazz musicians just as later the groupies liked sleeping with rock people. They were very loyal to us when we were in their area, we were their boyfriends until we moved on and they took up with somebody else from another band. I remain friends with some of them to this day, elderly ladies now, mostly rather respectable but not against the odd memory of times in Bradford or Oswaldtwistle in digs where the landlady used to say 'You married?'"

Senator Joseph McCarthy, very likely a closet homosexual, made America identify homosexuality with Communism.

McCARTHY AND HOOVER

During the Second World War, America was jittery about subversive activities and J. Edgar Hoover established a network of 60,000 volunteers to glean information about their neighbours – immorality was regarded as a likely sign of political degeneracy. The FBI bugged the high-class establishments where foreign diplomats went for sex and was not above a little sexual blackmail. The fear of communism spilled over into peace-time. In 1947 the House Un-American Activities Committee began questioning the patriotism of its fellow Americans, concentrating on Hollywood, the simple deduction being that communism equals decadence equals sex equals the movies. A number of stars came out against the "Red Tide" and – to their eternal shame – named names; more than 300 actors, writers and directors were blacklisted. Radio, television and others areas of society came under investigation; more lives were ruined. Then in 1950 – when the invasion of South Korea by the communist North drew the United Nations into a three-year war – an obscure senator from Wisconsin escalated anti-communism into a national witch-hunt.

Joseph McCarthy claimed to have a list of 205 names of prominent communists being harboured by the State Department, accused the Truman administration of being "soft on communism" and the Democratic party of a record of "twenty years of treason." He was unable to substantiate his claims; nevertheless, when

Eisenhower got into the White House three years later, McCarthy was elected chairman of the powerful Permanent Sub-Committee on Investigations and by hectoring cross-examination, damaging innuendo and guilt by association, he arraigned a large number of innocent people. Television audiences became hypnotized by his grating voice asking: "Are you or have you ever been a member of the Communist Party?"

What was ghoulish was that McCarthy, who was probably a homosexual, quickly made America specifically identify communism with homosexuality. In this he was helped by Hoover, whose closet queenery is in no doubt. Hoover said there were 3,500 "sex perverts" employed in the federal bureaucracy and later told Congress that the FBI had incriminating dossiers on 14,000 federal employees.

Hoover was a wilier man than McCarthy: he never went so far that he could not pull back. McCarthy overreached himself when he accused the army of "coddling communists," was ultimately condemned by the Senate and died in disgrace. But for four years this "pathological character assassin," as Truman called him, held America in the grip of a paranoia – a paranoia that resulted in a number of measures of censorship as the country attempted to root out degeneracy. Congress created a Select Committee on Current Pornographic Materials, its chairman saying it would go after "the kind of filthy sex books sold at the corner store which are affecting the youth of our country." It was the lurid covers on books by the likes of Hank Janson which outraged the moralists. Police confiscations, and prosecutions, became common in this climate of repression. A New York psychiatrist, Fred Wertham, latched on to the "pollution" in children's comics, warning that where pornography attracted perverts, comic books were making them. The way breasts were drawn upset Wertham particularly:

> One of the stock mental aphrodisiacs in comic books is to draw girls' breasts in such a way that they are sexually exciting. Wherever possible, they protrude and obtrude. Or girls are shown in slacks or

"The kind of filthy sex book" targeted by the Select Committee on Current Pornographic Materials.

The cover lines for **Hush-Hush** *(opposite) and* **Whisper** *magazines promised more than they delivered – but they led the way for the salacious* **Confidential.**

negligees with their pubic regions indicated with special care and suggestiveness.

The comic industry was forced to create a Code not unlike Hollywood's, prepared with help from Roman Catholic, Protestant and Jewish leaders.

Unintentionally, Kinsey contributed to the homosexual panic of the Fifties, but his assertion that ten per cent of men had some overt homosexual experience was only extra fuel: the fire was already alight. His report got Kinsey on to Hoover's hit list, the FBI opening a file on him and his institute; a special committee of the House of Representatives investigated charges that his research served communism by undermining the American family.

Kinsey was also unintentionally a factor in the launch of the most scurrilous scandal magazine America had seen: *Confidential*, which "Tells the Facts and Names the Names". "Kinsey was making people talk about sex," explains *Hollywood Babylon* author Kenneth Anger. "Robert Harrison who started *Confidential* said 'They want sex magazines? I'll give them sex magazines.' So he put them out there: *Whisper, Titter, Hush-Hush* – titillation, nothing hard-core. But the terrorist attacks by the likes of McCarthy, which didn't just want to know if people were Reds – asking whether they were sleeping with a communist spy led to whether they were dirty in bed – got Harrison thinking. The political thing had turned into the sexual thing and the sexual thing was much more interesting. The public wasn't that interested in who was a Red."

Harrison was right when he said that "Americans like to read about things they're afraid to do themselves." And he tore apart the lives of the country's most famous citizens who *were* doing such things, concentrating his efforts on Hollywood. Using telephoto lenses, infra-red film and the services of models, bit actresses and call girls who haunted the bars on Sunset Strip and made themselves

PRESLEY Does NOT Love 'Em TENDER!

WHISPER

PDC

June 25c

JAYNE MANSFIELD'S OVERNIGHT MICKEY

DANE CLARK'S BEDTIME STORY • THE REDHEAD UP IN RUBI'S ROOM
• LINDA CHRISTIAN'S CHUMMY CHA-CHA-CHA •
BILLY DANIELS AND THE CALL GIRL • HOW TO SPOT A SEX PSYCHO

Another soft-core title, available at the corner store, which the US authorities tried to ban.

sexually available – with miniature tape-recorders in their purses – Harrison told his readers that Frank Sinatra consumed a bowl of Wheaties between sexual encounters, that Errol Flynn had a two-way mirror in his bedroom, that Dan Dailey liked to dress in drag (so did Hoover, but no-one knew that at the time), that Lana Turner shared a lover with Ava Gardner, that Liberace liked boys, that "The Best Pumper In Hollywood" was "M-M-M Marilyn M-M-Monroe!" *Confidential* reached a circulation of four million, something never before achieved by any American publication, before its stories became such reckless tissues of lies that, like McCarthy, it combusted. In 1957, a number of stars including Dorothy Dandridge, Robert Mitchum and Maureen O'Hara – who was alleged to have had sex in a cinema with a Latin lover, "stretched out on three seats, the lucky South American occupying the middle chair" – sued. On the night before she was due to give evidence, one of *Confidential*'s editorial staff killed herself: she had been selling secrets to the prosecutor. Soon after the trial the magazine's editor-in-chief shot his wife in the back of a cab and then turned the gun on himself.

It was into this curious maelstrom of repression and hypocrisy, ultra-conservatism and sexual curiosity, that Kinsey dropped *Sexual Behavior in the Human Female*, five years after his first study. The basis for this second volume was now over 17,000 case histories; more importantly it was from a wider cross-section of the population: Kinsey had been criticized over *Sexual Behavior in the Human Male* because his findings had been based on all-white under-thirties from a cluster of six north-east states – which had probably skewed his results without invalidating them.

Now America learnt that:
- 50% of women lost their virginity before marriage (almost half to their fiancés, but a third had experience of intercourse with two to five partners and 13% with six or more)

The sex appeal of Jayne Mansfield (opposite) was a exaggerated as a painting on a wartime bomber.

- 34% of women who were still single at twenty-five had sex (compared with 14% of single women born before the turn of the century)
- 20% of married women over thirty-five were unfaithful and 40% of those who were younger
- 62% masturbated
- 66% had nocturnal sex dreams
- 13% had at least one homosexual contact that resulted in orgasm
- 3.6% had at least one sexual contact with a lower animal

In 1938, Lewis Terman, the creator of IQ tests, had looked into marital happiness in an intimate study of 792 couples and found that a third of women rarely, if ever, reached orgasm. This he considered "one of the most puzzling mysteries in the psychology and physiology of sex." Fifteen years later, Kinsey found that a quarter of women could not reach orgasm in the first year of marriage but that the figure was only one in seven by the tenth year. About half of all wives reached climax every time they made love.

The failure of many unmarried women to reach orgasm, Kinsey said, often inhibited their sex lives after marriage. It was clear to him that a woman's response to sexual stimulation was therefore learned behaviour. "Early orgasmic experience may, therefore, contribute directly to the sexual effectiveness of a marriage," Kinsey wrote, his message clear: pre-marital sex was

Squeaky-clean sex: Doris Day and Rock Hudson in **Pillow Talk** *– in two separate baths, of course.*

American comedy, **Father of the Bride,** *with Spencer Tracy and Elizabeth Taylor, captured all the pressures of a daughter's wedding – in the days when daughters got married!*

good practice for achieving good orgasm and a woman who saved herself for marriage was likely to be orgasmically inadequate. He dismissed the view, held by almost all psychologists who took a doctrinaire stand on the subject, that a climax achieved through clitoral stimulation was "juvenile" while vaginal orgasm was "mature". Vaginal orgasm was all but physiologically impossible.

He demolished the knee-jerk arguments against premarital sex with numbers. In a sample of 2,094 single white females, who between them had had intercourse some 460,000 times, only 476 resulted in pregnancy – one pregnancy for every 1,000 copulatory acts. In a sample of 1,753 women who had had premarital intercourse, only 44 had contracted venereal disease.

Kinsey reported cases of husbands encouraging their wives to have extramarital sex: "In some instances it represented a deliberate effort to extend the wife's opportunity to find satisfaction in sex relations. In not a few instances the husband's attitude had originated in his desire to find an excuse for his own extra-marital activity." He did not disapprove. But he did believe that a stable marriage depended on both partners having a good sex life, however it was achieved. Two-thirds of the marriages he investigated were in danger at some point because of sexual dissatisfaction. This observation was borne out by the number of men and women who sought aid from marriage counsellors. As the Fifties began, the infant Marriage Guidance Council in Britain expanded its clientele by a third to 18,000 people – and it would only counsel those who were married. Twice as many women as men sought divorce, and the divorce rate was rising steadily. In 1950 there were 385,000 in the US, compared with 264,000 in the last pre-war year. Britain's pre-war divorce rate had quadrupled to 32,000. The Royal Commission on Marriage and Divorce which reported in 1955 was so concerned by the British trend that it demanded less permissiveness, or there would be social disaster. "It may become necessary," it wrote, "to consider whether the community as a whole would not be happier and more stable if it abolished divorce altogether."

The hostile reactions that *Sexual Behavior in the Human Female* attracted like iron filings were predictable: the vocabulary of morality is limited. The Reverend Billy Graham concluded that it was "impossible to estimate the damage the book will do to the already deteriorating morals of America." Henry Pitney Van Dusen, head of the Union of Theological Seminaries, said Kinsey's view of sex was "strictly animalistic" and depicted "a prevailing degradation in American morality approximating the worst decadence of the Roman Empire." Dr Iago Galdson, a New York public health official, wanted to know "What magic is there in premarital coitus that is missing from the legitimized act. Why can't the female learn as well by one as the other?" (Had he read the book? Surely not.) Congressman Louis Heller from Brooklyn demanded that the Post Office refuse to handle *Sexual Behavior in the Human Female*, accusing Kinsey of "hurling the insult of the century against our mothers, wives, daughters and sisters."

Gauging the public's reaction was a trifle confusing: a Gallup poll found a three-to-one majority who believed it was "a good thing rather than a bad thing to have this information available," whereas a ratio of five to one had been in favour of the first report. On the other hand, 200,000 copies sold in two weeks rather than in the two months of its predecessor and thousands of women wrote to Kinsey – many more than the men who had responded in 1948. Some of the letters brought tears to Kinsey's eyes, revealing as they did lives blighted by sexual ignorance: of the sex act itself even, a full forty years after Margaret Sanger had begun to campaign, of basic birth control. Some women wrote seeking advice about the preferences of their men which they found perverse. One woman whose husband liked "intercourse through the mouth, if you know what I mean" asked: "What am I to say? Shall I agree? Or is it something wrong … I want to please him, but I do not want to go against nature or do anything unnatural."

The postbag alone convinced Kinsey that a liberating crusade might begin, but it was naive of him to think it was that easy to achieve what he wanted: to nail "the Victorian image of female sexuality." America was still too ultra-conservative, too wedded to cultural orthodoxy. As James H. Jones commented in his biography, *Alfred C. Kinsey: A Public and Private Life*: "Kinsey was a prophet without an organized feminist reform movement to take up his cry."

The Press generally was disappointed that *Sexual Behavior in the Human Female* had no shock-horror revelations. "Little that is startlingly new," said *Cosmopolitan*, not a "shattering blast." The consensus appeared to be that, even if women were more sexually active then they had been (only eight per cent still kept their nightie on to make love, Kinsey said) they were not as sexually active as men. They did not become fully sexually responsive until near thirty, by which time their sexuality was for the most part safely channelled into raising a family. They experienced fewer orgasms from all sources. They had fewer sexual partners. So all was

Anthropologist Margaret Mead said that Kinsey gave a man little to choose "between a woman and a sheep".

right with the world, after all. Britain agreed. The papers quoted the juicier bits from *Sexual Behavior in the Human Female* but told readers that Kinsey's interviewees were "abnormal" (a word, incidentally, that he never used other than when quoting the gynaecologist Robert Latou Dickinson who maintained that "there are only three kinds of sexual abnormalities: abstention, celibacy and delayed marriage"). Well-adjusted women, the British Press concluded, were not promiscuous.

Among the voices raised against Kinsey's second study was Margaret Mead's; she was now taking Kinsey to task for what she called an ill-conceived attack on conformity which, if removed, would mean that young people had no need to keep their "previously guaranteed reticence." Perhaps Mead should have been listening to Billy Graham. That reticence was shredding. The phenomenon of the American teenager was already part of the culture – and with it the generation gap.

Pop history suggests that the Fifties invented teenagers, forever in sulky telephone conversation with boyfriends or girlfriends, or "necking" in automobiles at the drive-in. But it was the Thirties that identified the species and coined the term – prompting Hollywood to put Mickey Rooney into the first of sixteen Andy Hardy movies that ran right through the war and out the other side.

The telephone and the automobile changed sexual relations right from the beginning of the century. B.S. Steadwell of the World Purity Federation worried in 1913 that the phone was installed in every brothel in the land "and therefore connects every house with these dens of infamy." The less febrile used the instrument to make less contentious sexual connections and, as E.S. Turner noted in his *History of Courting*:

A girl lying in bed could hear the voice of her boyfriend on her pillow, a voluptuous thrill which would have been regarded as wildly improper in days of prudery. The man might be standing in a drafty telephone box, but in fancy he was right there on the pillow with his voice.

The automobile was a far more dangerous sex aid. As early as 1902 advertisements were proclaiming that "To Have A Good Time Get A Girl And An Auto". The word "Joyride" carried connotations. By the Twenties the auto was widely regarded as "sin on wheels": it made getting away from prying eyes and social constraints all too easy. Car sales declined dramatically during the Depression, but sex and the automobile were inextricably entwined in the American mind. A sociologist who in 1936 made a study of the tourist cabins outside Dallas found in one sample that out of 109 guests who visited one site, only seven gave their correct names. Genuine travellers were unpopular because they stayed all night; site operators liked the couples who came (so to speak) and went in an hour or two. What was different about the Fifties was that affluence put the auto into the possession of most young people, not just the older well-off. And a car guaranteed a sex life. Teenagers cruised the streets, fetched up in drive-ins and secluded spots, and petted to messy orgasm in the back seat. In post-war America the auto was the surrogate bedroom where most sexual encounters took place. In a treatise on sex and the auto in the Twenties Peter Ling wrote :

John Travolta and Olivia Newton John at the drive in, in **Grease.** *Affluence in the USA during the Fifties put the auto into the hands of most young people who could use it as a surrogate bedroom.*

Each of the phases of petting came to be associated with a corresponding emotional stage in a couple's relationship. Kissing, while not automatic, was all right if the two merely liked each other: deep or French kissing indicated romantic attachment; breast-touching through the clothing heralded that things were becoming serious, and continued under the brassiere if the feelings intensified. Finally, explorations below the waist were reserved only for couples who considered themselves truly in love.

These stages had not changed by the Fifties and did not usually end in intercourse, either. "The trick was to stay very, very popular without going 'all the way'," wrote Janet Harris in *The Prime of Ms America.* "Like most girls of my generation, I managed to graduate from High

Right from the beginning of the century, advertisers have used pretty young women to sell the motor car – as here in the Fifties – overtly establishing a link with sex.

School with my virginity intact." There was still the fear of pregnancy. Contraception was still denied outside wedlock – clinics even demanded a wedding dress receipt from a bride-to-be sensible enough to seek precaution before her wedding night. But with hormones and libidos raging, reluctant to go all the way and yet desperate for naked sex, the young rushed into early marriages, the average age of brides dropping to eighteen. Of every five girls who found themselves pregnant without having reached the altar, one got a ring as well as a baby; four opted for abortion.

Until the Fifties, teenagers shared their parents' world. They watched the same films, enjoyed the same songs on the radio, shared the same values. In the Fifties the pieces flew apart: the young were not prepared to be cut-down versions of their parents. The uncertainties of the post-war years seemed to demand rules: parents imposed them; teenagers rejected them.

The Blackboard Jungle *the seminal rock 'n' roll–teenage movie.*

M-G-M's EXPLOSIVE DRAMA OF A BURNING PROBLEM!

BLACKBOARD JUNGLE

'X' CERTIFICATE

STARRING GLENN FORD · ANNE FRANCIS · LOUIS CALHERN

METROSCOPE

WITH MARGARET HAYES Screen Play by RICHARD BROOKS · Based on the novel by EVAN HUNTER · Directed by RICHARD BROOKS · Produced by PANDRO S. BERMAN · An M-G-M Picture

Teenagers everywhere identified with the confusion of James Dean (left) in **Rebel Without a Cause.**

Teenagers looked at their parents and found them as square as the TV sets in front of which they slumped night after night downing highballs; parents looked at their teenagers and could not penetrate their inarticulacy. The breakdown of family communication was often tinged with aggression on both sides. Teenagers stormed from their homes and sought identity through their own sub-culture with its own idols, own films, own music. Sex and rebellion were one. A generation identified with the confusion of James Dean in *Rebel Without a Cause*. It, too, felt that it was being torn apart. And with Marlon Brando in *The Wild One*. "What are you rebelling against, Johnny?" "What've ya got?" Juvenile crime that stemmed from feelings of angst-ridden alienation characterized an age on both sides of the Atlantic. British censors were as worried by attacks on the social order as they were about morality. *Rebel* was heavily cut, *The Wild One* refused release.

Black music, banned by the networks but beating out from the new small stations, was the common denominator of American teenage rebellion. Teenagers listened to black music day and night and parents were baffled by it. And troubled. For those young enough to hit the wavelength, black music was sex, earthy and raw. Hank Ballard's *Working with Annie* exemplifies what was on offer. It had nothing to do with the Ford assembly line in Detroit where Ballard started as a fifteen-year-old during the war. Work was ghetto slang for sex, just as jazz had been. Ballard would have got away with that because the meaning was obscure in the wider community, "but what bust me was another line, 'Annie please don't cheat, give me all my meat'. We didn't get no air-time, but they were tearing down the door at the record stores, that song stayed number one for six months, that was all you could hear on the juke boxes." Black music: dark teenage secrets. And then came Elvis Presley, a white man who sang black, a fusion that sent teenage America wilder than Sinatra ever had. Ballard, best known for writing The Twist, was downtown in Charleston, West Virginia, buying some guitar strings when he happened to see Presley on a TV in a shop window: "Saw this dude singing a song called *Heartbreak Hotel*. I saw this dude jumping with his guitar, shaking his leg … I never seen a white man doing it, scared the hell out of me. I went back to the hotel and I said, 'Man, I don't know his name but I just saw a white dude on TV acting like a black dude. Gonna be a superstar.'"

At a time when America was trying to desegregate its schools, Presley and rock 'n' roll might have been a force for racial harmony – Lloyd Price began a concert with black and white kids segregated at the beginning who were dancing together at the end. But Middle America did not hear the music as a redemptive power. Middle America saw phallic symbolism. When Presley made his first television appearance on *Ed Sullivan* the camera was

If you're looking for trouble: Marlon Brando's **The Wild One** *so worried British film censors it was refused release.*

2000 | 1990 | 1980 | 1970 | 1960 | 1950 | 1940 | 1930 | 1920 | 1910 | 1900

allowed to show him only from the waist up.

If music was ready to cross the racial divide, sex was not. A fourteen-year-old black boy in Chicago whistled at a white woman in a store and wound up in the river with a bullet in his brain. One of those responsible boasted: "As long as I live and can do something about it, niggers are going to stay in their place. Niggers ain't gonna vote where I live … They ain't gonna go to school with my kids. And when a nigger even gets close to mentioning sex with a white woman, he's tired of living." In Britain, the first black immigrants were arriving from the West Indies: before the Fifties were over the country would have to start resolving its own racial conflicts.

In the meantime, rock 'n' roll swept the land and made young people come alive.

Post-war Britain was a drab and impoverished country divided by class and beset by social strictures where youth, in the words of writer Frederic Raphael, "was indoctrinated by a combination of Tin Pan Alley slop and Christian piety." Schools were still single-sex. There was not much opportunity for boys and girls to meet, except in dancehalls and the new coffee-bars where the Gaggia espresso machines hissed. Few young men had cars – and those that were on the road were pre-war scrapheaps, however lovingly looked after; small, draughty and utilitarian, they were not accommodating of sex. Warm-hearted promiscuous girls who met jazz musicians may have had penetrative sex: and some of those who lived in the ports where the US navy and the great passenger liners berthed, sending ashore young men far more knowing than their British counterparts: and the more adventurous who went on holiday to Butlin's. For most, however, sex was a snog at the bus-stop waiting for the last bus, or a fumble in a shop doorway, unless there was an

New meeting places for the young: espresso coffee houses spread across Britain.

opportunity while baby-sitting younger siblings when mum and dad were at the pub or the pictures. Again, fear of pregnancy stopped most encounters short. Condoms were available in barber shops but most British young men were too inhibited to meet the discreetly asked "Would there be anything else, sir?" with anything but a shake of the head.

Rock 'n' roll dragged British youth out of its conformity. Immorality, lewdness, blatant sexuality – the words peppered the headlines. The emergence of the Teddy Boy – a working-class peacock in a parody of Edwardian dress of drape jacket, velvet collar and drainpipe trousers who prowled in gangs and carried a flick-knife – was blamed on rock. Certainly the Teds liked Bill Haley's *Rock Around the*

Elvis Presley: "A white dude acting like a black dude – gonna be a superstar," said Hank Ballard.

Clock: when the soundtrack to *The Blackboard Jungle* began to thump, they were on their feet hollering and slashing the cinema seats. "Rock turned the whole concept of young people on its head," George Melly observes. "Rock absolutely gave them a charter to behave wildly and, in the view of the establishment, badly. And quite right, too. Generally speaking, Britain was a cheerless, puritan place for most people. Young men, remember were waiting to go into the Armed Forces for eighteen months or two years National Service. Until rock came along they were wasting their time at a period when their hormones were raging." He rather liked early rock because it was "ferocious – and Presley had something remarkable until they turned him into a middle-of-the-road sentimentalist."

While Hollywood, still bound by the Production Code, was mesmerized by big-screen techniques and was working out a finite seam of musicals, continental film-makers were bringing adult stories to the screen fleshed with sensuous women: Magnani, Moreau, Lollobrigida, Loren, Bardot. The Sex Kitten Brigitte: for a generation of young men her pout, her ponytail, her black-mascared eyes made her the most desirable creature on the planet, and tens of thousands of young women attempted to be her clone. A sophisticated audience for foreign realism grew up on both sides of the Atlantic. ("When these people talk about realism, they usually talk about filth," Joe Breen said.) But overall, film audiences were in decline: television knocked the cinema hard. The way to staunch the haemorrhage was obvious, but Hollywood was too timid to turn to sex as it had in the Depression. And then *And God Created Woman* – Bardot, directed by her husband Roger Vadim – hit the screen, savaged by the censor's scissors but clearly showing America had to go with the flow. Vadim was to write, claiming, perhaps, too much:

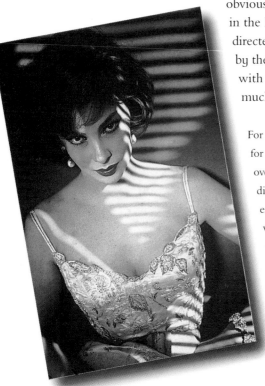

> For the Americans it was the first declaration in a film that love for pleasure is not sin. Even in France, which had been permissive over books and plays, films were treated surprisingly strictly. The difference between the way we saw life as young people – especially the amoral attitude to sex – and the conventional way of portraying it on screen was so great that I knew we were on the verge of a big change. After *Et Dieu …* they accepted the idea that love could be filmed erotically without being pornographic. Today, of course, it is a film for children.

Hollywood entered a period in which rows with the censor meant that as much as a third of film footage routinely ended up on the cutting-room floor. British cinema, too, was tangling with the censor in the fight for survival wrought by the arrival of television. It was less the sex, which was still not overt, but the

Gina Lollobrigida: an actress who brought sensuousness to the screen.

With And God Created Woman, *Roger Vadim created an international star of Brigitte Bardot – and changed Hollywood's attitude to sex.*

social realism which was being portrayed. The new "kitchen–sink" genre was "too real" for chief censor John Trevelyan. The first of the breed, *Room at the Top*, portrayed a working–class hero calculatedly seducing the daughter of a rich businessman in his North Country town to climb over the class barrier. "Oh Joe, wasn't it super," she breathed afterwards. Not much – but real sex had come to British cinema.

In his memoir *What the Censor Saw* Trevelyan wrote:

> In retrospect one can see that [it] was a milestone in the history of British films … Up to this time the cinema with rare exception had presented a fantasy world; this film dealt with real people and real problems. At the time its sex scenes were regarded as sensational … Ten years later these scenes seemed very mild and unsensational … There was no nudity or simulated copulation, but there was rather more frankness about sexual relations in the dialogue than people had been used to.

Sex arrived in British film – but social realism worried the censor.

**The first American nudie
The Garden of Eden.**

Nudity was still not part of mainstream American or British cinema, but the way was opening. The nudist film arrived, shot in the healthy outdoors with lots of volleyball – breasts jiggled, women were devoid of pubic hair and men's backs were always to the camera. The first American nudie was *The Garden of Eden*, sponsored by the American Sunbathing Association. British men in macs queued round the block. The first British attempt in the genre, *Naked as Nature Intended*, was sold to the censor before shooting began on the pretext that it was a genuine film about British naturism. In *Doing Rude Things: The History of the British Sex Film*, David McGillivray quotes the film's maker, Harrison Marks, telling John Trevelyan: "I'm going to be waving the banner for nudists." "You were lying?" McGillivray asked Marks and got the reply: "Well, of course I was. I didn't have a script. I only had an idea. All I knew was that I wanted to put nudes on the screen." After it had been made, Trevelyan refused the film a certificate as he had *The Garden of Eden*, but it did no good: local authorities were taking a more relaxed view. In 1959 Hollywood adopted a half-way stance over nudity, making two versions of a love scene between Linda Cristal and John Saxon in *Cry Tough*. *Playboy* published stills. A police chief in California pulled copies from the news-stands.

Playboy began life on the kitchen table of an ex-GI, failed cartoonist and *Esquire* copy-writer who had a dream and took out a loan against his furniture to realize it.

Ignoring the "tit 'n' bum" titles that emerged during the war – and were shipped to England is vast quantities right through the Fifties – the magazines that dominated the American post-war men's market placed an emphasis on the great outdoors, appealing especially to those who missed the camaraderie of their service days. In *Argosy* and *Stag* guys did guys' things like hunting and fishing; when they did come indoors it was to play poker with each other. What the magazines also did, Hugh Hefner noted, was exclude women – this despite the new wonder ingredient in marriage, "togetherness", a term coined by *McCalls* to indicate that a man's place was in the home every bit as much as a woman's. That was the advertisers' favourite line, even if it was a bill of goods.

When he went back to college as a psychology student after the war, Hefner wrote an essay on *Sex Behavior and the US Law* in which he said:

> It is impossible to undo the mistakes of centuries in a few years, but Krafft-Ebing and Freud have started the work and Kinsey's statistics will undoubtedly help too. Let us see if we cannot begin to find our way out of this dark emotional taboo-ridden labyrinth, and into the fresh air and light of reason.

Hefner wanted to produce a magazine that at some level did that, a magazine that allowed men to celebrate sex and appreciate woman but within

Hugh Hefner launched **Playboy** *and urged men to forget domestic bliss and get themselves a succession of playmates.*

2000
1990
1980
1970
1960
1950
1940
1930
1920
1910
1900

a world in which they could care about finer things. That was *Playboy's* manifesto. But Hefner did something subversive, too. Effectively he told men to forget aspirations of owning a ranch house and living in domestic bliss, and get themselves an apartment – and a succession of playmates.

Hefner redefined masculinity. As it was joked, Kinsey told men to feel good about their sexuality and "Hef" did the PR. *Playboy* reached a million circulation and became the most imitated magazine in the world. The first nude Playmate was Marilyn Monroe who had posed for a calendar, curled up on red velvet "with nothing on but the radio." The calendar company had been afraid to send out in the mail for fear of falling foul of the Comstock Act. Every month a different Playmate was delivered – clean and wholesome, air-brushed if necessary to perfection. Comedian Mort Sahl joked that a whole generation of males grew up believing that women folded in three places and had staples in their navels.

Recalling its launch forty-five years later, *Playboy* quoted Barbara Ehreneich, author of *The Hearts of Men: American Dreams and the Flight from Commitment*:

> The real message was not eroticism, but escape – literal escape, from the bondage of breadwinning. For that, the breasts … were necessary not just to sell the magazine, but to protect it. When, in the first issue, Hefner talked about staying in his apartment listening to music and discussing Picasso, there was the Marilyn Monroe centerfold to let you know there was nothing queer about these urbane and indoor pleasures. And when the articles railed against the responsibilities of marriage, there were the nude torsos to reassure you that the alternative was still within the bounds of heterosexuality. Sex – or Hefner's Pepsi-clean version of it – was there … to prove that a playboy didn't have to be a husband to be a man.

Playboy added:

> Her tone is oddly sexist: Hefner wanted to liberate males. When feminists borrowed the same blueprint a decade later (in finding their identity outside the home), it was hailed as heroic.

The first issue of *Playboy* carried no cover date – Hefner did not know if there would be a second. The obvious reason is that men might not have been hooked by his message. The less obvious reason is that the Post Office might have put him out of business – no magazine containing nudity was being sent through the mail at the time. As it happens, he was prosecuted, but only fined, which might have been taken as an indication that the laws on obscenity would soon be relaxed. That would have been premature: Samuel Roth had to be jailed first.

Roth was America's one-man sexual underground who for decades sold bootleg copies of ancient classics of eroticism like the *Kama Sutra* and *The Perfumed Garden* and smuggled in copies of Frank Harris and Henry Miller from Paris. Having already served three years in the slammer for sending "obscene" material through the mail he now posted out his circulars first-class – Post Office investigators could not

Marilyn Monroe, Playboy's first Playmate. Comedian Mort Sahl joked that a generation of men grew up believing women folded in three places.

legally open them. In December 1953, the month after *Playboy* went on sale, Roth wrote in his newsletter, *American Aphrodite*:

> While I have no wish to offend persons who seem to me both prudish and unrealistic, neither have I any wish to trim my sails to their faint breezes. I want freedom of speech as a publisher. I know that people are interested in sex, as they are interested in all other aspects of living, and I believe that this is healthy, normal interest – vigorous and creative. Those people who think that sexual love is dirty may leave my books alone. I do not publish for such as those.

Less than two years later Roth was busted again and sentenced to five years. The case went on appeal to the Supreme Court, where the prosecution put its thumb on the scales by bringing in a box of pornography that had nothing to do with Roth, whose conviction was upheld. The Post Office mounted a purge on those using its mails to traffic in "obscenity", with the support of Hoover who warned the nation that "millions of innocent children are exposed in their formative years to reading matter and art depicting shocking sexual travesties."

But Hoover and the Post Office were not listening carefully to Justice William Brennan who presided at Roth appeal:

> Sex and obscenity are not synonymous. Obscene material is material that deals with sex in a manner appealing to the prurient interest. The portrayal of sex in art, literature and scientific works is not itself sufficient reason to deny material the constitutional protection of freedom of speech and press ... The test is not whether it would arouse sexual desires or sexually impure thoughts in those comprising a particular segment of the community, the young, the immature or the highly prudish, or would leave another segment, the scientific or highly educated or the so-called worldly-wise and sophisticated, indifferent and unmoved ... The test in each case is the effect of the book, picture or publication considered as a whole, not upon any particular class, but upon all those whom it is likely to reach. In other words, you determine its impact upon the average person in the community.

The courts, however, *were* listening – and not to Hoover who was now frothing about obscene materials "creating criminals faster than jails can be built." Cases began to be thrown out and new case law established. Female nudity was not obscene. The discussion of homosexuality was not obscene. Male nudity was not obscene. Ordinary men and women were listening, too. When 55 independent news vendors in Chicago were hauled up for selling girlie magazines, a jury of five women and seven men voted to acquit them, "uninfluenced," as Gay Talese reported in *Thy Neighbor's Wife*, "by a church group that sat in the courtroom holding rosary beads and silently praying." The judge had a heart attack and was rushed to hospital.

The story of impatience with "obscenity" prosecutions was following a similar pattern in Britain.

For a hundred years the Campbell Obscene Publications Act had given magistrates the power to have destroyed as obscene whatever materials the police presented to them. Down the decades thousands of books and magazines went into the incinerator – or policemen's inside pockets. At the time the Act became law in 1857, Lord Campbell had gone out of his way to give assurances that it did not apply to art and literature – it was aimed at those who sought "to corrupt the morals of youth." As, however, the average copper (or Customs and Excise inspector) was as qualified as Anthony Comstock to make the distinction between literature and pornography, quantities of books by writers such as Rabelais, Defoe and Zola went into the flames.

At the start of the Fifties, when smutty books were on the increase, the Home Office, in co-operation with the Director of Public Prosecutions and the police, began a crackdown on pornography. This became excessively enthusiastic, sucking in contemporary writing and putting respectable publishers in the dock – instead of simply seeking destruction orders as in the past, charges of obscenity were now being laid.

Most of these prosecutions failed. As the climate became more liberal an exasperated

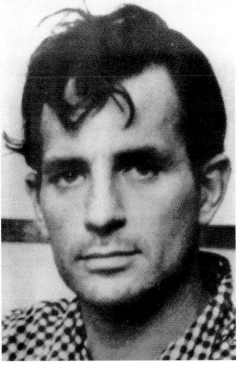

The middle classes went **On the Road** *with* **Jack Kerouac** *– at least in imagination.*

magistracy took a more robust view than in the past. A number of prominent authors wrote to *The Times* about police censorship. There was frank public ridicule. The result was a new Obscene Publications Bill that became law in 1959 offering a trade-off: increased police powers of search and seizure in return for a defence of publication for "the public good" – an all-things-to-all-men clause that would soon be exploited and keep edging back the barriers.

In America, other catalysts to sexual liberalization were emerging. The hip comedians politicized their gags and ridiculed the Establishment's beliefs. The Beats, whose manifesto was "disengagement", just dropped out.

At a time when comics appeared on stage in tuxedos (often with a line of showgirls behind them), Mort Sahl stood on stage wearing a sweater and carrying a rolled up newspaper to deliver his anti-establishment monologues. These were brave exercises in free speech when Joe McCarthy was still on the loose and it was un-American to mock. The intelligentsia and the campuses latched on to what Sahl, Shelley Berman and, in a different way, Tom Lehrer, were doing – their LPs were prized among the chattering classes in Britain, too. The authorities called the movement "sick humor"; some less questioning citizens called Sahl a communist and waited outside theatres to try to beat him up. But hip humour was more subversive than Hefner. It made people laugh – and it gave their laughter an edge of anger. Sick humour put repression of all kinds into some sort of perspective – and it was a factor in the destruction of

Allen Ginsberg, king of the Beats, who believed in "disengagement".

McCarthy and what Tony Hendry, a founding editor of *The National Lampoon*, called "his cherished vision of a rigid-with-fear, screwed-shut, dumbly obedient, boot-in-the-mouth America." Soon, if people were looking under their bed it was for their lovers' clothes, not Reds.

The Beats ridiculed authority, too, but they also advocated the abandonment of all social and moral imperatives. They dressed unconventionally, borrowed the language of the black ghettos, smoked dope and promoted sexual licence. Numbers of the middle classes followed their lead, albeit timidly, and turned hippie, at least at weekends – it would be the next decade before the world caught up. The middle classes also read *On the Road*, Jack Kerouac's rambling gospel of drifting and casual sex, in which he declared that

The only people for me are the mad ones, the ones who are mad to live, mad to talk, mad to be saved, desirous of everything at the same time, the ones who never yawn or say a commonplace thing, but burn, burn, burn like fabulous yellow roman candles, exploding like spiders across the stars.

Yeah, man – that was one spaced-out cat, Kerouac. No less bugged by convention was Allen Ginsberg, writer of the best-known Beat poem *Howl*, an incantatory love poem to his homosexual lover which brought him an obscenity charge on which he was acquitted.

George Melly first encountered Ginsberg when he found the Beat poet in his flat – Melly's flatmate had lent Ginsberg his room. The following evening Ginsberg accompanied Melly to a gig at South Harrow Jazz Club, "reciting William Blake all the way on the Tube." Adds Melly: "We went into the bar at the British Legion Hall where I was performing with Mick Mulligan and all these old soldiers, some of them from the First World War, were drinking their pints. Alan said to me, 'George, you don't get enough love, you should get your dick out and masturbate over the whole audience.' Of course these old men choked in their beers." Social comment takes many forms.

Momentous changes in human affairs take time to bed themselves in: but the seeds of sexual liberalization were being sown – too late, however, to save Wilhelm Reich, scourge of Nazism, the man who saw healthily expressed sexuality as the basis of political reformation. After leaving Germany in the early Thirties, Reich lived in Denmark, Sweden and Norway, where he taught, conducted experiments in measuring electrical responses on erogenous skin surfaces under sexual stimulation, and caused controversy which always moved him on. In 1940 he fetched up in a little town in Maine, USA, where he continued his research into the source of all sexual energy, which he believed to be the orgasm. In 1947 *New Republic* magazine explained:

> Until Reich, says Reich, it had been naively assumed by nearly everybody that the sexual orgasm was nothing more than a tricky bit of sugar coating devised by Mother Nature to make sure that the race survived … The orgasm, said Reich, was far more important than a lure to procreation. That was simply a sideline use. The real function was to release sexual tension built up by sexual energy … According to Reich, though, only a very few individuals were blessed with orgiastic potency. Society's general anti-sexual attitude, compulsive morality, legally enforced monogamy and family pressures on behalf of pre-marital chastity had so inhibited man's natural sexuality that most of the world was now peopled, said Reich, with orgiastic cripples.

The good news, however, was that released orgasmic energy, which Reich called orgone, floated in the atmosphere where it could be collected and harnessed. He believed concentrated exposure to orgone could cure impotence, frigidity and a range of medical conditions from cancer to the common cold and he built orgone accumulators – six-sided, zinc-lined, coffin-sized boxes – in which patients sat to cure themselves by directing orgone at their genitals.

Physical scientists said Reich was talking utter claptrap. Most psychoanalysts looked askance but said nothing, in deference to Reich's international reputation. In the Fifties Reich built up a large following. Even today 200,000 orgone boxes are in use, principally in Germany, Brazil and Mexico; ergonomic models are purchasable over the Internet. As to their benefits, Dusan Makavjev, who in the Seventies made a semi-documentary film inspired by Reich, *W.R.: History of the Organism* (the additional brace of letters in the significant word a sop to censorship), is cautious:

> I talked to a number of people who used orgone accumulators, some of them are even known and famous, some actors, who were definite in telling me that it helped them. I have learned about people losing headaches or fever or flu. I tried it a few times. Something was happening, a little ticklish feeling in your skin … You feel the presence of some energy around you.

In 1957 Reich felt the presence of the American Food and Drug Administration. Agents came and destroyed his boxes with axes. Reich had been renting them out, thereby breaking the law: the boxes were not approved. Copies of all his books were confiscated and dumped in a New York City incinerator, most of them, Makavjev points out, "written before Reich even thought of orgone accumulators – it was a part of the McCarthy kind of operation, the silencing of somebody who was politically suspect." Reich was charged with fraud but did not show up in court; he did not think the government, never mind the judiciary, was competent to judge him. He went to prison for contempt where he died soon after, diagnosed as a paranoid.

2000

1990

1980

1970

1960

1950

1940

1930

1920

1910

1900

Prostitute and prospective client in Soho. Legislation in 1959 largely removed the street-walkers from the street.

Kinsey was already dead, destroyed by the same dark forces of human sexuality.

Sexual Behavior in the Human Female put Kinsey's face on the cover of *Time* magazine, but, time was running out for him. The Indiana Provincial Council of Catholic Women asked, "in the name of more than 150,000 women – most of them mothers, many of them with sons and daughters of college age," whether Indiana University was "still a place fit for the educating of the youth of our State." The university teetered but held firm. The Rockefeller Foundation which funded Kinsey – and which itself was being looked at by a committee investigating tax-exempt foundations – did not, anxious that continued support might prejudice its position. An axe just as effective as those that demolished Reich's work fell the year after the second report was published. Kinsey was "cut loose". He began planning his next project on sex offenders, but spent most of his time unsuccessfully chasing other backing. He was now very ill with heart trouble and he was unable to sleep.

In 1955 Kinsey and his wife Clara paid a first visit to Europe. Stopping off in London, he went to Soho and Piccadilly Circus on a Saturday night where he counted over 1,000 prostitutes. "I have never seen so much nor such aggressive behaviour anywhere else," he said. From London, Kinsey moved on to Paris, then Italy, where one of Kinsey's guides was Kenneth Anger who was living there at the time. Kinsey was unable to climb stairs without effort and Anger followed him around the hotel with a chair in case he fell. Anger took him to observe what was going on in several of the legalized brothels; Kinsey thought most of the women enjoyed their work. Anger also took him to "cruisy movie houses in little towns" where he would stand, steadying himself against the wall in the balconies, watching "the kind of musical chairs of the all-male audience, boys and men." Once, Anger remembers, Kinsey wrote in his notebook "seventy-two orgasms in two hours." Kinsey was enthralled by the Coliseum at night where there was "outrageous cruising in the moonlight where the

Christian martyrs had died." Kinsey, Anger adds, saw things that he missed: "'Did you see that priest over there, and over there?' And you'd have to peer because the priests were completely in black and like crows would swoop down on these soldiers and disappear again when they knelt down during fellatio. The soldiers would just be standing there in a nonchalant way, you wouldn't realize there was a priest at their feet."

Kinsey's reputation remained intact on his death the following year. What was not known was that he had not been entirely the arm's-length scientist he purported to be, gathering information only by means of his exhaustive questionnaires.

There is plenty of evidence that Kinsey came to sex research as a prude (He was fond of saying that he would rather die than not put in a hard day's work). His attitude changed, however, from the occasion on which, during an interview with a black prostitute in Indianapolis, in response to her mentioning that her "spur tongue" (clitoris) was two inches long, he paid her an extra dollar to have a look. Soon, to disprove current medical literature on male orgasm which maintained that semen squirted, he was watching 500 men – mostly recruited with the help of a male prostitute – while they masturbated (Three-quarters "dribbled", as Kinsey supposed, if you have a need to know). He also watched women masturbate and sessions of hetero- and homosexual intercourse.

Had any of this been known outside the inner circle of the institute – and in view of the various investigations into what he was doing it is astonishing that it was not – Kinsey would have been fired. Had it been known that his desire to record the actual physiology of sex ultimately made him engage in a merry-go-round of sexual activity with members of his inner circle and their wives, as well as with carefully chosen outsiders – encounters that were filmed in the attic of his home – it is very likely he would have gone to jail.

One of Kinsey's intimate colleagues has spoken of his attitude to his research as "high on the scientific-objective and high on the prurient." James H. Jones, whose 1997 biography revealed the full extent of Kinsey's sexual pursuits for the first time, acknowledges Kinsey's faults – his menacing attitude to those who opposed him, his unsavoury coercion of the wives of staff into being "team players" – but does not condemn him. In an article that appeared in the *New Yorker* Jones wrote that Kinsey was:

> A strong-willed patriarch who created around himself a kind of utopian community … In other ways, he was perhaps even more like one of those protean eccentrics of the nineteenth century – a self created visionary with a burning belief in his mission (and his ability) to change the world.

You can take Kinsey or you can leave him. But no-one is untouched by what he did. He forced the Western world to confront its sexuality in all its guises, to understand that while knowledge about the sexual impulse raises anxieties, they are less damaging than ignorance and denial. He set out to bring sexual enlightenment. He believed that he had failed, as others before him. That was not so. It was just that the fuse of the sexual revolution which he lit was still burning when he died.

THE SEXUAL REVOLUTION

SEXUAL INTERCOURSE

BEGAN IN 1963

WHICH WAS RATHER LATE FOR ME.

WROTE THE POET PHILIP LARKIN WRYLY.

SEX IS LIKE THE WHEEL: THE YOUNG OF EVERY DECADE INVENT IT, OR THINK THEY DO. THE SIXTIES WAS THE DECADE IN WHICH INVENTION WAS NOT CONFINED TO THE YOUNG. THE SIXTIES WAS ALSO — AS HAS BEEN OBSERVED, EQUALLY WRYLY — THE DECADE THAT DID NOT HAPPEN UNTIL THE SEVENTIES. WHATEVER THE TRUTH, THERE WAS PROBABLY MORE SEXUAL EXPLORATION, MORE CELEBRATION OF SEX IN THE TWENTY OR SO YEARS UP TO 1980 THAN IN ANY COMPARABLE PERIOD IN HISTORY. THIS WAS A PERIOD IN WHICH THE OLD TIES OF FAMILY, COMMUNITY AND CHURCH BROKE DOWN AND SEX ASSUMED A MORE EXPLICIT ROLE IN PEOPLE'S LIVES BECAUSE OTHER THINGS WERE MISSING.

The counter-culture arrived — a network of separate tunnels beneath the pavements of society, going in different directions, criss-crossing, sharing a common ideology of "sex 'n' drugs' n' rock' 'n' roll". Sex became a political act. Revolutionary politics tried to absorb the ideology of sexual freedom, as if sleeping with everyone in a political cell was a first step towards bringing down the state. Students from Paris to New York rioted and thought that sex was a blow against bourgeois morality. The Hippies dropped out further than the Beats — in India, Tibet — believed that such a thing as Flower Power existed and exhorted the world to "Make Love Not War". It may have been empty idealism, but the slogan meant something when it was taken up by those

Make love not war: recently married John Lennon and Yoko Ono hold a bedside press conference in their hotel room in Amsterdam.

protesting against what was happening in Vietnam. In his hippie phase, with hippie naivety, John Lennon took off his clothes and staged a public love-in with Yoko "to give peace a chance". Once the feminist and homosexual movements got into their stride – literally, since they, too, marched for their beliefs – they showed how sex could be effectively politicized; but by then no-one was wearing flowers in their hair.

In practice, sex was never as free as distance suggests, though there was a sharp increase in conventional (that is to say, furtive) adultery. But those who tested the outer limits of sexual possibility did change social attitudes both to sex and gender. Some marriages became "open", with partners at least theoretically accepting the other's right to have sex outside the relationship. Some tried group marriage or communal living. Others toyed with bisexuality. For some, tantric sex came back along the Hippie Trail, bringing mysticism and a stab at spirituality. A sizeable minority took to extremes the pleasure-pain principle which is inherent in sex and got into sado-masochism with nipple and genital clips, whips, handcuffs and black leather. Kinsey had found that one in five men and one in eight women responded sexually to "S & M" stories. A masochist capable of violent self-brutality, Kinsey always said that he felt sorriest for people like himself: it was almost impossible for them to meet. By the Seventies that was not a problem: S & M was a phenomenon, even a cult. There was also sex for the young – good, old-fashioned sex, but first experienced at a younger and younger age as time progressed. Ellen Steinberg, who hit the road with her first lover at the age of seventeen, was hardly typical, but she was not perhaps untypical either.

We went to Tucson, Arizona, and we lived in the desert in an artist community for six months. I loved Van, but I left him so I could try sex with other people. In the following six months I had sex with fifty-two guys. I kept a list of their names and a brief description of what we did sexually. The desire to document my sexual experiences was there from the start. It was fun, creative, liberating, each time was a discovery, and it felt so darned good.

Pop singer Marianne Faithfull, introduced to casual sex by a man named Jeremy Clyde, was very typical of her generation:

It was great sex, and in the morning I must have looked a bit dewy-eyed and wistful. Jeremy, I could see, was a bit concerned I was going to fall in love with him. It must have been obvious I didn't know the ropes of this game and in his sophisticated way he tried to clue me in. My lesson concluded with a friendly if diffident: "Lovely being with you, Marianne, perhaps we'll run into one another again soon." I somehow got the picture, and yet I didn't get it. I'm very obedient, and good at being told what to do, but I've spent most of my life trying to grasp that particular bit of sexual etiquette, without success.

Marianne Faithfull, in a scene from the film **Girl on a Motorcycle** *with Alain Delon, did not understand the sexual etiquette of the Sixties.*

Some women who thought that marriage was still worthwhile took the plunge but refused to accept "honour and obey" in their wedding vows. Marriage itself fell into a state of disrepair. Divorce became easier – no need to prove adultery as was usual in the past, irrevocable breakdown was enough to send couples their separate ways. By the mid-Seventies, as James McMillan wrote in *The Way It Changed,* the British divorce rate had increased five-fold and "was moving towards the American pattern of one divorce for every two marriages". Changes in abortion law were much slower on both sides of the Atlantic: by then, however, termination on demand had come, causing numbers to rise swiftly. In Britain in 1977, teenage abortions were

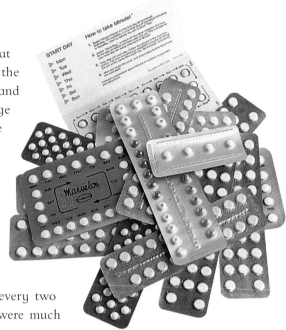

The Pill released women from the fear of pregnancy, changing their sexual attitudes.

28,000. Illegitimacy had increased three-fold, the total of births to unmarried mothers in the country reaching 97 per 1,000 – overtaking the century's highest figure, 93, which came at

Despite an array of contraceptive means, illegitimacy increased three-fold.

the end of the Second World War. Helen Brook, a member of the British Family Planning Association, became so impatient with the refusal to give contraception to unmarried women that she set up her own advisory centres, seeing those aged under twenty-five, married or not.

Sex remained an uneasy face-off between the progressives and the moralists but, as discussing sex in public became a non-stop activity, society gradually accepted behaviour it would once have considered disgraceful. Many still disapproved about motherhood outside wedlock, but now it was more likely to be with a shrug. An illegitimate child was no longer a "bastard" (the word virtually dropped out of the language other than as invective) but became "extra marital", like the sex that created it. This term itself was later replaced, more humanly by "child of a one-parent family".

The issue of cohabitation also changed accordingly. "Trial marriages" became acceptable: then "stable relationships" which promised long-term commitment:

*Marriage began to go into decline in the late Sixties. But some still considered it worthwhile –
including this nudist couple.*

then "living together", which promised no commitment at all. All of these states caused
problems of nomenclature: how were people within them referred to? "Lover" was for the
brave and defiant; but it rather palled for others if the relationship settled down. "Significant
other" was an Americanism which caused British toes to curl; in the UK, people preferred "my
other half", a description of awkward Britishness which carried irony, too. Most eventually
settled for "partner", and a better word has not been found.

In 1938, when he was conducting his investigations into marital happiness, Lewis Terman
noted that, whereas 87 per cent of women and 50 per cent of men in his study who were born
before 1890 had been sexually inexperienced when they married, that applied to only 30 per
cent of women and 14 per cent of men born after 1910. This led him to speculate:

If the drop should continue at the average rate shown, virginity at marriage will be close to the
vanishing point for males born after 1930 and females born after 1940. It will be of no small interest

2000

1990

1980

1970

1960

1950

1940

1930

1920

1910

1900

to see how long the cultural ideal of virgin marriages will survive as a moral code after its observance has passed into history.

Terman's projection may have been a tad precipitate, but by the Seventies virginity as a moral code was history. So was the *sine qua non* of chastity. In 1962, a Scottish psychiatrist, Professor G.M. Carstairs, tried to put the matter of chastity into a realistic framework when he delivered the prestigious and influential Reith Lectures on BBC radio. Suggesting that in the eyes of Christ the cardinal virtue was charity, not chastity, he said:

A pill a day keeps conception at bay – with the days of the week to remind the forgetful.

It was his intemperate disciple Paul, an authoritarian character, who introduced the concept of celibacy as an essential part of Christian teaching, and centuries later it was the reformed libertine St Augustine who placed such exaggerated emphasis upon the sinfulness of sex. It has always been those whose own sexual impulses have been precariously repressed who have raised the loudest cries of alarm over other people's immorality.

The advent of the female oral contraceptive – the Pill – raised such cries to a screech.

THE PILL

That it was possible to inhibit ovulation and thus prevent pregnancy had been known from the beginning of the century. Indeed, veterinarians used a substance secreted by the ovaries of cattle to make them barren. In the Thirties, Margaret Sanger, the pioneer of American birth control, visited the Soviet Union to see experimental work then being conducted into chemical contraception for humans. This work was abandoned as the Russians, like the Nazis, encouraged the idea of state breeding. By 1945 the hormone progesterone had been identified, but scientific institutions were reluctant to move the matter forward, not least because of the violent opposition of the Catholic Church. Sanger, however, as persistent as ever, talked the biologist Geoffrey Pincus into beginning research in 1951, financially backed by her wealthy friend Katherine McCormick, who had helped smuggle diaphragms for her back in the Twenties. The first trials were conducted successfully in Puerto Rico and Haiti and by 1961 – when Sanger was past eighty – the Pill was being prescribed.

The condom had always been regarded as slightly unsavoury: its use had a built-in restraint. What caused the moralists anxiety was that, as Paul Ferris wrote in *Sex and the British,* whereas the condom carried an inhibitory "reminder of the penis in action", the Pill "sounded like medicine". No, it was more: it was not, as one doctor said at a London symposium, "just an anti-baby pill. It is more a wafer of love". Sex: the Pill would make it a secular religion.

Men, of course, welcomed the Pill: it gave them freer access to women's bodies and, indeed, took away from women a major excuse for saying no. That angered feminists, not yet an organized group, who saw the balance of sexual power tilt even further in men's direction. They quickly compensated by advocating that the Pill gave women for the first time the licence to behave sexually as badly as men. And then came Masters and Johnson, the successors to Kinsey, an element of whose research could be subverted to the view that men were superfluous to women's requirements.

THE NEW KINSEY

William Masters and his research associate Virginia Johnson picked up where Kinsey left off: they got men and women to remove their clothes, attach electrodes to their bodies and engage in sexual activity that was monitored and filmed. Despite what Kinsey had done, there was still no accurate information about the physiology of sex. Masters, a professor of obstretics at the medical school of Washington University in St Louis – and a pioneer in infertility – wanted to find out even if, as other told him, he was committing professional suicide. He got off to a bad start, refused the only textbook on human sexual anatomy in the university library on the grounds that he was "only an assistant professor of obstretics, not a full professor", but he was not to be denied. With the tacit agreement of the local police, he used male and female prostitutes as laboratory subjects – until he discovered that many of the women were physiologically abnormal, the demands of their occupation causing chronic congestion in the blood vessels of the pelvic region. So he placed notices on the bulletin boards around the university and was inundated by students eager to earn a few dollars. Altogether, Masters and Johnson observed some 700 men and women perform coitus and self-manipulation. With the aid of the "Penis-Cam", an artificial penis of clear plastic that contained a light source and a camera, they filmed the vagina in orgasmic contractions and the effects on it of injected sperm.

In April 1966, after an eleven-year study, Masters and Johnson published *Human Sexual Response,* a love story in four acts – excitement, plateau, orgasm, resolution – that involved every part of the body as well as the brain. They confirmed Kinsey's finding that there was no such thing as a vaginal orgasm. More radically, they indicated that most women did not reach orgasm without clitoral stimulation. More radically still, they showed that, "As contrasted with the male's usual inability to have more than one orgasm in a short period, many females, especially when clitorally stimulated, can regularly have five or six full orgasms within a matter of minutes."

Human Sexual Response rectified a number of misconceptions. The clitoris was not a kind of penis which became erect during arousal; rather, it withdrew into a protective foreskin as orgasm

*Husband and wife sexologists Virginia Johnson and William Masters –
the first to document the physiology of sex.*

approached, its length decreasing by half. Women did not discharge at climax – a myth perpetuated by pornographic novels down the ages. Intercourse was not dangerous during pregnancy or menstrual periods. Anal intercourse was neither dangerous nor perverted. Humans could maintain sexual activity into their nineties. Baldness was not a sign of virility. And, hammering home another of Kinsey's messages: there was nothing harmful about masturbation.

But two conclusions overshadowed all others: the penis was not necessary to produce a fulfilling female orgasm – and in intercourse its size was irrelevant, "unless the woman thought it was relevant". In deference to those men who might think that their penis was too small – something that Masters and Johnson said bothered every man at some time – *Human Sexual Response* omitted any data on average dimensions, merely observing that smaller organs showed a greater proportional increase in arousal. According to John Heidenny, author of *What Wild Ecstasy*, "there is no evidence that Masters and Johnson asked any of their female subjects whether penis size mattered. If they did, the answer was never recorded. It's possible Masters and Johnson were so anxious to make their political point that they ignored any evidence to the contrary." The fact of the matter was to be irrelevant to militant feminism: Masters and Johnson had dethroned the penis and elevated the clitoris to sexual supremacy – and had told women they were no longer dependent on men for sexual pleasure.

Human Sexual Response was so badly written it might well have been in Sanskrit; Masters apologised for that: "You must remember that in publishing this book we were concerned primarily with acceptance. This is the reason it wasn't written in 'English' … In fact, we rewrote it to make the language as technical and non-inflammatory as we could. In retrospect it was probably a mistake." Never mind, it outsold Kinsey.

From sexual function, Masters and Johnson now turned to sexual dysfunction. A man who in his work with infertility "really saw couples stripped down to their relationship's bare bones", knew what he was talking about when he argued publicly that sexual inadequacy was the great cause of divorce. "And I would estimate that 75 per cent of this problem is treated by the psychologist, the social worker, the minister, the lawyer," he said. "Medicine really has not met its responsibility." At an educated guess, he added, half of the forty-five million married couples in America were sexually incompatible to some degree.

It was couples whose sexual incompatibility was bringing their marriages to the end of the line that Masters and Johnson set out to help: women with an inability to reach orgasm, either all or some of the time, men with primary impotence (a life-long inability to achieve vaginal penetration), secondary impotence, or premature ejaculation – "the most frequent problem," observes Johnson today. "When some young men develop their sexual opportunities under pressure – back seat of a car, hurry up, don't get caught – they're very susceptible to the problem. And then the wife has a problem. And the relationship."

Masters and Johnson would only treat married couples referred to them through the proper channels, and only together. "There is no such thing as an uninvolved partner in a sexually distressed marriage," Masters said. There was nothing complicated about the treatment. Couples came to St Louis for a fortnight and were seen daily as out-patients. They were encouraged to explore the latent capabilities of their bodies, touching and stroking themselves, then their partner. Therapy did not always involve intercourse: "Just going from A to B may be enough," Johnson said at the time. "It is not always necessary to go from A to Z." The aim of the "healing process" was to expel from the bedroom two invisible spectators: "The man worrying whether he will be successful this time, the woman concerned about her own chances of pleasure in so precarious a situation." However simple the technique, Masters and Johnson achieved with it an overall success rate of 80 per cent, maintained after five years. With vaginismus (a form of muscular spasm which makes intercourse difficult or impossible) the success was 100 per cent, with primary impotence 40 per cent – which Masters and Johnson considered "a clinical disaster".

All of this was documented in *Human Sexual Inadequacy*. But Masters and Johnson also had some general advice to offer, stemming from their research. They showed how to delay any man's ejaculation by employing a "squeezing" method (learned from prostitutes who know how to stop a client coming so quickly that he might feel he had not got his money's worth). They also demonstrated that it made sense for the female "superior" position to be used more often in coitus, not only because it offered a woman a better chance of achieving orgasm but because, if a man was not functioning at his best, his partner could compensate by virtue of

A drawing from Alex Comfort's **The Joy of Sex,** *still a best-seller more than 25 years after first publication.*

having more freedom of movement. Sex therapist Mark Schwartz, who did his postgraduate training with Masters and Johnson, watched them "work their magic": "One couple hadn't had sex for fifteen years, but were making love again before they left St Lewis. Another couple had lived together for two decades without consummating their relationship – they'd tried but had stopped because it hurt her so much. Then they gave up. We helped them overcome their inhibitions. Their only regret was that they hadn't found out how to do it sooner. We saw people who had zero income, people who were millionaires. It was breathtaking to see a sheikh walk in with five wives or something because he had erectile problems. Being rich didn't stop you having to struggle with the same issues."

Human Sexual Inadequacy was another big seller. But one element caused great controversy: the use of "partner surrogates" in treating single men. To many, this practice was unpaid prostitution. Masters said he saw no other way of helping men who otherwise would remain "societal cripples".

By the end of the Seventies there were thousands of sex therapists – Masters and Johnson had single-handedly created an entire industry.

It was then, however, that cracks began to appear in the eminence which the husband and wife team had enjoyed for 15 years. A third book on homosexuality, which was possibly outside their area of competence and in which they took a position that homosexuality was a learned behaviour, led to a re-examination of their previous statistics. Within another decade financial problems led to the closure of their foundation. By then the sex therapist had been largely put out of business. The bookshop shelves were aswamp with self-help books – including the *Joy of Sex*, written by an Englishman, Dr Alex Comfort, which promoted "loving, unselfconscious intercourse" and was illustrated by exquisite line drawings (ten million copies later, it is still selling). People were also more likely to see a gynaecologist or urologist who could prescribe the new medical treatments that had become available for some sexual problems including premature ejaculation.

"There's not that much sex therapy to do any more," says Schwartz, who now specializes in treating sexual abuse. "In 1970 I had thirteen therapists working for me and we had a huge client waiting list. Now a sex therapist can't make a living." He laughs. "Maybe no-one is having sex any more."

He defends Masters and Johnson for beginning sex surrogacy: "If a man was impotent and you said to him 'If you can't have an erection, how is that going to affect your life?' he'd say, 'Well, if I can't have an erection, then I can't find a partner. If I can't find a partner then I have to live the rest of my life alone. If I have to live the rest of my life alone, then I might as well be dead.' Catch-22. These men were living in virtual isolation, extremely depressed, inhibited. Some men were terrified of women and thought they were gay because of a homosexual experience. Kinsey had published and said that having a same-sex experience after puberty was not abnormal or even unusual, statistically speaking. But a lot of men coded that to mean they were gay, when the truth was they had some bisexuality but a lot more heterosexuality. Whatever their sexual dysfunction, they couldn't reverse it until they had someone to have sex with – and so the idea of the surrogate came up. What was remarkable was that we found out such men had problems with intimacy in a relationship. It wasn't just their erections. When they got close to a woman they got scared and when they got scared they began to act in very dysfunctional ways. In a clinic you'd only see a person for a matter of hours. Surrogates lived with these guys twenty-four hours a day seven days a week for two weeks. Out there with them they got to know how they acted on the streets, in restaurants, at close quarters. In actuality men learned ten times more out of the bedroom than in the bedroom – and a lot of us learned this along the way."

Surrogacy led to very few emotional problems, Schwartz adds, "because the boundaries of the relationship were always clear from beginning to end. It was a two-week relationship, period. Some men did have a hard time letting go, but what we found was that within two or three months they found another person. Emotionally awakened by a surrogate, they were able to transfer to a new partner. The results we got with surrogates were so remarkable that you wouldn't believe it if you couldn't witness it with your own eyes."

SWINGERS

Few surrogates work in the field now – in the age of AIDS the treatment has largely lost its appeal. Marilyn Fithian, who with her late husband opened a centre for marital and sexual studies on the West Coast thirty years ago, thinks this is regrettable. She worked with male and female surrogates and found them particularly helpful with virgins. "Surrogates aren't as

acceptable as they were in the Seventies – but that's true of the whole field of human sexuality," she observes and adds: "There's a general assumption that sex is a normal, natural behaviour and that you don't have to teach anybody how to have sex. We know through research that isn't so. It's a learned behaviour. There's a lot more to sex than putting a penis in a vagina, believe me. But we're getting more and more conservative views and values, for whatever reason. It's been much more difficult in terms of people teaching sex education courses; showing films that were readily acceptable a number of years ago are difficult to show in schools now. Until we do something more realistic about sex education most men are going to carry on learning about sex from *Playboy*."

A blow against bourgeois morality? This hippie couple are oblivious to the world.

When she was conducting a study of nudism, Fithian discovered that some nudists were involved in "swinging" – sex with strangers, purely for kicks. That brought her into contact with Sandstone, a retreat where, Gay Talese wrote in *Thy Neighbor's Wife,* founder John Williamson "wanted to assemble a large membership of stable couples, young middle-class sensualists who believed that their personal relationships would be enhanced rather than shattered by the elimination of sexual possessiveness."

Esquire in October 1972 had much the same sense of veneration in its voice when, describing life at Sandstone – a ranch house with teakwood floors and walls and an Olympic-sized indoor swimming pool, set in fifteen acres in the Topanga Hills of southern California, overlooking the Pacific – it told readers:

> In the evening … people without clothes sit around the fireplace talking softly, touching gently, singing sometimes to the tunes of a bearded guitarist – and, when the mood suits them, a few of them will leave the living room and go downstairs to make love. They make love openly … unconcerned by the lack of privacy, unashamed and unintimidated by things that might inhibit outsiders. It is a fundamental concept at Sandstone that the human body is good, that an open expression of affection is good, that sexuality is a positive force toward greater intimacy and understanding … More than four hundred people – among them doctors, lawyers, actresses, factory workers, artists, housewives – pay $240 annually to visit Sandstone during the day to sunbathe and swim in the nude if they wish, and to remain on the estate at night to attend one of the many parties that sometimes continue until morning. People do as they wish at Sandstone, where the atmosphere is free, open, guiltless.

Opposite: Nipples, once air-brushed from magazines, became a familiar sight once some British newspapers introduced the "Page Three" Girl.

Whatever turns you on. Or off. "That huge swimming pool," says Fithian, "probably had the highest sperm count of any pool in the world." She expresses no censoriousness: "We attended a number of their parties and took out people who wanted to do sex therapy. Alex Comfort was another when he came over to see us. We would see maybe fifty couples on any occasion having various kinds of intercourse – behaviours we would never have seen in the research laboratory. I mean daisy chains with a number of people, for example. It was helpful in relation to doing therapy. When you're working with a client and they talk about some things they've been involved with, you understand what they're talking about."

On the opposite seaboard of America access to public sex was available in New York clubs

The hippie culture embraced not only a "dropout": minority in the Sixties. In the Seventies their displays of public sexuality were overtaken in America by the affluent.

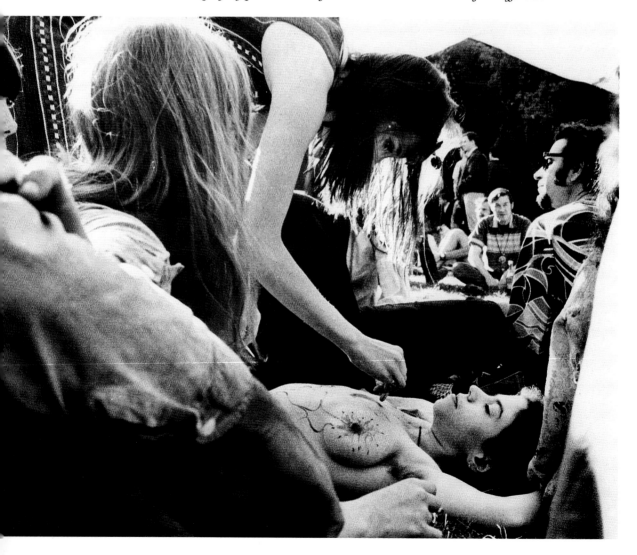

and bars, some of them extreme like the Hell Fire Club which catered for deviancy (if deviancy existed any longer) and made a speciality of S & M. But in terms of popular excess there was nothing like Plato's Retreat, the ultimate gathering place for swingers which offered a disco, a free bar and buffet, and a labyrinth of rooms filled with mattresses or waterbeds for anyone to have sex with anyone who said yes, in whatever combinations. The swimming pool, Jacuzzi and steam room were for sex, too. You could keep your clothes on in Plato's but most wore nothing more than a towel. Or a smile.

Michael Perkins, a writer of erotic fiction and a leading authority on modern erotic literature, remembers "the visceral feeling" when you walked into Plato's for the first time: "Your heart rushed, you could barely breath because in those days everyone smoked marijuana. The atmosphere was dense with sexuality, sexual sweats and juices and smoke. It was something like a haze over the rooms. And then if you looked below the haze, all these bodies moving. It violated, no matter how liberated you thought you were, every taboo. You realised at the time that, 'Boy, I sure have been conditioned, because this is really difficult to look at.' I think that's how most people felt. It never became something you took for granted." Approaching a woman to invite her to have sex was something else that could not be taken for granted – the cardinal rule of swinging was that men were supposed to take no for an answer. "The discomfort was part of the excitement of it," Perkins says. Homosexuality was forbidden – it was just bad for business; straight men needed the guarantee that they would not be propositioned. The wildest swinging happened when there were more men than women in the crowd, because women became abandoned when group sex occurred and that turned men on: "You would often see many men around two or three women who were active – we were not into victim feminism in those days. Men, by nature at times, are pathetically horny and will do anything to get close to a willing female. The pack chases a willing female. What will ever change about that? But after a while it seemed repulsive in a way. You wanted to say to these men, 'You rutting fool, why don't you try talking with them first?'"

Perkins embraced the sexual revolution – "it was the sexual equivalent of storming the barricades." His first venture into swinging was when he and his wife tried a four-way marriage with a bisexual called Marco Vassi – a man who "was spiritually tormented, who could never quite outgrew his Catholicism, no matter how many hours he sat in Zen monasteries" – and the woman he was then living with. "Of course it was preposterous, but we were sincere about it," Perkins says. "My wife and I had our own home, we had children and all the problems of trying to survive a bourgeois life. Marco was a free will-o'-the wisp. For him it was play – serious, but play."

Less adventurous Americans were swinging in the suburbs, joining clubs where they exchanged names, addresses and Polaroids. A swing club might be purpose-built but most were just someone's home opened up on a Saturday night. Even in bread-and-butter swinging the Jacuzzi was de rigeur. As the *Etiquette of Swinging* booklet published by the North American Swingers Club Association put it, "Being nude in comfortably hot water is conducive to making friends." And try to forget about the sperm count. Most swinging occasions, *Esquire* wrote when it got its sense of irony working, were "depressingly alike: potato-chip and onion-

2000

1990

1980

1970

1960s

1950

1940

1930

1920

1910

1900

The Ice Storm, *a 1998 film that looked back to the sexual explicitness and swinging in the suburbs that occurred in the Seventies.*

dip breaks, with some clumsy rolling around on wall-to-wall Acrilan carpeting." Bob McGinley, founder of Wide World of Contemporary People which evolved into the NASCA, considers the scene to have more dignity. "Swinging is a social, sexual recreation for middle- to upper-middle-class Americans who have no need to intersperse their talk with swear words," he says. And should such words as "infidelity", "adultery" or just "promiscuity" hover in your mind, McGinley adds that swingers do not consider their recreation to be extramarital: "An affair is extramarital, apart from the marriage relationship. Whereas in swinging it's part of the marriage relationship – a major difference there. Swingers don't consider swinging much different than going to a dance and dancing with somebody else's spouse."

He confirms Perkins' view that swinging, while instigated by men, is maintained by women: "Every experienced swinger knows that the ideal ratio for a swing party has more men than women, since women become so aroused in that situation. Females have a capacity for sexual enjoyment which I think transcends that of the male. I remember talking to one woman who told me she wore contacts – without them she could only see blurs. 'So when I go into this group room activity I take my contacts out. I can't see them so it doesn't matter what they look like. It only matter how they make me feel.' And women have much more of a tendency to be bisexual. Now I'm not using the term as a psychologist would use it. I'm using it in the sense that women also enjoy other women's bodies. Their love object is the male, they are heterosexual, but they appreciate another woman's body, they enjoy touching another woman's breasts and perhaps having oral sex. You get a couple of women sexually enjoying one another and their husbands are watching and are turned on by this. The women know that they're turned on by it. So there's a strong heterosexual component in their same-sex activity. Turn it around. If two men started touching, the women would be offended. Swinging is not a homosexual-orientated activity."

As far as McGinley is concerned, AIDS is not and never has been a threat to the swinging community, even though his members do not use condoms (A NASCA newsletter carried an article stating that "Unless your partner is suspected of being from a high-risk group, or is known to be infected, using condoms to prevent AIDS is like putting on a seat belt when moving one's car from the driveway into the garage for the night – the risk is too low to warrant the need for the protection"). "I'm not aware of any person ever having contacted AIDS due to swinging – and we're in personal contact with every swing club in the world at least once a year," McGinley says. "AIDS has never been a factor in swinging and for very good sociological reasons. We have a very responsible group of people."

In the middle Eighties, the AIDS scare cut swingers by half, but the numbers were back up within five years. "It amuses me that *Time* magazine once wrote that swinging had died," says McGinley. In recent years his association – which today has over 400 swing clubs, takes swing tours to Japan, Fiji and the Caribbean and attracts 4,000 people to its annual lifestyles convention – has had a big push from the Internet, "which let's people get away from the small town feeling." The association is affiliated to others in Canada, Germany, Belgium, France, even Russia. "There aren't many clubs in England," McGinley adds, "because of the British official mentality which is rather anti-sexual. Swinging is strictly underground there."

SWINGING LONDON

Britain trailed in America's sexual wake. Wife-swapping

A taste for some in S & M? In Louis Bunuel's Belle de Jour, *Catherine Deneuve is a bored housewife who submits to sexual degradation.*

The James Bond movies promoted sex without commitment – Ursula Andress (opposite) in **Dr No** *was just one of those to fall for 007's chauvinist charms.*

A mini-skirted girl in Carnaby Street – the centre of Swinging London.

seemed a vogue for a little while, but it never developed into full-blown swinging. "Swinging London"? At the time the term was coined – by an American journalist – it only meant that the place was abuzz in fashion, pop music and the visual arts, and that the whiff of sexual possibilities to come was in the air. Mary Quant – who, George Melly wrote in Revolt Into Style, "recognized the irrelevancy of looking like a virgin" – and her imitators drew on elements of pop culture and of "the 'child-woman' whose first and most authoritative example was Brigitte Bardot [and] the 'kinky' clothes of the recently suppressed street walkers" to design female garments of such colourful skimpiness that staring men were seen to walk into lamp posts. Quant's mini-skirt, for all that by the end of the Sixties it was no more than eight or so inches long and commonly referred to as a "fanny pelmet", stretched around the world. Briefly, hippie culture spilled over into the popular to produce a period of fancy dress – kaftans, beads, Indian prints, Red Indian drag, Afghan coats, cannibalised military uniforms, long hair and often long boots – during which the sexes were sometimes indistinguishable. A new generation of photographers including Bailey and Lichfield brought movement and impact to the fashion shoot, which had been as formal and artificial as wedding-cake icing. Mannequins gave way to the first of the younger "models" like Jean Shrimpton, who were neither haughty and sedate, but lively and desirable. The same style of photography, using frequently sexual imagery, made advertising erotic. The Beatles, the biggest thing since Presley, were the acceptable face of pop, despite it being apparent that the tens of thousands of girls who turned out to greet them in London, New York and Adelaide were experiencing something close to orgasm. The leering, explicit Rolling Stones were not acceptable – the difference between wanting to hold hands and wanting to spend the night together.

Sex became a topic on everybody's lips: how to do it, how to attract someone to do it with, how to improve doing it. Thanks to Masters and Johnson, masturbation was not only permissible it was positively good; some psychologists and pyschotherapists recommended

*What's fit for the goose turned out not to be fit for the gander: when **Cosmo** featured male centrefolds like Burt Reynolds, female readers stopped buying.*

pornography as an aid and French novelist Alain Robbe-Grillet wrote: "An adult needs pornography as a child needs fairytales." Sexual fantasy was recognized as being indispensable in both masturbation and intercourse. A cartoon in which a couple are humping with evident dissatisfaction gave men and women everywhere a line of bedroom dialogue: "Can't you think of anyone, either?" A major survey conducted on behalf of the Playboy Foundation discovered that sexual liberalization was so advanced that four out of five couples were now indulging in oral sex. Furthermore, four in ten claimed to have sampled rear-entry sex – a practice virtually unrecorded by Kinsey.

STARS OF THE CENTREFOLD

Some tabloid newspapers began to publish topless pin-ups; toplessness was a fashion, too, for a while, at least for those capable of passing the pencil test. Some women's magazines tried a female version of the centrefold (Burt Reynolds was *Cosmo*'s first) until they discovered that sales fell – many women, however liberated, found photos of male "dangly bits" unedifying. Pubic hair, once the measure of an obscenity charge, was openly on display. Hefner's Playmates showed their pudenda, if discreetly, forced to do so by competition from the UK-produced *Penthouse* – which in turn was leapfrogged by Larry Flynt's *Hustler*, where the photographs were strictly gynaecological. "By the time the fifth issue came around, Flynt wrote in his biography, *An Unseemly Man*, "I had developed my own philosophy of what our models should look like."

"The Shrimp", Jean Shrimpton, the best known of the models to replace the haughty mannequin.

I wanted them to be the "girl next door". *Playboy*'s Hugh Hefner had always said that he

wanted that same look, but every woman who appeared in his magazine were the archetype for the unattainable … It seemed to me that the working stiffs I knew had fantasies about women who were a little more attainable.

Flynt dispensed with Hefner's rounded view of sex within a range of cultivated activities. "If a guy is going to jerk off looking at a centerfold, does he care about what kind of stereo to buy?" he wrote.

The November 1974 issue was a watershed, the first in which *Hustler* featured a so-called "pink shot". My idea of featuring female genitalia was fully realized. In the November issue the model's genitals were explicitly photographed, her vagina open like a flowering rose, fragile and pink.

Still from **The People vs Larry Flynt** – *them man who outdid* **Playboy** *in explicitness.*

SEX AND THE SILVER SCREEN

Theatre pushed the nudity envelope with the musical *Hair*, the erotic review *Oh! Calcutta!* – a happening that made the British Lord Chamberlain's Office relinquish its role in stage censorship – and *Che* (Guevara, the Cuban revolutionary) in which the cast was not only nude but simulated intercourse (which also got them arrested in New York). But cinema remained the real barometer. Female pubic hair, once the measure of an obscenity charge, appeared (a mere flash) in Antonioni's *Blow-Up*. Soon there was full frontal female nudity (first in the Swedish *Hugs and Kisses* – the British censor removed the scene, then put it back). The following year *If …* was showing male genitalia.

It was what was being done with male genitalia that caused the censors and the moralists the greatest anxiety. Simulated

Blow-Up: *the sexual themes of this Sixties film ensured it played to packed houses.*

2000

1990

1980

1970

1960

1950

1940

1930

1920

1910

1900

Hair, *the musical, advocated free love and featured full-frontal nudity of both sexes, playing to packed theatres. Milos Forman later brought* **Hair** *to the cinema.*

sex became so detailed that it was hard to tell it from the real thing. And sometimes was the real thing – Julie Christie and Donald Sutherland allegedly were not faking it in *Don't Look Now*, neither were Mick Jagger and Anita Pallenberg in *Performance*, both films by Nicholas Roeg. He was made to destroy the negative of the *Performance* love scene, under supervision. Then, after a cluster of ever more sexually explicit releases, came Bertolucci's *Last Tango in Paris* with its graphic frontal nudity, savage bouts of loveless intercourse, masturbation and sodomy with the aid of butter. "The most erotic move ever made," the *New Yorker* said. It seemed that mainstream cinematic sex was unlikely to go further. In *Sex on the Screen*, Gerard Lenn wrote that "the erection remains part of the specialized cinema." Not for long: *Deep Throat* crossed the line.

The first hard-porn movie to be seen worldwide in legitimate movie theatres, *Deep Throat* was different from the hardcore that proceeded it, in that it had a sense of humour and a storyline, which concerned a woman's inability to have an orgasm until she finds out that her clitoris is misplaced and she achieves satisfaction through oral sex. *Deep Throat* depicted seven acts of fellatio (besides four of cunnilingus and a choreographed orgy of male ejaculation reminiscent of Peckinpah's slow-motion shoot-outs in *The Wild Bunch*) and required Linda Lovelace to perform feats of which no sword swallower would be ashamed. "*Deep Throat* was one piece of pop culture that changed the way America thought about a major sexual practice," says Michael Perkins, who wrote the book of the film ("in two weeks, it supported some serious writing" – and sold a million). "The impact is difficult to describe to people in these blasé times of Monica Lewinsky. But it loosened all the other ties about sexuality."

There had been numerous prosecutions of mainstream films for obscenity. Most of them were overturned on appeal, but it was not surprising that *Deep Throat* found itself in New York criminal court. Among the prosecution witnesses was Ellen Steinberg, subpoenaed because she happened at the time to be working as a

The first widely distributed hard-core film was prosecuted for obscenity.

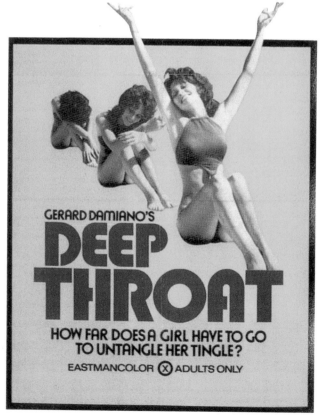

GERARD DAMIANO'S

DEEP THROAT

HOW FAR DOES A GIRL HAVE TO GO TO UNTANGLE HER TINGLE?

EASTMANCOLOR Ⓧ ADULTS ONLY

Benny Hill and a typical bevy of underdressed women.

popcorn girl in a theatre where the film was screened. Among witnesses for the defence was Marilyn Fithian, whose opinion was that *Deep Throat* "had a lot of socially redeeming value – and it was educational," and Dr John Money, professor of medical psychology at John Hopkins University, who said that people would be less likely to get divorced if they included films like it in their sex education. *Deep Throat* dispelled "the Victorian ethos that sex above the belt is fine and shows love, whereas sex below the belt has something nasty about it." The film, he said, put "an eggbeater in people's brains."

After considering 1,000 pages of testimony, Judge Joel Tyler called *Deep Throat* "a feast of carrion and squalor," and added: "This is one throat that deserves to be cut." The judgement gave the film even more street cred. Rochdale College in Toronto held illegal screenings and offered free entry to anyone who came in the nude. College president Bob Nasmith was the projectionist, because "there was a little heat involved and some people were concerned that

the law might get involved – I didn't give a damn." On one occasion the "Happy Hooker" Xaviera Hollander came to give deep throat demonstrations "and as a bonus gave a bit of lip service to the projectionist."
When *Deep Throat* got to the Supreme Court on appeal the conviction did not stick. A wave of "porno-chic" movies followed, including *The Devil in Miss Jones, The Story of Joanna* and *Behind the Green Door* (starring Marilyn Chambers, a former model in Ivory Snow detergent ads) which became the most successful hard-core movie of all time.
It says something about the British that while they liked hot screen sex they were fond of Benny Hill on television being endlessly chased by a bevy of under-dressed women, rather like a McGill postcard come to life, and to the nudge-nudge bawdy of the *Carry On* films. "English farce and low comedy ... coarse, iconoclastic and often scatological," Phillipe Daudy

Nudge-Nudge: one of the many **Carry On** *films, this one being* **Carry on Camping.**

2000 1990 1980 1970 1960 1950 1940 1930 1920 1910 1900

Christine Keeler, who played a part in the scandal that brought down the War Minister John Profumo.

wrote, with French aloofness in *Les Anglais: Portrait of a People*. "It is women who provide the greatest store of jokes ... This barrack-room humour is made up of adolescent frustrations translated into a virile buffoonery that unrelentingly ridicules all shameful temptations."

THE PRICE OF PUBLIC OPINION

In the immediate post-war years, morality seemed to have absolutes. As the years progressed things were less clear. However much private morality was changing, public opinion, a force unto itself, demanded that when War Minister John Profumo was caught with his pants around his ankles he had to pay a price. He had had an affair with Christine Keeler, who, as luck would have it, was also having an affair with a Soviet naval attaché. Keeler spilled the beans to the newspapers. A security enquiry soon revealed that no state secrets had been endangered and that the titillating coincidence between the bedroom antics of the politician and the Soviet diplomat (and possibly spy) were of no consequence. But the relentlessness of the press, which continued to hound Profumo long after suspicions of treachery were shown to be unfounded, led him to commit an unpardonable sin – he told the House of Commons that he had never had sexual relationships with Christine Keeler.

This *opera buffa* doubtless has a familiar, current ring. Thirty and more years later, public opinion still has much the same appetite for retribution. Until Profumo, newspapers either ignored tales of indiscretion or treated them with respect. But the sexual revolution had removed the journalistic gloves. One wonders how the libidinous Jack Kennedy – who turned the White House into a kind of Whitehall farce, with floozies being escorted out the back door as Jackie came in at the front – would have fared had he not been cut down in Dallas in the year that Profumo retired from public life. Marilyn Monroe, who had arrived late at a microphone to sing "Happy birthday Mr President" – prophetically introduced by Peter Lawford as "the late Marilyn Monroe" – was already in her grave, as much a victim of fraternal Kennedyism as of the Hollywood that had ruthlessly exploited her.

SEX IN PRINT

In the Fifties, if you wanted a book with dirty words in it, you got it from a back-street bookshop in a plain wrapper; it was, of course, de rigeur for the avant-garde to smuggle back copies of *Tropic of Cancer* and *Lady Chatterley's Lover* from Paris. In 1960, to coincide with the thirtieth anniversary of Lawrence's death, Penguin decided to publish his oeuvre in paperback and that, of course, included *Lady Chatterley*.

Lawrence's quasi-religious tract, recounting the salvation of the wife of the impotent Sir Clifford through

Marilyn had to be stitched into her dress before singing "Happy Birthday Mr President" to John Kennedy.

"the mystery" of gamekeeper Mellor's phallus (a favourite Lawrentian word) had appeared in America the previous year, been prosecuted and acquitted; British publication was to be a test of the "public good" provision of the 1959 Obscene Publications Act.

In his opening address, Mervyn Griffith-Jones, QC, hoped to shock the jury by telling them that the book involved thirteen acts of sexual intercourse, thirty "fucks" or derivations, fourteen "cunts", thirteen "balls", six "arses", six "shits", four "cocks" and three "pisses". He attempted to denigrate the sexual couplings by emphasizing that they took place "on the floor of a hut,

2000
1990
1980
1970
1960
1950
1940
1930
1920
1910
1900

in the undergrowth, in the forest." In the same address he made the farcical remark that was to follow him for the rest of his life: "Is it a book that you would have lying around in your own house? Is it a book that you would even wish your wife or your servants to read?"

Critics, clergymen, writers and a motley of others with an opinion trooped through the witness box. Griffith-Jones reduced a lady professor of English from Cambridge to tears, which infuriated social historian Richard Hoggart who gave evidence after her and "with a sudden excess of provincial bravado" said that *Lady Chatterley* "was virtuous and puritanical" – a view he defended against Griffith-Jones' bullying, although he was thinking, "My God, what a load of old tripe". The most extraordinary support for Lawrence came from Dr John Robinson, Anglican Bishop of Woolwich (who later wrote *Honest to God,* an attempt to interpret religion for modern man which scandalized conservatism). He described the book as "Something sacred … an act of holy communion. Lawrence's descriptions of sexual relations cannot be taken out of the context of his quite astonishing sensitivity to the beauty and value of all organic relations. I think the effect of this book is against, rather than for, promiscuity." A book Christians ought to read? "Yes, I think it is."

The jury brought in a verdict of "not guilty".

Today Hoggart describes the trial as "theatre, farce. A judge who didn't know whether he was coming or going – if he read *Horse and Hound* that was about his limit; his wife sitting at the back of the court with *Lady Chatterley* in a little case she'd knitted so that it wouldn't be seen when she was carrying it; a prosecutor who might have been carved out of solid rock, embodying all the worst of the old attitudes; and a jury which took three days to read the book in advance, one of them I think penning it out with his finger." But he adds: "It showed that people were much further ahead than what we might call establishment figures."

Fast-forward a decade to another courtroom and we find another trial, but one which was more comedy show than theatre: the trial of Australian Richard Neville and two colleagues, accused of publishing an obscene issue of their magazine, *Oz*. There were a number of underground publications like *Oz,* attacking the establishment, advocating drug use, promoting sex as a revolutionary weapon that would wrest power from the men in suits. Produced with a *Private Eye*-ish sense of humour, *Oz* had printed a few pictures of Mick Jagger's censored love scene from *Performance* (Neville was at the screening, sneaked into the projection booth and snipped out a few frames). What put the trio in the dock, however, was a "schoolkids" issue, edited by teenagers, which, James McMillan wrote in *The Way It Changed,* showed "Rupert Bear forcing a passage into his grandmother [and] teachers presented as sadists and sexual perverts, displaying gargantuan private parts."

Comedy show? Neville was to write:

Detective Inspector Frederick Luff took the stand.
"Having now read the magazine several times, is your mind a seething cauldron of depravity?"
The chubby-chops crusader fidgeted and mumbled.
"Speaking as a mature man – I don't know."

A "schoolkids": edition of **Oz** *magazine (opposite) led to the longest obscenity hearing in Britain.*

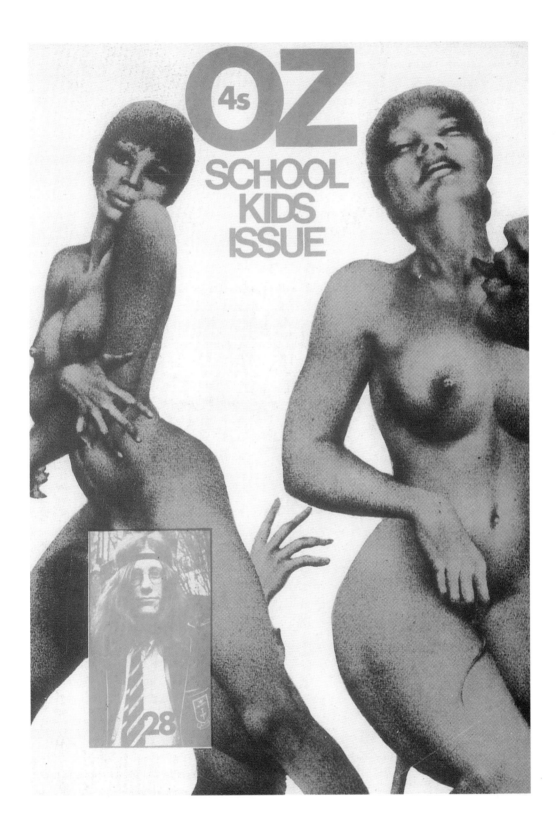

2000

1990

1980

1970

1960

1950

1940

1930

1920

1910

1900

"What are the worst bits?"

"The masturbating teacher," he said, referring to a full-page illustration of a pipe-smoking military type fingering himself and a schoolboy. "And the advertisement for *Suck* newspaper." This was three inches of text, describing a fancy version of fellatio.

"Has that corrupted you?"

"Perhaps. It had a tendency to make me think about sucking penis."

The gallery hooted.

Among witnesses for the defence were the wall-eyed comedian Marty Feldman and George Melly, then film critic of *The Observer* who says: "*Oz* was a bit rude, I mean, Rupert Bear with a big dick sticking out and so on, but it was the kids, that's what kids all want." On the stand, Melly was asked to turn to the page with the advertisement alluded to by Detective Inspector Luff, "which said that one way to make your oral sex even more enjoyable was to fill your mouth with ice cubes for a bit, then remove them and start on the oral sex and then fill your mouth with hot coffee and swallow it and return to the oral sex – the contrast between ice cold and hot, you know. I was asked what I thought this meant. I used the word cunnilingus and the judge said, "Mr Melly, the jury have not necessarily been enabled in their life by

classical education, would you mind explaining in ordinary words what cunnilingus means." I went right over the top. I said, "Well, sucking off or going down or gobbling or, to quote an expression we used to use in the navy, yodelling in the canyon." The whole jury collapsed with laughter. I was told sternly that this was not a musical. After listening to all this rubbish, hours of it, I went to New Merlin's Cave which is where I used to sing … with the John Chiltern Feet Warmers and I looked round all these families from Islington, men with beards, kids, and I thought, 'There are still human beings about.'"

Neville and his co-defendants were given prison sentences, but had their conviction quashed on appeal. "A sledge hammer to crack a nut, no, a popcorn seed," Melly says of the six-

Richard Neville and his fellow co-founders of the underground magazine **Oz**.

Moral minority: Mary Whitehouse and Malcom Muggeridge, at the Festival of Light Rally, 1971.

week trial, the longest obscenity hearing in a British court. He sees the *Chatterley* and *Oz* trials like "a pair of bookends" at either end of British repression – with the latter "the last kick of puritanism." In 1976, when a prosecution against the publication of *Inside Linda Lovelace* failed, even the police said it was no longer possible to press obscenity charges against the written word.

Moralists on both sides of the Atlantic had a tough time of it. Yet, in Britain, set-backs did not seem to diminish Mary Whitehouse's appetite for the fight. A Shropshire housewife, she had been on a crusade from the early Sixties to salvage the nation's morals. She was against pornography; mothers who let young daughter go on the Pill; Dr Martin Cole, who for a number of years made some attempt to establish sex surrogacy therapy in Britain; sex outside marriage; public displays of sex. But most of all she was against BBC television which she saw as a sink of inequity. Besides allowing "torrid love scenes" and "foul language", the BBC had allowed theatre critic Kenneth Tynan – who had staged *Oh! Calcutta!* – to be the first person on British television to say "fuck". George Melly and Jonathan Miller who watched Tynan's appearance – in a debate in which he said he would allow sexual intercourse on the stage of the National Theatre – "sent him a telegram of congratulations, instantly."

Whiter-than-white campaigner Mary Whitehouse demanded the resignation of the British board of film censors for passing Last Tango in Paris.

Whitehouse announced she was writing to the Queen and started a "Clean Up TV Campaign" (which turned into the National Viewers and Listeners Association).

There were other battlers for moral propriety, notable among them the Catholic Lord Longford and the television sage Malcolm Muggeridge. In *Revolt Into Style*, Melly declared his irritation with the television pundit Muggeridge,

> a one-time radical, whose views, tempered by a healthy cynicism, were rational and whose behaviour was all too human [who] has transferred his undeniable wit and professionalism to the service of a form of Christianity based on the rejection of pleasure, the suppression of sex and the denial of appetites. Where once he puffed smoke across the studio like a steam train, he now sits tobaccoless and celibate, castigating the whole age with an obsessive relish.

"St Mug" as Muggeridge was popularly known, was at least funny a lot of the time. "Lord Porn", who peered about him through milk-bottle lenses that evidently magnified the filth on which they alighted, was not. However, when the government set up a committee to investigate pornography, "the fastest-growing industry in the West," according to James McMillan's *The Way It Changed*, Longford was the only man for the job of chairing it. His 500-page report appeared in 1972 – a year in which Customs and Excise confiscated some

2.5 million pornographic items, 50 times the 1960 figure. Britain, Longford concluded, was suffering from a "neurotic sexual preoccupation which almost reached a point of perversion," and recommended that obscenity should be legally defined as that "which outrages contemporary standards of decency or humanity accepted by the public at large" – a definition through which a John Mortimer, QC, could have driven a double-decker bus. Not that the recommendation was even considered because, as Paul Ferris pointed out in *Sex and the British:*

> A scholarly essay by a liberal-minded psychologist, Dr Maurice Yaffé, printed as an appendix, concluded that there was little evidence about the effects of pornography. This effectively demolished the entire report.

In the States, Nixon's presidential commission on pornography not only declined to pronounce against it, finding no evidence of its harm, but voting to repeal all federal, state and local laws against the sale or exhibition of sexual materials to adults – much to the disgust of the occupier of the Oval Office who rejected the recommendation. "Pornography will corrupt Western culture and civilisation," he raged, before he was consigned to the margins by his own brand of immorality.

There can never be a consensual view about something so diverse as sex: people's opinions eddy and flow and depend on their age, class, experience, wealth and religious belief. Even as permissiveness appeared to have laid waste to all around it, something of a backlash occurred. On both sides of the Atlantic there was talk about "a moral majority". In Britain a "Festival of Light" rally held in Trafalgar Square attracted the largely middle-aged women of Christian conviction who supported Mary Whitehouse. She (bearing a message from the Pope), was supported by Muggeridge and Longford, as well as the chaste pop singer Cliff Richard. In America, *U.S.News & World* reported, "After years of growing license for eroticism, many people across the US are fed up. Crackdowns are beginning on blatantly pornographic books, movies, stage shows – even radio programs." The magazine went on to list some of the actions taken: the closure of a sex bookstore in De Kalb County, Illinois, by a new ordnance prohibiting such businesses from opening within 200 yards of a church, school or house; the seizure at Newport Beach, California, of 1,000 reels of obscene films, packed in cartons labelled "Mother's Cookies"; the picketing of a Detroit theatre by protesters carrying placards reading "What Happened to Family Pictures?" More widely there were moves to prohibit X-rated movies at drive-ins where the screen was visible to passers-by, notice of suspension of alcohol licences was served on bars employing nude waitresses and entertainers, and police started making arrests in bars where sexual intercourse was being staged as part of the entertainment. In New York City Mayor John Lindsay began sweeping the peep shows, porno movies and prostitutes out of Times Square.

None of these things would put the genie back in the bottle but as the Eighties arrived the world seemed jaded by the heavy commercialisation and cynicism which had turned the sexual revolution into the sexual marketplace. Genital herpes, virulent relative of the common cold, had knocked on the door and sent the promiscuous scurrying to the clinics for check-ups. And AIDS, "the gay disease", was suddenly realized not to be just a striker-down of homosexuals. Headlines like the *Wall Street Journal's* "New, Often-Fatal Illness Seen In Gay

Men Now Affecting Women, Heterosexual Men" and others – "How Heterosexuals Can Get Gay Disease", "Now No-One Is Safe!" – put a crimp in the public sex scene, while sending sales of condoms soaring. Among those who died was Marco Vassi. "AIDS did not end swinging, but it ended my participation in it and most of the people that I knew," says writer Michael Perkins. "It was the death-knell for real swinging. Ending with AIDS is perhaps metaphorically what should have happened."

A lot of people re-examined their lives. Many who tried to prove that emotion was mere sentimentality and that recreational sex did not endanger emotional ties had been hurt. One was Marianne Faithfull, Mick Jagger's girlfriend when he filmed *Performance* and had on-set intercourse with Anita Pallenberg:

Having intercourse with Anita Pallenberg on set during the making of **Performance** *irreparably damaged Mick Jagger's relationship with Marianne Faithfull.*

I pretended everything was okay. Anita was my dearest friend and Mick was the man I loved. I was expecting his baby. I guess I knew by then things weren't right between Mick and me, but I didn't know what to do about it. It was terrible. And anyway, who was I to talk? I'd had my blazing affair with Tony Kent the year before. It was like that then. If it felt good, you did it. That was part of our creed. It would have been hypocritical not to sleep with someone simply because they were involved with someone else! But Anita was my friend, my only friend really – that was betrayal.

Never from the beginning a true believer in the promiscuity in which she indulged, Faithfull wrote a sad song, *Why'd Ya Do It* which contained a line that spoke for a million betrayals: "Every time I see your cock, I imagine her cunt in my bed".

There were other self-selected victims, including Sandstone regulars John and Judith Bullaro who, John Heidenny noted in *What Wild Ecstasy,* were major characters in *Thy Neighbor's Wife,* Gay Talese's examination of sex in America:

In one long scene, which Talese believed to be the most sexual he would ever write, he recalled how Bullaro watched Judith make love to John Williamson. Although just moments before Bullaro himself had made love to Barbara Williamson, he collapsed, finding the sight of his wife making love to another man unbearable.

The Bullaros' marriage collapsed soon after. So did the marriage of Jonathan Dana who made the film about Sandstone (it grossed $1 million in 1975) and who had taken part in the retreat's lifestyle with his wife. "Jealousy is a green-eyed monster," he says. "I think a lot of people got hurt." Like Tom Hatfield, a member of Sandstone's inner commune who produced the retreat's magazine. His girlfriend stopped having sex with him when she started having sex with one of the film crew and, Hatfield admits, "I got a little hysterical." Michael Perkins was another whose marriage was destroyed by permissiveness: "Jealousy is an emotion that is like poison, and you find it seeping into your emotional relationship and you can't stop it, it's like an addiction," he says. "It came in two stages. The first kind was a simple sexual jealousy: she touches someone else in a sexual way, she wants someone else, then I must be nothing to her. That can be easily gotten over – no, not easily, there were scenes, fights, quarrels. And that can actually be a spice to lovemaking, to feel a little frisson of jealousy. But the second stage of jealousy comes when the other person stops making an emotional commitment and that's when the relationship inevitably breaks down. We lasted about four years I guess before it broke down for us and she found that she was more interested emotionally and sexually in other people. She found sado-masochism which I didn't condemn or judge in any way, it simply did not appeal to me. And so we split. End of that experiment."

Perkins saw "a lot of freak-outs at Plato's, where "men couldn't handle their jealousy and the bouncers had to hustle them away." In retrospect, he thinks that open sexuality was "wonderful in concept, difficult in execution, and ultimately impossible." He adds: "In my older age I begin to think that moderation is probably the best path. Sexual obsessiveness can be damaging. It's numbing like anything else. And unless there is emotional commitment, what's the point?"

2000

1990

1980

1970

1960

1950

1940

1930

1920

1910

1900

IDENTITY IS
DESTINY

SIXTIES GRASS-ROOTS POLITICAL AGITATION AGAINST WAR, FOR NUCLEAR DISARMAMENT AND, IN THE STATES, FOR BLACK CIVIL RIGHTS, GAVE BIRTH TO FEMINIST AND GAY PRIDE. BOTH MOVEMENTS WANTED THE SAME THING: EQUALITY. FEMINISM STARTED WITH A SMALL, EDUCATED ELITE; GAY PRIDE WAS A SOUND THAT CAME UP FROM THE STREET.

Gay: purloining the word in the 1950s robbed the language of something for which there is no exact synonym and upset linguistic purists and others, including Kenneth Anger, the homosexual film-maker. "The loss of a perfectly good word," he says. "And it trivializes the homosexual experience." For most non-heterosexual men and women, however, the word was important, not just because it embraced both sexes comfortably, which "homosexual" did not, but because it defined rather than disparaged.

In Oscar Wilde's time, "the vice that dare not speak its name" really had no name – the pejorative term was "invert": homosexuality was usually referred to in euphemisms. "Homosexual" had been coined in the mid-nineteenth century, but it did not come into usage until the century's end, when the medical profession was dividing into specialities that were marking out their territory. When Wilde stood trial, homosexuality was regarded as a weakness of character, a vice. To several of the new branches of medicine it was an illness or a psychological disorder. In the decade from 1898 to 1908 a huge literature of more than 1,000 papers were published on the subject, much of it nonsensical and contradictory.

While what men did sexually together was covered in law, what lesbians did was entirely their affair. (It was said that no legislation was suggested in Victoria's reign because none of her ministers wished to explain the matter to her). An attempt was made in 1921 to bring lesbianism within the law, but nothing happened: it was better not to let people become aware that there was such a thing as female same-sex sex. Novelist Radclyffe Hall ("John" to her friends) wrote *The Well of Loneliness* to disabuse the public and "to encourage inverts to face up to a hostile world in their true colours" and "to bring normal men of good will to a fuller tolerant understanding." The book was prosecuted in the most famous literary trial in Britain before *Chatterley* as likely to

"deprave and corrupt those whose minds are open to such immoral influences". The publisher was fined twenty guineas and copies seized and destroyed. As Radclyffe Hall, who appeared in court in a Spanish riding hat and a leather motoring coat with Astrakhan collar, emerged, the women who had occupied the gallery shook her hand. Anyone who has tried to read *The Well of Loneliness* is likely to agree with Virginia Woolf's assessment of it as a "meritorious dull book … one simply can't keep one's eyes on the page." Nonetheless, for many lesbians, the court case concerning it "was an affirmation of their existence."

For some – the intellectuals, artists, actors, the well-to-do – it was chic to be gay in the Twenties and Thirties: bohemianism was attractive; for many students it was a guise, a form of rebelliousness. Women in men's clothing like Tallulah Bankhead in London or Gertrude Stein's salon in Paris, who affected monocles, jodhpurs and boots, were regarded as an exotic *divertissement*. Camp, personified by Noel Coward, only just over the border from heterosexuality, was acceptable and amusing. For most ordinary homosexuals, theirs was a secret world, hermetic – and largely safe, if one did not go importuning in public places – with its own meeting places, the pubs and clubs which tolerated them. At various times homosexuals had ways

Oscar Wilde: imprisoned for two years for homosexual offences, he died in exile.

"John" Radclyffe Hall: her prosecuted novel struck a blow for lesbians.

of recognizing one another, until these passed into the mainstream and were abandoned: brown suede shoes, a pink shirt or a ring on the little finger were to the two decades what the earring was to be to the Seventies and early Eighties. In the interwar years, an outrageous few like Quentin Crisp (who famously declared himself "one of the stately homos of England") simply did not care who knew what they were and dressed and acted accordingly. "In an era where gay men and lesbians could only define themselves in terms of the heterosexual world," Alkarim Jivani wrote in *It's Not Unusual*, a history of 20th century British homosexuality, "the ones who were relatively open about their sexuality felt that they had to present themselves as parodies of that world." Explains Crisp:

The roughs were the boys who pretended to be more masculine than they were and the bitches were the boys who pretended to be more feminine than they were. And in this way we parodied the masculine/feminine – it was a pseudo-normal life. We couldn't imagine a life in which two women who are fond of one another live together – it had to be that one was a pseudo man and one was a woman. And it was the same with the boys – we had to have a pseudo-normal relationship.

The armed forces have always been nervous about homosexuals in its ranks. When World War Two was declared, they attempted to screen them out. US army psychiatrists at induction stations watched for signs and used words or phrases from homosexual parlance to see if they were was a flicker of recognition; men were asked if they had homosexual feelings or experiences. Absurd diagnostic tests were devised. One, published in the *American Journal of Psychiatry* after the war, was based on the belief

Quentin Crisp: turned down for war service because of sexual perversion.

that homosexual men did not display a gag reflex in response to the application of a tongue depressor; another, devised jointly by the US army and navy, supposedly could detect a specific reaction common to all those "confirmed to the practice of sexual oralism". During the course of the war, some 4,000 US servicemen were discharged for sexual "abnormality" and an unspecified number were released as "neuropsychiatric cases".

The British forces screened out the most outrageous homosexuals and during the war conducted more courts martial for "indecency between males" than for any other category of offence, although the numbers were few – 48 in 1939, 324 in 1945. Generally speaking, however, the services turned a blind eye, particularly the navy, where many even extravagant homosexuals found a place to fight for their country. *It's Not Unusual* related the story of a coder on a ship whose action station was to relay the messages from the captain to the forward guns who would simply repeat, "Open fire, dear," making the crew collapse.

"Some gay soldiers who were sent abroad were amazed by what they found," *Newsweek* wrote in 1994. "A 26-year-old army captain from Cincinnati was dumbfounded in 1945 when he first walked into the Boeuf sur le Toit in Paris: "It was a great gay nightclub," he remembered. "Beef on the roof! Suddenly you realized the size of homosexuality - the total global reach of it. There were hundreds of guys there from all over the world in all kinds of uniforms: there were Free Poles dancing with American soldiers; there were Scotsmen dancing with Algerians; there were Free French; there were Russians. It was like a United Nations of gays."

Some homosexuals who did not get into uniform had their own experiences to relate. Quentin Crisp – who turned up for an army medical arrayed in his trademark velvet suit and hennaed hair and was given his exemption papers which said he suffered from sexual perversion – was one. The GIs who thronged London could not credit him. They would seize his hands, inspect his long varnished nails and call out to each other to come and have a look. They were fascinated by Crisp's voice, too, and continually asked him to "say something." Crisp adds: "And whatever you said was wonderful and I thought 'I'm the toast of the regiment!'"

George Melly was an active homosexual

Boeuf sur le Toit: "a great gay nightclub".

2198. Marine Militaire Française   Le Bal à bord d'un cuirassé

French sailors dance together. During both world wars a percentage of basically heterosexual men displayed various levels of homosexual behaviour when deprived of women.

when he volunteered for the navy near the end of the war. He went to the recruiting office from Stowe public school "wearing pink corduroys, sandals, and an open silk shirt with some art-school scarves I'd nicked from the still-life drawers. I don't think I was wearing any make-up or if I was it was very discreet." An admiral asked him why he wanted to join the navy and he replied: "I think the uniform is so much more amusing, don't you?" He got in, trained as an able seaman and, when D-Day arrived and the navy "pulled out those they found the least promising", found himself at Chatham on an "overflow" ship with not much to do except take lovers in the crew and in London where he frequently went. He remembers catching "crabs" ("the navy called them minge mice, mechanized dandruff, mobilized blackheads – I loved those expressions") and he passed them on "to this gang of rich gays I was involved with, who weren't best pleased. One of them I remember lying in a bath in great luxury complaining bitterly and I said, "That'll teach you to sleep with the lower deck.'"

After the war Melly went to work in an art gallery for a Belgian poet called E.L.T. Mesens and one day ended up in bed with him and his wife Sylvia – "a kind of bridge, I suppose between total homosexuality and heterosexuality." Once he launched himself into the jazz world, Melly gradually began to have girlfriends as well as boyfriends "and eventually no boyfriends at all." His second marriage has lasted thirty-six years. One wonders how Kinsey, who ruled that homosexuality was not a fixed entity and recorded the wide diversity of bisexuality in much homosexual behaviour, would have scored Melly on his famous scale – a scale on which he scored Kenneth Anger "a perfect six". Says Anger:

> When I asked him what that meant, he said a seven was exclusively homosexual, a six meant that I
> would be attracted to some women, and that's right. I've slept with some women. I was deeply in love
> once with a married woman but she went back to her husband. In the hippie days one witch claimed
> I was the father of her baby which may be true. But basically I'm homosexual and I'm proud of it.

During the Second World War, gay men and women experienced the same sexual liberation as everyone else, returned with an idea of the extent of homosexuality – which had never before been apparent – and perhaps expected to capitalize on what they now knew. But, like women who had similarly profited, they had to be put back in their place. When fear about the Cold War was at its height in the US, McCarthy arrived on the scene to equate communism with "deviancy" and stoke a moral panic. Homosexuals were targeted as security risks. "Those who engage in overt acts of perversion lack the emotional stability of normal persons," a Senate committee said. Almost every government department equipped itself with a polygraph. No politician would associate himself with the conservative Mattachine Society, the "ties-and-jackets" gay-rights movement.

Unquestionably, Alfred Kinsey was a factor in what became almost a pogrom. Before him, most people thought that homosexuality was rare; after him, most people thought that homosexuals were everywhere. In fact, Kinsey had not quite said what popular belief held – his statement that ten per cent of men had more than a casual homosexual contact was shorn of its important if muddled qualification that the percentage was "exclusively homosexual for at least three years between the ages of sixteen and fifty-five". The fact that elsewhere in *Sexual Behavior in the Human Male* he put the figure of males who were exclusively life-long homosexuals at four per cent (which subsequent studies have largely indicated is about the case) was somehow lost. That horrified Kinsey. But he refused to speak out in public: "The upheaval that would follow would be hardly less disrupting than if the communists were to take over the administration of the Federal Government," he said, which from a man who knew he was under FBI scrutiny sounds like a bit of special pleading. Kinsey's silence allowed the "10 per cent" to become common currency, even among homosexuals. One homosexual group in Madison, Wisconsin, called itself the Ten Per Cent Society and for several decades the figure was regularly used by groups like the National Gay and Lesbian Task Force.

In the climate of fear the post-war years engendered, homosexuals began to congregate for protection and support in their own ghettos: in Greenwich Village in New York, in Chicago, Los Angeles, San Francisco, New Orleans, Miami. A "gay manifesto" pamphlet from the time said:

> San Francisco is a refugee camp for homosexuals. We have fled here from every part of the nation, and
> like refugees elsewhere, we came not because it is so great here, but because it was so bad there. By the
> tens of thousands, we fled small towns where to be ourselves would endanger our jobs and any hope of
> a decent life. We have fled from blackmailing cops, from families who disowned or "tolerated" us; we
> have been drummed out of the armed services, thrown out of schools, fired from jobs, beaten by punks.

*Gay actor Rock Hudson – here with Elizabeth Taylor in the 1956 film **Giant** – was to die of AIDS but, to the end, refused to come out of the closet.*

2000

1990

1980

1970

1960

1950

1940

1930

1920

1910

1900

In Britain the same climate of fear was fuelled, largely in response to American pressure and the humiliation felt by the country over the defection to the Soviet Union of the homosexual spies Burgess and Maclean. Arrests and convictions shot up. In 1938, the last full year before the war, 956 men were prosecuted; in 1952, the figure was 3,757, almost a four-fold increase. When masturbation and oral sex, whether in public or private, were "gross indecency" and carried a maximum jail sentence of two years, and anal sex could mean life, a gay man was advised not to give anyone his surname or address or keep a diary: any gay men coming to police attention would have his possessions turned over and his friends questioned – and they were likely to finish up in court with him. Just speaking to another man in the street, even innocently, could result in arrest for importuning. *It's Not Unusual* quoted one man who was alleged to have stopped three separate men in the street (the police did not produce them as witnesses) who said of his conviction and fine:

Homosexual spy Donald Maclean defected to the USSR in 1951.

I felt dirty, I felt that they had sort of disfigured me – I really did feel as if they had torn half my face away and... [I had] all these gangling nerve ends. And I was terrified to go out ... even just to the shop. I was terrified that I was going to be picked up again by another police car, that they were after me, and of course my sex drive disappeared completely.

It is a sad reflection on the time that homosexuals were held in such contempt that the police on both sides of the Atlantic felt that they had a perfect right not just to set them up but to fit them up, too. The public was not prepared to listen to cries of injustice or worry that many convicted homosexuals lost their jobs. In fact, a suggestion that homosexuals should be sent to remote Scottish islands like St Kilda where "the natural and bracing climate would strengthen their resolve" received strong public support. To be homosexual in the postwar years was to be paranoid; 90 per cent of all blackmail cases in the era involved homosexuals.

Kinsey's biographer James H. Jones believes that the sexologist Havelock Ellis did not consider homosexuality to be an illness, but suspected the public was not prepared to accept a more enlightened view. "At least for the time being, the disease model offered the best hope for winning tolerance for homosexuals," Jones wrote. Unfortunately, homosexuality was thereafter regarded as something which could be treated and in the postwar years medicine became determined not to be thwarted. During the Fifties and much of the Sixties a number of therapies were offered to, and sometimes forced on, homosexuals. Those making a court appearance were often told they would receive a lesser punishment if they underwent treatment. Usually this was aversion therapy – alcohol combined with drugs made a patient vomit while he looked at erotic gay literature or slides; sometimes electro-convulsive shocks were administered; occasionally, shockingly, lobotomies were performed. One who agreement to hormone treatment was Alan Turing, a mathematician who, as a cryptographer at Bletchley during the war, helped to crack the Nazi Enigma codes and went on to produce the first modern computer. The treatment caused depression as a result of which he poisoned himself. As late as 1963 psychiatrists were said to have "overwhelming evidence that homosexuals are created not born".

Authority was particularly keen to make an example of "names". A Labour MP was entrapped by the police and his career was ruined. The actor Sir John Gielgud made an embarrassed court appearance. On the evidence of two sailors who later said their statements were false and forced from them by the police, the book reviewer of *The Sketch* newspaper, the novelist Rupert Croft-Cooke, was sent to jail – where he wrote a book, *The Verdict of You*

A group of homosexuals dressed as women are loaded into a police "paddywagon" after a raid in New York in 1939.

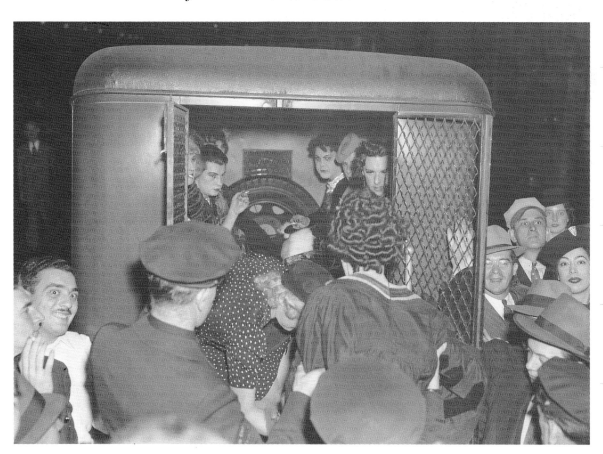

The arrest of actor John Gielgud caused the Press to call for his new knighthood to be withdrawn.

All, exposing what was in effect a government witch-hunt that "dragged men of probity from useful life" and "put them stunned and baffled in prison." A few weeks after his release, Croft-Cooke received an official letter demanding the return of his war decorations. He refused. Then, within a month of Croft-Cooke's conviction, the police netted "the big one" – a peer of the realm. Lord Montagu of Beaulieu, his second cousin Michael Pitt-Rivers and the journalist Peter Wildeblood also went to jail, on the evidence of two RAF servicemen who had taken part in consensual acts but whose evidence bought them immunity. In *Against the Law*, Peter Wildeblood later wrote:

> I am no more proud of my condition than I would be of having a glass eye or a hare-lip. On the other hand I am no more ashamed of it than I would be of being colour-blind or writing with my left hand.

It was evident from the Montagu trial, with its manifest hypocrisy and double standards, that this state of affair could not go on. In 1954 the British government appointed Wolfenden to consider prostitution and homosexuality; when the Committee reported three years later, its recommendation concerning homosexual behaviour was that what happened in private between two consenting adults over twenty-one should be decriminalized – the first progressive piece of proposed legislation relating to homosexuality for five centuries. However, Home Secretary Rab Butler considered Wolfenden to be "in advance of public opinion" – and the recommendation was not implemented for another ten years. By then homosexual decriminalization in America was under way as a result of the Model Penal Code which recommended the repeal of state sodomy statutes (as well as those relating to adultery and fornication), because it was no longer the government's place "to enforce purely moral or religious standards". Illinois was the first state to fall into line on homosexuality – something that just under half the states still have not done.

Sixties fashion, which brought the genders closer together, allowed many lesbians to dress less obviously as men and allowed some gay men to express their sexuality more openly in clothes that a decade previously would have got them assaulted. In the Seventies, as a reaction

First as a play, then as a film, **Boys in the Band** *dealt with homosexuality asa contemporary subject, making the public begin to view it with more understanding.*

to decades of being told that they were surrogate women, many homosexual men sought to establish an identity of their own in the "gay clone" look still prevalent today – a look which at the beginning of the Eighties had the *London Evening Standard* asserting that "gay men these days are manlier than the straights." Popular culture was also acknowledging homosexual culture and plays like *Boys in the Band* and films like *Victim,* both dealing with homosexuality as a contemporary subject, had an impact on the thinking of straight and gay alike. In his survey of cinematic homosexuality, *The Celluloid Closet,* Vito Russo commented that *Victim* "creates a gay hero with credentials enough to get into heaven, let alone society," but Dirk Bogart who played the barrister whose marriage and career are threatened by blackmail over a brief homosexual affair puts it in a more significant light: "It was the first film in which a man said 'I love you' to another man. I wrote that scene in. I said, 'There's no point in half-measures. We either make a film about queers or we don't.'"

Gays became increasingly visible as they began to network, to set up their own action groups, to meet in their own clubs and bars. But self-belief did not come in a rush. Even as the world loosened up around them, many in the gay community felt such guilt and self-loathing that even their own organizations tolerated speakers who savaged them. As late as

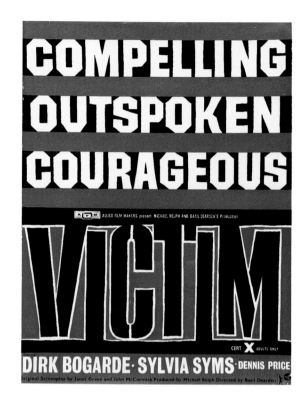

COMPELLING
OUTSPOKEN
COURAGEOUS

ALLIED FILM MAKERS present MICHAEL RELPH AND BASIL DEARDEN'S Production

VICTIM

CERT X ADULTS ONLY

DIRK BOGARDE · SYLVIA SYMS · DENNIS PRICE

Original Screenplay by Janet Green and John McCormick Produced by Michael Relph Directed by Basil Dearden

1963 psychiatrist Albert Ellis told a gay group that "the exclusive homosexual is a psychopath." It was difficult to be "out". Most homosexuals led a double life, their straight friends and business associates unaware of their true sexuality. Some homosexuals denied their own inclinations even to themselves like Jim Fourett, a prime mover in the Youth International Party (the Yippies), a political movement whose aim was to make "politics and anything held sacred look absurd". Once, defending a Black Panther text, he insisted that "faggot" was black argot for a powerless man, not a homosexual. Eventually he came to realize he was denying his own nature and "outed" himself on the David Soskine TV show in the late Sixties. "Virtually nobody dared to be 'out' in the late Sixties, early Seventies," he says. "There was no such thing as a gay actor in Hollywood. Most of the

Victim, *starring Dirk Bogarde (below, right) was the first film in which one man told another "I love you".*

Peter Finch, who made a film playing Oscar Wilde and then appeared in **Sunday Bloody Sunday** *(above, left with Murray Head) was unafraid to take on gay roles.*

people who were 'out' had to give up their career track. You couldn't be a gay doctor or teacher or whatever - and what does that do to a person, having to separate his sexuality from the rest of the way he presents oneself to the world?" Bob Kohler, another veteran gay activist, had no such problem: "I've done more so-called butch things than most straight men I know. I fought in a war, I spent eight months in a hospital I was so fucked up. I don't know what makes 'a man;. I had no problem with either my feminine side or my masculine side but a lot of people did, constantly being told 'You're less than a man, less than a man.'"

But, bit by bit, things did change. The Washington branch of the Mattachine Society issued a statement: "In the absence of valid evidence to the contrary, homosexuality is not a sickness, disturbance or other pathology in any sense, but is merely a reference, orientation or propensity, on a par with, and not different in kind from, heterosexuality." The American Psychiatric Association, previously a hostile enemy, removed homosexuality from its list of mental disorders, at last recognizing homosexuality not as an illness but a state of being. When the Kinsey Institute asked homosexuals if they would take a "magic pill" to turn them into heterosexuals the vast majority said no.

STONEWALL AND BEYOND

Years of struggle went into making gayness proud. But sometimes a single moment defines a cause and that moment came on June 28, 1969, when a sleazy dive on Christopher Street in

New York 1962: a drag queen is taken away from a public gathering – for masquerading as a woman.

Greenwich Village, the Stonewall Inn – a well-known gathering place for gay men, lesbians and transvestites – was raided. Gay bars across the US were used to being rousted: the cops usually dragged away the most flagrant queens and anyone wearing three or more items of the opposite sex's clothing. There was nothing significant about the Stonewall raid – and yet it suddenly turned into a riot in which, for the very first time, the gays fought back.

Jim Fourett was on his way home late from the record company where he then worked: "As I came round the corner I saw the police car pull up in front of Stonewall. They brought out this very butch woman, you know, a 'diesel dyke', a 'bulldagger' were the kinds of words that were used. There's a park opposite where a lot of gay street kids lived and they started taunting her as the police put her in the car. She was thrashing around - first she got out of the cuffs, then she threw herself against the door and suddenly she tumbled out and started pushing her body against the car - she actually moved it, to the cheers of the crowd. And suddenly things escalated from a sort of camp comedy and ignited. For me, being a political person, it was a moment not to forget." The police retreated into the bar. Parking meters were uprooted and thrown in after them, as well as trash cans.

Bob Kohler, who was walking his dog to the park, remembers: "The kids started throwing change at the cops and calling then Alice Bluegown and Lily Law. I saw nothing that I can say to you caused a riot, but suddenly there was a lot of anger and eruption and the cops backed into the Stonewell. Somebody tried to bash down the door with a parking meter. Glass was smashed. Fires were started in every trash can. But there was still humour. A fire hose peeked out through an opening because the cops were going to fire-hose everybody, but only a trickle of water came out, which was very humiliating. And again lots of laughter.

"On the second night, when the Tactical Police Force came in buses and helmets like stormtroopers, the kids formed a little line and they had a little song they sang, 'We are the

2000

1990

1980

1970

1960

1950

Stonewall: the first time that gays fought back – and began the Gay Pride movement.

Stonewall girls, we wear our hair in curls. We don't wear underwear, we show our public hair.'
And they would do Rockette kicks and the TPF would run after then and when they turned
around another four would be coming from the other direction and doing the same Rockette
thing again. At one point a young good-looking Puerto Rican cop tripped and fell and a
queen grabbed his club and she said, 'How would you like this up your Puerto Rican ass?'
Well, we're going back 30 years now, that cop was ready to kill. Fairies weren't supposed to
talk like that, fairies weren't supposed to fight back, fairies weren't supposed to do any of the
things that fairies were doing. It got bloody and a lot bloodier after the first night. A lot of
ordinary people got hurt, too."

The moderate Mattachine Society wanted to calm things down; they called for peace
and a candle-lit procession. The rioters were not interested – and their leaders formed the
Gay Liberation Front, "based on the North Vietnamese," says Fourett. Within twenty-four
hours the boarded-up windows of the Stonewall were plastered in political slogans, among
them "Support Gay Power". The day after the riots, the first pamphlets were given out: "Are
homosexuals revolting? You bet your sweet ass we are." Within six months the GLF had
spoken at 175 campuses. The notion that of necessity homosexuality for most people had to
be a matter of secrecy began to unravel.

1940

1930

1920

1910

1900

Ten years on from the first gay parade, in the city that styles itself the most gay-friendly in the world.

A year after Stonewall, the first Gay Pride week was inaugurated and the first march held. Up to 15,000 gays went from Greenwich Village to Central Park, while similar marches took place in San Francisco, Los Angeles and Chicago. "It's hard for people today to understand how important and terrifying that march was," says Fourett. "It's one thing to walk in Greenwich Village where it's safe to hold your boyfriend's hand or your girlfriend's hand. But it's another to march up Fifth Avenue. Homophobia and bias are irrational responses and the potential for violence was there. I got spat on. I'd been spat on after a war demonstration, but being spat on as a gay person is very different. The police certainly just looked the other way. But the high of what we were doing! It was like being on acid even if you weren't on acid."

Kohler remembers everybody being asked to take off belts, jewellery, kerchiefs - anything that could be grabbed in a fight. "Collectively we didn't think we were going to make it," he says. "We were determined to have this march, but we were all scared to death."

Stonewall was described as "the hairpin drop heard around the world" and the message came in loud and clear in Britain. The same conflict of the old and the new occurred between the established, conservative Homosexual Law Reform Society (which became the Campaign for Homosexual Equality) and the emergent Gay Liberation Front. There was only ever going to be one winner. Homosexuality was a classification, gay promised to be a lifestyle. The first British Gay Pride march did not happen until 1972, but by then gays had made themselves heard – and seen. Adopting the feminists philosophy that "the personal is the political" the British GLF demonstrated against those it perceived as its adversaries in exactly the same way as all the left-wing movements. The most notably clash occurred with the Festival of Light, which saw the "forces of evil" in open homosexuality. The Front infiltrated the organization, sent out fake mailing lists, forged tickets, and arrived at a gathering in Central Hall, Westminster, some in drag under their clothes, others dressed as clerics and nuns and Ku Klux Klansmen. Once the signal was given, they turned the meeting into chaos.

Within ten years a gay culture existed that was complete. Gay parades were being held to coincide with Stonewall, which was rivalled by Sydney's Mardi Gras and the London Gay Pride Festival. In San Francisco gay men and lesbians were beginning to win political office. It was OK to be gay. The British *Sunday Mirror* ran a spread on the new gay visibility:

"Rockette" kicks on parade": it was with this routine that gays taunted the police at Stonewall.

For some the subject is strictly taboo. For others it provokes sniggers and embarrassed jokes. But like it or not the speed with which homosexuals – or "gays" as they prefer to be known – have organized themselves is nothing short of a social revolution. Yet ten years ago homosexuality was outlawed in Britain. Today there are homosexual campaign groups, political societies, trade union groups and a gay

A transvestite hugs a policeman during Berlin's gay pride celebration in 1997, an event that attracted 60,000 homosexuals and lesbians.

newspaper. There are clubs, discos and phone-in organizations which will help members find anything from a gay pub to a gay plumber. And more and more people are "coming out" which in gay language means admitting in public they are homosexual … the gays are probably Britain's most powerful and vocal minority group.

THE BIRTH OF FEMINISM

The gay and feminist movements should have been natural allies – after all, both saw heterosexual men who ruled the world as the common foe. The problem from the feminist perspective was that when it came to power, gay men were no more accommodating than their straight brothers. The leaders of all the radical movements were men, happy to have women on board but in the traditional roles. Famously, black activist Stokeley Carmichael brushed off women's libbers with the remark that "The only position for women in the Student Nonviolent Coordinating Committee is prone." "Women? I

Sydney's gay Mardi Gras, which started in 1978 as an event for 1,000 "misfits and wierdos", now rivals San Francisco in size and is even more outrageous.

2000
1990
1980
1970
1960
1950
1940
1930
1920
1910
1900

guess they ought to exercise pussy power," Eldridge Cleaver said. The only alliance that most male activists were prepared to make with women's lib was in bed.

Novelist Rita Mae Brown, who had protested against everything - "you know, the war, racism, you name it, I dropped the leaflet" – was at Yale when she heard what Carmichael said and remembers "the white hot rage that just shot through my body. Like, fine, buddy, you can face the white man all by yourself if that's what you think, because this little girl's taking her white ass out of here."

She found herself feeling the same about the Gay Liberation Front to which she turned, not just because women were expected to make the coffee and lick the envelopes, not even because the brothers insisted on leading all the marches and making all the speeches, but because women "were truly beside the point." And so the women left there, too. "Some women were devastated, because they really thought that gay men were going to be their brothers, but I wasn't. I have yet to see any man that's willing to give up male privilege to help women."

But for a second time gay women were to find themselves spurned. Heterosexual women in the feminist National Organization of Women were hostile and evasive and tried to incorporate lesbianism into some "broader issue". Being a lesbian in the National Organization of Women was "like being the daughter of Adolph Eichmann," Rita Mae Brown says. "They thought we were going to crack open the movement in some way, give men all the ammunition they needed to destroy the women's movement." Her rejoinder was, 'They're going to call you a lesbian whether you are or whether you aren't. If that one word can scare you, you aren't going to do squat.' They threw me out."

Betty Friedan, head of NOW, called lesbians "The Lavender Menace." Lesbians were not invited to either the first or the second Congress to Unite Women. Some retaliated by writing ideological position papers, but Rita Mae Brown, who, Jim Fourett describes as then being, "as feisty as hell," got together "a bunch of gay women to have some fun," had T-shirts stencilled with "Lavender Menace" and sneaked backstage at the congress, where they doused the lights. When the lights came back, "we were all there in the aisles, on the stage, behind them all." Brown adds: "It was not violent or anything like that. We basically just said, 'You can't deny us any more, let's have a little heart-to-heart, sister.' Some were just horrified and threw their purses on the ground and did that kind of girl stuff. But the rest of them really got it. We woke up a lot of the straight women who thought they could get along without us."

The seeds of feminist discontent found focus when, as Rosalind Miles wrote in *The Women's History of the World*, "activist women saw that there was a subject class more in need of liberating than the occupied Vietnamese, nearer to them in oppression than their own blacks – themselves." Inspired by Simone de Beauvoir's statement that "One is not born a woman, one becomes one" – an indication that the inferior status of women was man-made – Betty Friedan wrote *The Feminine Mystique*. In it, she strove to define the modern married woman's sense of emptiness:

> It was a strange stirring, a sense of dissatisfaction, a yearning that women suffered in the middle of the twentieth century in the United States. Each suburban wife struggled with it alone. As she made the beds, shopped for groceries, matched slip cover material, ate peanut butter sandwiches,

2000

1990

1980

1970

1960

1950

1940

1930

1920

1910

1900

chauffeured Cub Scouts and Brownies, lay beside her husband at night, she was afraid to ask even of herself the silent question, "Is this all?"

Domestication was a lie, Friedan told women, they were prisoners of their traditional roles as wives, mothers and housekeepers, and they were economically dependent on men. She dismissed Freud's adage that anatomy is destiny and replaced it with another: identity is destiny. Women, she said, would always find something missing in sex until it was sex between equals. The book, initiated the post-suffrage phase of the women's struggle. It was quickly followed by Helen Gurley Brown's *Sex and the Single Girl,* which had a different answer to women's dilemma – stay single and have a career *and* a better sex life than your married friends. Soon, journalist Gloria Steinhem gave feminism the cutting edge it needed and the movement, which had stumbled to its feet without a true ideology, began to question Western society's basic psychological, cultural and biological assumptions – and the contradictory roles that men asked women to play: that of home-maker and seductress, two stereotypes previously kept separate. Steinhem, who had got herself hired as a Playboy bunny to expose the sexist world of Hef, became founding editor of a magazine whose title indicated that a woman had a right not to be identified as a "Miss" or a "Mrs" but as a *Ms.* Steinhem was blonde, beautiful and smart and she knew how to make use of her assets. "She knew that how you look is more important than what you say – sad but true," says Rita Mae Brown. "She was so beautiful men couldn't dismiss her. I watched with glee as she twisted interviewers around her little finger."

Feminist talk turned to action early in 1968, when WITCH (the Women's International Terrorist Conspiracy from Hell) invaded the New York Bridal Fair wearing black veils. Later that year the New York Radical Women protested against the Miss America pageant because it was degrading to women, "enslaved [them] by ludicrous beauty standards". The protesters crowned a sheep and liberated women were invited to throw items of clothing that symbolized oppression – stiletto-heeled shoes, suspender belts, bras (which, unlike Vietnam war draft cards, were not burnt) – into a trash can. In Britain women disrupted a Miss World contest with football rattles and stink bombs and Prince Charles

Helen Gurley Brown advised women to stay single – have a career AND a sex life.

Protest outside the 1968
Miss America contest
LEFT: Hugh Hefner among
the Playboy bunnies. Feminists
said he was sexist.

displayed his sensitive side by remarking: "Basically I think it's because they want to be men."

A flood of books with a variety of feminist perspectives began to be published. Two that came out within months of each other remain among the most influential and certainly among the best written. Both were academic and serious, but where American Kate Millett's was earnest, Australian Germaine Greer's was mischievous.

In *Sexual Politics,* Millett broke new ground by showing that, throughout history, men had ascribed an importance to the penis which they denied to the vagina, and used that importance as an ipso facto right to power and domination in everything from religion to the bedroom. She illustrated her point with some descriptions of sexual activity in contemporary literature, exposing the chauvinism of writers like Henry Miller, Norman Mailer and D.H. Lawrence.

Millet quoted one of the couplings between the gamekeeper Mellors and Lady Chatterley in which he "concedes one kiss on the navel and then gets to business":

And he had to come into her at once, to enter the peace on earth of that soft, quiescent body. It was the moment of pure peace for him, the entry into the body of a woman. She lay still, in a kind of sleep, always in a kind of sleep. The activity, the orgasm was all his, all his; she could strive for herself no more.

The scenes of sexual intercourse in *Lady Chatterley,* Millet noted, "are written according to the 'female is passive, male is active' directions laid down by Sigmund Freud. The phallus is all; Connie is 'cunt', the thing acted upon, gratefully accepting each

Bras, seen as a symbol of female oppression by many a radical feminist were burnt in the 1960s.

manifestation of the will of her master." Considering the single act of anal intercourse in *Lady Chatterley* (which, for whatever reason, the prosecution in the British trial had chosen to ignore) Millett derided Connie Chatterley's expressed belief that she needed this "phallic hunting out" – the incident, she wrote, was merely an expression of Lawrence as male supremacist; but at least it was written without hate. Millett reserved her contempt for Norman Mailer whose hero in *An American Dream,* Stephen Rojack (having just killed his wife) twice sodomizes his maid despite her resistance. It was, she said, Mailer's way of

A movie version of **Lady Chatterley's Lover,** *the novel that feminist writer Kate Millett said showed that D.H. Lawrence was a male supremicist.*

"expressing contemptuous mastery." She delineated the scene. Rojack goes to the maid's room, finds her masturbating, gets "a pure prong of desire to bugger, there was canny hard-packed evil in that butt, that I knew." And is the maid outraged by this penetration? No, she is in awe: "You are absolutely a genius, Mr Rojack." Millett concluded:

> Mailer's *An American Dream* is a rallying cry for a sexual politics whose diplomacy has failed and war
> is the last political resort of a ruling class that feels its position in deadly peril.

Millett drew no attention to Lawrence's obvious hatred of the clitoris and of a woman who might reach orgasm without the male propulsion. As the feminist movement, in the wake of Masters and Johnson, was now promoting the clitoris as the new seat of power – "the only organ in the human body purely for pleasure" (in *Re-Making Love* Alix Shulman would tell women: "If the vagina was the stronghold of Freudian, male-dominated sexuality, the clitoris is the first beachhead of feminist sexuality.") – it is worth quoting from this scene in *Lady Chatterley* in which Mellors tells Connie about his runaway wife:

> She'd never come off when I did. Never! She'd just wait. If I kept back for half an hour, she'd keep back
> longer. And when I'd come off and really finished, then she'd start on her own account, and I had to
> stop inside her till she brought herself off … she'd sort of tear at me down there, as if it was a beak
> tearing at me. By God, you think a woman's soft down there, like a fig. But I tell you the old rampers
> have beaks between their legs, and they tear at you with it till you're sick. Self! Self! Self! All self!

All self. And why not? The movement's slogan was simple: "Think clitoris!"

In *Sexual Politics,* Millett brought her greatest firepower to bear on Freud, who formulated the opinion that women's role in coitus was to be passive, that vaginal orgasm was "adult" whereas clitoral orgasm was "immature", and that "masturbation, at all events of the clitoris, is a masculine activity". Millett particularly took Freud to task over his theory of "penis envy" which happened when girls discover they are "castrated" – a "momentous discovery which little girls are destined to make":

> They notice the penis of a brother or playmate, strikingly visible and of large proportions, at once
> recognize it as the superior counterpart of their own small and inconspicuous organ, and from that
> time forward fall a victim to envy.

Observing that there were several unexplained assumptions in this ("Why is the girl instantly struck by the proposition that bigger is better? Might she just as easily, reasoning from the naivety of childish narcissism, imagine the penis is an excrescence and take her own body as norm?") Millet wondered how, in an age when nudity was virtually non-existent, little girls even got to see a penis. She concluded that "the real tragedy of Freudian psychology is that its fallacious interpretations of feminine character were based upon clinical observations."

THE CLITORIS FIGHTS BACK

The fundamental insight of Germaine Greer's *The Female Eunuch* was that women had been systematically robbed of productive energy by society's insistence on confining them to a passive sexual role. She argued that women might break through the crippling stereotype by casting off the shackles of marriage and sexual repression (She put that more baldly and slightly differently in *Oz:* "A woman's best interests mean junking monogamy and fucking for sex instead of ego and prestige"). She was for sex between men and women, but warned that for the women's movement to demand liberty from men was to perpetuate the estrangement of the sexes (liberty, in any case, was something one took without asking); and she was for the involvement of the whole person, not "the substitution of genitality for sexuality." She wrote:

> The process described by the experts, in which the man dutifully does the rounds of the erogenous zones, spends an equal amount of time on each nipple, turns his attention to the clitoris (usually too directly), leads through the stages of digital or lingual stimulation and then politely lets himself into the vagina, perhaps waiting until the retraction of the clitoris tells him that he is welcome, is laborious and inhumanly computerized.

Greer (whose working title for the *Female Eunuch* was "The Clitoris Fights Back") challenged the idea of the clitoris as being supreme, warning that "If we localize female response in the clitoris we impose upon women the same limitation of sex which has stunted the male's response." But she spoke up for female genitalia, noting that some of a woman's modesty about her private parts stemmed from actual distaste. "The worst name anyone can be called is *cunt*," she wrote. "The best

Germaine Greer: one-woman wrecking crew who sought equality while having plenty of sex and laughs.

thing a cunt can be is small and unobtrusive: the anxiety about the bigness of the penis is only equalled by anxiety about the smallness of the cunt. No woman wants to find out that she has a twat like a horse-collar." Women, she pointed out, did not always feel that shame and quoted a seventeenth-century female ballad:

> You'll find the Purse so deep
> You'll hardly come to its treasure

    Aggressively heterosexual, media-savvy, imposingly tall and arresting, Greer was a one-woman wrecking crew, brilliant and unpredictable. Unlike many feminists who took up the battle and treated men as the enemy, Greer set out to achieve equality for her gender by having lots of sex and plenty of laughs. *Maclean's* magazine commented that:

> Unlike the drab stereotypes of feminists – women in overalls with bad skin and lank hair, which she frequently lampoons, Greer appealed to men as well as women – a feminist who wore feather boas, flaunted her promiscuity, posed in the nude for the pornographic magazine *Suck*, and actually claimed that she was having *fun*.

    Greer taught English at Warwick University, but to *Suck* (which she helped edit), she was "Doctor Gee" who edited a "Cunt Power" issue of *Oz* and organized a Wet Dreams erotic film festival in Amsterdam, where she screened an uncut print of the Jagger film *Performance*. When she took part in a New York City Town Hall discussion – the panel including the unrepentantly unevolved Norman Mailer, who described feminists as "legions of the vaginally frigid, out there … with the souped-up, pent-up voltage of a clitoris ready to spring" – a man in the audience stood up to ask her what sex would be like after liberation. "Why even ask?" Greer replied. "Because I don't know what women are asking for," the man said. "Well, you can

Underground magazine* Suck, *published in English in Holland advocated unrestrained sexual activity.

relax," Greer snapped, "because whatever we're asking for, it's not from you."

Oz editor Richard Neville was to write of his first meeting with her:

> At a party I met a striking young woman whose hair escaped in a shock of dark anarchic curls. Tall and voluble, she flashed her IQ like a searchlight. My Hawaiian shirt, all the rage, was fetchingly unbuttoned to show off a tan.
>
> "Aha, a male nipple." She took hold of it between thumb and forefinger. "See how it grows? Just like a dick."
>
> "Ouch," I said.
>
> "Nipples are a mass of erectile tissues," she continued, as I tried to ignore the glances of onlookers. "You should learn to masturbate all your male parts."

"She could behave like a very badly behaved man, if she wanted to," observes English journalist Anthony Haden-Guest, who was once her next-door neighbour. "As an Australian she saw it as her right."

Early feminism took on men with a sense of humour. They promoted masturbation as "the safest sex" and suggested replacing men with the well-calibrated vibrator – as one remarked, "the penis can't rev 3,000 times a minute." In *The Dialectic of Sex,* Shulamith Firestone put forward an ironic vision of a manless society in which an ovum could be fertilized by electrical charge rather than sperm. But when it came to male violence as a problem between men and women – this at a time when Vietnam was on television in newly arrived colour and the body bags were coming home – the message took on a harder edge. "The only genetic superiority that men have is their capacity for violence," Germaine Greer wrote in *The Slag Heap Erupts.* Much later in *The Rites of Man: Love, Sex and Death in the Making of the Male,* Rosalind Miles would put forward a reasoned general argument:

> We need to acknowledge that the seeds of violence are in every man, therefore their education should be devoted to training that out, not beating it in; that aggression is contagious, and that watching it, taking part in it, reading about it, and expressing it will never reduce it, and consequently that all arguments for "letting off steam", "just enjoying a bit of a rough-house" … are spurious and corrupt; that the passion of violence will always, must always, demand a victim.

In the late Seventies, much less reasoned feminists narrowed the argument to sex, projected women as the eternal and only victim and denounced "the phallus [as] the eternal root of all the evils in the world". For Andrea Dworkin even consensual heterosexual intercourse was "genital theft" committed by men. The mechanics of coitus meant degradation because it was a kind of invasion, the conquering of a woman "defined by how she is made, that hole, which is synonymous with entry." In *The Demographic Revolution,* Jane McLoughlin predicted that soon women would wear men as fashion accessories like alligator handbags and wrote: "One of the anthropological pleasures of the 1990s will be watching how men cope with a new role – that of the redundant male."

Women on both sides of the Atlantic were already demonstrating against the huge increase in pornography and picketing sex shops, but pornography and rape were now linked – the basic content of pornography was male violence against women. Susan Brownmiller wrote *Against Our Will*, promoting the idea that rape is a crime of power. Robin Morgan in *Sisterhood Is Powerful* moved the argument on down the line: "Pornography is the theory; rape is the practice." In the States feminists tried to have pornography defined as a form of sex discrimination, thus allowing individuals to sue pornographers in court. In 1984, the city of Minneapolis approved a local law (drafted in part by Andrew Dworkin) only to have it declared unconstitutional by the Supreme Court.

Next, rape was linked to marriage and men were depicted as beasts, despoilers inflamed by vicious fantasies filled with hate, "running amok," as Neil Lyndon put it in *No More Sex War: The Failure of Feminism*, "with his priapic proddings and pokings, threatening the survival of the planet with his phallic imperatives and his imperious demands for cold meat-loaf, warmed slippers and accommodating vagina." In conciliatory voice Lyndon also wrote:

> If criminal rape includes a drowsy Sunday morning leg-over where neither partner is fully conscious and one of them may be wishing for a few more minutes of uninterrupted snoring, I suppose we may all, men and women, say that we have been rapists and victims. If criminal rape includes those occasions when both of the couples have taken on such a load of intoxicants that neither is fully capable of a clear-headed declaration of consent or refusal, yet intercourse is completed withal, we may all acknowledge some rueful degrees of guilt.

Much to the unease of moderate feminists, the extreme propaganda spread. In Britain the London Rape Crisis Centre published *Sexual Violence: The Reality for Women*, describing rape "not as an abnormal act but … part of the way men treat us as women"; and the American Presbyterian Church produced a report on human sexuality, *Keeping Body and Soul Together*, claiming that "wife-battering is rampant and almost 40 per cent of rapes happen inside heterosexual marriages." The bisexual feminist Camille Paglia called the report grotesque and commented in *Sex, Art and American Culture*:

> The idea that feminism is the first group that ever denounced rape is a gross libel to men. Throughout history, rape has been condemned by honourable men. Honorable men do not murder; honourable men to do not steal; honourable men do not rape … Men have provided for women. Men have died to defend the country for women. We must look back and acknowledge what men have done for women.

Feminism had begun to lose its way. It is important, however, to pay tribute to what the movement had already achieved, as Reay Tannahill has in *Sex in History*:

> Those of its spokeswomen who attracted most publicity in the Western world were combative, vociferous and frequently silly, but there was enough truth in what they said to trouble the consciences of even the most lukewarm liberals. The extremist wing of the movement aimed to sweep away all the social attitudes that had developed out of 5,000 years of male supremacy, but its more practical members saw the struggle for equality

2000 1990 1980 1970 1960 1950 1940 1930 1920 1910 1900

with men as, by and large, a legal one, and hoped that when laws were liberalized other problems would gradually disappear ... the feminists could claim to have accomplished as much in seven years as their Suffragette predecessors had done in seventy.

To that one could add that the second wave of feminists had not needed to resort to arson and bombings either.

If feminists who thought like Germaine Greer extended the fight for equal rights into the bedroom and had a high time doing it, it was as nothing compared to the hedonism which homosexual men enjoyed in the Seventies' wild expansion of discos and bathhouses. Only a few years earlier gay men and lesbians met in dingy bars and basements in small numbers and under constant threat from the police. Now, as the discos spread out of the black gay clubs of Manhattan into the white gay clubs (and later crossed into the straight world), men and women who had hidden their sexuality were able to be open about it. Dancing was

Scene from **The Killing of Sister George** *(with Beryl Reid and Susannah York on right) was filmed in the most famous real-life lesbian club, The Gateway, Chelsea.*

symbolic of their new-found freedom.

While lesbians partied on the disco scene – and benefited from some of the concessions feminism won from men, particularly in the workplace and in terms of discrimination law – they did not experience the sense of sexual liberation felt by gay men. Firstly, their sexual behaviour had never been subject to law; secondly, unlike most homosexuals, they were more likely to be drawn into long-term relationships rather than promiscuity; and thirdly, according to Rita Mae Brown, "lesbians are still women raised as women and still sexually repressed. Being a lesbian doesn't automatically help you with those demons you have to unleash."

In terms of her own intimate life, she remained "tremendously isolated" in the disco years. She adds: "I could always get people to go to bed, I mean they'll always come in your door in the middle of the night if they're attracted to you, but I didn't get to spend time with anybody until I turned thirty. I was always the dyke that would bust your career. And that was hard. Even then the person I was in love with was an actress and she thought her career would be ruined. We were never seen in public. That part was devastating."

Dress – and behaviour – in New York's Studio 54 exemplified the open sexuality of the Seventies.

Gay men had no such problem and for them the bathhouses – full to bursting during the 1976 New York centennial celebrations when the world came to party – were an even greater liberalization than the discos. Bathhouses became, according to Bob Kohler (who managed New York's Club Baths), "the new community centres, legitimate places to go. They were safe. They were clean. You knew people. We had cute little Latinos bringing you towels, coffee, you were waited on. We had double rooms, we had deluxe rooms. Before bathhouses were legitimate, most gays had nowhere to go but bars. You would be at a bar three or four hours. 'I'll wait for one who's prettier than that, I'll wait for the next one, maybe he'll be prettier' – then suddenly its 4 am. No wonder we had such an extremely high rate of alcoholism in the gay and lesbian community."

For many gay men, every day was Christmas and birthday rolled together. The levels of

2000

1990

1980

1970

1960

1950

1940

1930

1920

1910

1900

promiscuity were prodigious. Marco Vassi would go to a bathhouse for two or three days, the writer Michael Perkins relates, and invite any man passing his darkened cubicle to come in and have sex. Many men had thousands of encounters, some even several tens of thousands in a life-time. "It was a smorgasbord" of sex, admits Kohler. "Two, three times a day was not uncommon. But what is promiscuous? Isn't that another word for freedom? Wouldn't any straight person have wanted to change places with us if they could?"

Jim Fourett thinks that "far too many people thought the meaning of the sexual revolution was more sex", but provides reasons if not excuses for the promiscuity: a"The ideals of the Sixties were lost. The Vietnamese won their war, Nixon became president, and the hope of changing the world went. So the people I knew dissipated the energy for change in multiple orgasms and got on by having a really good time. From revolution to let's be fabulous, you know?"

"In the disco era, gay men lived with total abandon," Kohler comments. "We just shook our tambourines, danced our asses off, took every drug we wanted – you could be up all night for a week on good speed – and if we got a little clap you just went to the doctor for a shot of penicillin. We thought we were invincible, we thought we would live forever. And then suddenly we were being decimated."

Wild celebrations at the first anniversary bash of Studio 54 – New York's "in" discotheque.

2000

1990

1980

1970

1960

1950

1940

1930

1920

1910

1900

The iconic gay disco band, The Village People, in performance.

THE ADVENT OF AIDS

In 1979 a drag queen called Brandy Alexander became ill with GRID, a gay-related immune deficiency, which was also called gay cancer. No-one really knew what the illness was, or how it was transmitted. The gay press ignored GRID - it was that rare. Then at the beginning of 1981 a thirty-one-year-old gay man checked into the accident and emergency of UCLA Medical Centre in Los Angeles because his oesophagus was almost completely blocked by a fungal infection. He developed pneumonia only seen in transplant patients whose immune systems had been artificially depressed to prevent their bodies rejecting the donated organs. His death was followed quickly by others, mostly in the big gay centres of New York, Chicago, Los Angeles and San Francisco. One who died was Marco Vassi, nursed by *Deep Throat* popcorn girl Ellen Steinberg who had long since become a porn star herself under the name Annie Sprinkle. Another was a young and good-looking airline steward from Quebec City named Gaetan Dugas. He had continued to visit the bathhouses after beginning to show symptoms, would have sex in a darkened cubicle, then turn on the lights to reveal his karposi's sarcoma lesions. "Gay cancer," he used to say in his French accent, "now maybe you'll get it."

Larry Kramer, who wrote for the gay newspaper *The New York Native* realized that the bathhouses were conduits for the disease and began a campaign to shut them down. Often he felt that he was acting alone in the face of enormous indifference – "the bathhouse owners

AUGUST 12, 1985

TIME

SMILES AT HELSINKI
A Diplomatic Debut

AIDS

The Growing Threat
What's Being Done

Virus, magnified 135,000 times, destroying T cell

Four years after the outbreak of AIDS began to decimate the gay community, the epidemic continued to spread — until anti-retroviral drugs arrested it.

At the height of the AIDS crisis, protests against the establishment were frequent.

were too busy making money to care that people were dying," he says. Bob Kohler thinks that Kramer's campaign was an act of hysteria. As the equivalent of community centres, bathhouses "should have been used as a rallying point, as centres for disseminating information."

The disease that came to be defined as AIDS arrived in Britain the following year – a thirty-seven-year-old computer programmer was the first to be found suffering from the same rare pneumonia seen in LA. When he died, a trust was set up in his name: the Terrence Higgins Trust. "US Disease Hits London" said a stark headline. In March 1983 there were six British cases, in October 1985, 241 – by which time the numbers of those who had died in the US had reached 5,500. Inevitably, AIDS induced a backlash against homosexuals. There were numerous outbreaks of "queer bashing". Bob Kohler remembers gangs of ethnic minorities "going up and down Christopher Street screaming 'Fucking white devils, bringing diseases to us.'"

In Britain in 1983, a survey found that 62 per cent of people did not approve of homosexual relationships; two years later it was 69 per cent; two years later still, 74%. Responding to what it believed was popular opinion, the Tory government introduced a clause into its Local Government Bill which forbade local authorities from promoting homosexuality, publishing homosexual material or teaching in any maintained school that homosexuality was acceptable "as a pretended family relationship". For many, straight as well as gay, the notorious Clause 28 was history going backwards and they opposed it. A number of homosexual protest groups like Act Up and Outrage were formed and the actor Sir Ian McKellen "came out", at the age of forty-nine, to help found Stonewall, for which he lobbied

2000

1990

1980

1970

1960

1950

1940

1930

1920

1910

1900

vigorously. Lesbian protesters infiltrated BBC Television Centre and chained themselves to the desks and cameras as Sue Lawley attempted to read the *Six O'Clock News.*

Clause 28 got on the statute books but was never enforced.

Today, anti-retroviral and combination-drug treatment allow AIDS victims to live longer and they hold out the hope of a cure. Bob Kohler welcomes the prospect but it does not banish the depression of the AIDS years:

> I was going to funerals of people, twenty-five, twenty-six, thirty. And you're not supposed to go to funerals for people that age. My lover died of AIDS, my closest friend died of AIDS, my friend Vito Russo the film historian died of AIDS. AIDS surrounded you, AIDS was your whole life. There was a lot of denial in the gay community, there was panic, they were running around closing bathhouses, they were saying it was the mosquitoes at Fire Island, that it was in the water someplace else. I had a friend who was convinced it was in the bread he bought from the Korean markets, you couldn't change his mind either. You had people who felt it was a government plot, which I believed for a while.

He thinks gay life "had reached the peak and, like the song says, it was too hot not to cool down. We were living on an edge, there was no two ways about that. But I think the punishment was far too cruel. It's the day the laughter stopped and I don't think it's coming back."

Perhaps that is too negative a view. Perhaps it is better to see something positive from the period, as John Bancroft has done in *Human Sexuality and Its Problems:*

> One of the most poignant lessons of the AIDS epidemic is the vivid evidence it provides of the love which exists between many gay couples as they contend with the disease. Anyone who has doubted that homosexual love can be of the highest order should doubt no longer.

A Thai poster depicting a condom and a syringe carrying an anti-AIDS message.

SEX SELLS

IT IS THE SORT OF FILM AWARD CEREMONY WITH WHICH WE ARE ALL FAMILIAR — THE MEN IN TUXES, THE WOMEN'S EVENING DRESSES DISPLAYING GENEROUS AMOUNTS OF BRONZED FLESH. THE ACTRESSES IN THIS AWARD CATEGORY ARE NERVOUS AS THE MC OPENS THE ENVELOPE: "AND THE AWARD FOR BEST ANAL SCENE GOES TO ..."

The American movie porn industry, the largest in the world, has become respectable. Respectable? What else? What could say more about an industry's respectability than the fact that with the Adult Video News Awards it has created for itself the equivalent of that bastion of American culture, the Film Academy Awards? Here in Las Vegas, before an audience of 3,000, the porn stars, producers, directors and distributors receive their "Emmys" in fifteen categories: most outrageous sex scene; best bisexual video; best gay solo feature; best all-girl; best group; best gang bang ... Respectable? Today's porn barons are legitimate businessmen who talk in terms of market niches, profit margins and maximizing product. Some even provide their staff with full medical care and life insurance. Hollywood technicians who once freelanced furtively on porn, now do so openly — in fact, it is considered kind of neat. On Hollywood's Sunset Boulevard, porn companies promote their wares on giant billboards, which had never happened before 1998. This was a year in which the industry, centred on the Californian San Fernando Valley, turned out 8,000 titles (twelve times Hollywood's output) and Americans rented or bought nearly 700 million hard-core videos — an average of six per household.

John Wayne Bobbit: porn attraction after a knife cut from his wife.

Porn existed almost from the very moment celluloid first clicked onto a projector's sprockets at the end of the nineteenth century. Within ten years sexually explicit shorts were showing in smoking room and brothels. There is no record in America or Britain of police confiscating such films — it would seem that the authorities looked the other way so long as they were being

Americans spend $10 billion a year on commercialized sex, including $700 million on hard-core videos.

screened for a selected audience. The earliest known example of "stag", made in 1915, is *Free Ride*, in which a man driving a car picks up two female hitchhikers. When they pull off the road, they engage in missionary and rear-entry intercourse – despite the male being encumbered in voluminous underwear and his trousers hobble his ankles – and the women appear to pass out with pleasure. In another film from the period, three naked girls agree to have sex with a naive young men, but only through a hole in a fence, on the other side of which the trio substitute a goat. "That the best girl I've ever had in my life!" proclaims the dialogue card. In another, a stage hand and an actress try oral sex, anal sex and then a "regular jazz", after which she complains, "Gee, I wish I could get a man with some pep". All of this seems hilarious to modern eyes – but the basic conventions of hard-core were already being defined.

When 16 mm film projection equipment became widely available in the Twenties and Thirties, men drove from place to place across America with porn in their trunks for showing to circles of businessmen in the know and to college fraternity houses, and side-show hucksters set up adults-only tents at travelling carnivals. Much of what was projected in them took advantage of small-town gullibility and showed little that was explicit – the original "exploitation" films. A group of independent film-makers known as the Forty Thieves took exploitation further, staying on the right side of the obscenity law by packaging its output as a series of cautionary tales. "Can a beautiful model stay pure?" asked *Secrets of a Model*. "It's the warning film for loose women!" proclaimed *Sex Madness*. The Forty Thieves even showed the sex hygiene film *Damaged Goods* under the come-on title of *Forbidden Desire*. The projectionist on the "Sucker Belt" circuit carried a "square-up" reel of hotter footage for emergencies when the crowd turned nasty. Thirty years on, Kodak's Super-8 movie camera made a significant difference to the pornographic landscape. The Super-8 was aimed at the average American family which wanted to record the kids playing in the backyard. Pornographers spotted the potential and produced thousands of shorts for home consumption – and unlike the old 16mm, they included sound. In the permissiveness of the late Sixties, the

Mafia bought hundreds of these shorts to show on public "loop" machines that had been developed in the Twenties for running children's cartoons on a continuous cartridge that did not have to be rewound. Two minutes of porn on a single machine could gross 10,000 dollars a year.

COMING CLEAN

By now America and Europe were producing full-length sex films and, unlike the exploitation genre, they made no attempt to hide their true purpose. In 1960 there were perhaps twenty cinemas in the US that exclusively screened adult pictures; by 1970 there were 750, many of them belonging to the Pussycat chain owned by David Friedman, a king of exploitation con from the old days. He removed every second seat in his cinemas "so that men would feel able to masturbate privately". Women rarely went to see porn films and usually found it a profoundly embarrassing experience when they did. That changed suddenly, if briefly, with

In **Deep Throat,** *the first mainstream hard-core movie, Linda Lovelace performed acts of which a sword swallower would have been proud.*

2000

1990

1980

1970

1960

1950

1940

1930

1920

1910

1900

Deep Throat and "porno chic" when, for the first time in the century, hard-core ceased to be strictly for the raincoat crowd and husbands took their wives. When *Time* magazine reported the phenomenon, the trend increased. Newsroom film showed ordinary women – always in pairs – entering theatres (albeit shielding their faces if they spotted the camera); old ladies stood in line with their shopping bags and were unconcerned. By the end of the Seventies, America was making and mass-marketing two hard-core porn movies a week and all the indications were that explicit sex had leapt into the mainstream and was about to be as acceptable as it was and has remained in most European countries, where hard-core is even available on terrestrial television. For the porno film-makers the world seemed to be their oyster. In fact, the oyster turned out to be a thwack in the face with a wet kipper – the industry fell foul of Richard Nixon's campaign against permissiveness.

Nixon's own commission on pornography had refused to come down against it but, refusing to be beaten, he found another route – he appointed to the Supreme Court judges sympathetic to his intentions. Soon, under Chief Justice Warren Burger, the court was making a case-law ruling: while "the sexual revolution of recent years may have had useful by-products in striking layers of prudery from a subject long irrationally kept from needed ventilation," it did not follow "that no regulation of patently offensive hard-core materials is needed or permissible: civilized people do not allow unregulated access to heroin because it is a derivative of medicinal morphine." It was ridiculous to suggest, the Burger ruling declared, that the Constitution protected the public exhibition of explicit sex acts any more than it would "a live performance of a man and woman locked in a sexual

"King of the Nudies" Russ Meyer, with one of his stars, Pandora Peaks – over endowed like all Meyer's stars.

Russ Meyer's **Kiss Me Quick**, *a typically pneumatic offering from the breast-obsessed director.*

embrace at high noon in Time Square." And the Supreme Court handed over matters of taste and decency to local prosecutors because "our nation is simply too big and too diverse for this court to reasonably expect that such standards could be articulated for all fifty states in a single formulation."

Until now any community could prosecute a national film or publication for obscenity, but that community had to apply national standards. By telling local communities to set their own standards Burger turned the law on its head – and it was open season on the porn brokers. It was not long before a number of men were on their way to jail, including *Deep Throat* director Gerald Damiano, hauled into court in Bible Belt Memphis. Little wonder that Russ Mayer, maker of porn for big-breast fetishists, cancelled his next production and told *US News and World Report:* "I think I'll go fishing."

THE VIDEO AGE

The porn movie business continued, in a highly nervous state. Cinema porn stopped being chic and went back to the grindhouses. Soon it was hardly there either, but not because the law had throttled it out of existence: the home video recorder had arrived. Video may have killed the radio star, but it was the wave of the future for porn. As more and more Americans bought VCRs – very largely, market research showed, to watch pornography – the chicken-and-egg of market forces made the machines cheaper. Soon video porn was everywhere and it was difficult for community watchdogs to draw a bead. But, from time to time, they did, as Russ Hampshire, president of VCA Pictures, one of the US's highest-profile production companies, knows only too well – he was arrested in Mobile, Alabama, and spent nine months in the slammer. "There was this big sting, they got a lot of different video companies," says Hampshire, a Vietnam war hero who brought his experience running McDonald restaurants in El Paso, Texas, to the porn business. He remains bitter. "What's ironic is there were about eighteen video stores in Mobile and fifteen of them had adult videos in them. And there was an adult theatre five blocks from the courthouse." The same kind of sting trapped Al Goldstein, editor and publisher of *Screw* magazine, which has surveyed the sex scene since the Sixties, in Kansas. He stayed out of jail on a plea bargain. Larry Flynt, publisher of *Hustler,* was trapped in Georgia, and went to hospital with a bullet in his spinal chord which left him paralyzed, fired outside the Fulton County courthouse by a white supremacist offended by an interracial photo-spread that the magazine had carried.

In the mainstream movie *Boogie Nights,* the porn film-maker Jack Horner, played by Burt Reynolds, at first refuses to move into video. "If it looks like shit, it is shit," he says. In the early Eighties that description fitted much of the output, particularly the amateur or "gonzo" lines for which ordinary couples set up a camera in their bedroom and recorded themselves having sex. "For that one minute it was hot and happening," observes ex-porn star Sarah Jane Hamilton who now directs for VCA. "It had a newness, a rawness, and it showed people actually getting it on and enjoying sex which a lot of old pornography hadn't – it was about domination. For a while people liked amateur so much it put the major porn business in the

Films like the 1998 release **Boogie Nights,** *starring Burt Reynolds, which is about the porn industry itself, has helped to make porn respectable.*

2000

1990

1980

1970

1960

1950

1940

Black-to-black: the costumes worn by Batman and Catwoman in the blockbuster movie Batman
Returns, *parody hardcore S & M, which enjoys widening sales in the mainstream.*

1930

toilet." The line retains a niche, but the ease and economy of video means there are niches for
any sexual taste. Dwarves? Bondage, S&M, flagellation? Fat women, pregnant women, older
women? You've got it. Kitty Fox did not get into porn until she was forty-eight, seven years
ago, when she met a producer at a Swingers' Lifestyle convention. "There's a lot of older
women, younger men stuff right now," she says. Very young-looking girls are always a big item
but, although in earlier years one of porn's biggest names, Traci Lords, took part in seventy-five
hard-core videos while she was under age, the industry has cleaned up its act and no girl less
than eighteen is employed by the legitimate companies. "Every girl's got to be eighteen and
have two IDs to prove it," says talent agent Jim Smith, who began World Modelling in the days
of silent sex-loops, when producers literally went out into the street to look for their "talent".

1920

1910

Smith has 500 porn performers on his books as well as another 250 who do nude magazine

1900

work. He gets thirty or forty inquiries every day from men wanting to break into porn movies and around a hundred inquiries a week from women, half of whom fix an appointment although only half again turn up for the interview and nude Polaroid session. Smith estimates he can find work for about 80 per cent of those who show. "I've had women in here from four foot ten to six foot two," he elaborates. "I've had women from 'A' cup to 'Triple E' cup. We had a lady with us who weighed 480 pounds and we got her a considerable amount of work. In this industry there's an opening for almost anybody." Smith has his standards. "I have this thing about religion. I won't supply anyone to portray a rabbi or a priest or a preacher – to me that's over the line."

At the high end of the market, only the beautiful people work for companies like Russ Hampshire's VCA or Steve Hirsch's Vivid, where quality counts and sex and production values are not mutually exclusive. "My niche is feature-quality films dealing with couples-type people – something a person can watch from beginning to end," says Hampshire. "We were the first company to get into special effects. Some of our films have morphing in them. We have CI computers which is unheard of in adult." Says Hirsch: "Give 'em quality and people will spent the money." Paul Thomas, a former actor seen on stage and film in *Hair* and *Jesus Christ Superstar*, now directing two dozen hard-core movies for Vivid each year, agrees, but puts things into honest perspective: "A film can be brilliantly scripted, acted and directed, but if it doesn't give you a hard-on, it's a failure."

Tracie Lords,
once one of porn's biggest names
and who appeared in many films while underage.

Hirsch, who runs Vivid like an old-style Hollywood studio and was the first to put his female stars under exclusive contract, is regarded as the cleverest marketing man in the industry. He makes eighty or ninety movies a year and, because he supplies cable channels like Playboy and Spice as well as several hotel chains, shoots them in hard and soft versions. The difference is basic. "Soft-core is the imagery of sex – hard-core is penetration, the actual act." At VCA, Hampshire's main marketing slogan is "More bangs for your bucks". He does not do compilation tapes, which represent half of the industry's 700 million annual releases. "Sex scene after sex scene after sex scene – guys sitting round four hours, six hours, who knows?" he says scathingly. Hirsch, however, puts out around fifty compilations every month.

The contents of all Vivid productions is broken down and fed through the computer so that it can be repackaged into concentrated explicitness that needs no fast-forwarding. Paul, who looks after this area of the company's affairs, is matter-of-fact: "A person's race, the size of their breasts, their penis, what the action is – if the girl's performing oral sex, if the guy's performing oral sex, what kind of penetration, what toys they're using, what body part of the woman the guy ejaculates on or in. And then the sexual positions – doggy, missionary, straddle, reverse straddle, spoon, sixty-nine, pile driver. We take all that and put it into the computer."

Oral sex sells well, he says, so does anal – "bought by guys to show their wives and maybe get lucky." If you can think of a combination of sexual possibilities it is likely that Paul has compiled it. "The wackiest was called *A Pussy in a Pussy*," he recalls. "It involved a woman's labia that was kind of large." Titles matter in porn. The photo shot for the video box cover is the single most important element for point of sale or rent, but the title has got to grab attention. Many are facetious echoes of mainstream box-office hits: *Sore Throat, Beverly Hills Copulator, Forrest Hump, Jurassic Pork;* once, there was even *E. Three, the Extra Testicle.*

EXPLOITATION?

Feminists who have campaigned against the exploitation of

Many hard-core videos grab attention by parodying the titles, and sometimes the content, of mainstream films.

The photo shoot for the box cover is the most important element in ensuring that a porn video sells or rents.

women in porn can only be surprised that, in the Nineties, is not the men but the women who take home the big bucks for their bangs. A top woman can command 10,000 dollars a movie, a top male get 500 dollars a day and that is it – "which is why you'll hear the expression 'gay for pay'", explains Sarah Jane Hamilton. "Straight men will perform gay because the money is so much more." Like the women, men can endorse products, but they cannot go on the strip-dance circuit, where the really big money is. That porn has moved over into respectability could not be more clearly underlined than by the fact that female porn stars now host their own shows on cable, act as spokeswomen for a variety of manufacturers and have featured in mainstream advertising. "We use them in a very natural, non-porn way," explain Rick Klotz, whose Fresh Jive company makes casual clothes. "It was just a kind of cool idea; 95 per cent of the people we sell to wouldn't know who they were, but the people who know, know. The campaign really did get us out in the marketplace."

All told, the very top women in porn, who are on exclusive contracts with the major producers and paid 30,000 dollars for so few as four movies a year, can pull in 200,000–300,000. A male star makes 40,000 if he is lucky. "Men are just necessary props in this business," says Hamilton. Confirms Jim South: "The girls absolutely run the industry. They not only make the lion's share of the money, they dictate who they'll work with and who they won't work with." He reels off daily rates: "A pro-am or gonzo, shot in a couple of hours, in and out, 350 dollars. Up the scale, girl masturbating, 100 dollars, blow job 200-250, girl/girl

300-500, boy/girl 400-700, boy/girl anal another 100, DP – that's double penetration – 100-150 more than that, but up to 2,500 for a star. A gang-bang of course pays the most – the average is about 3,000 dollars."

Double vaginas have also been done and a triple anal, for which rates are by negotiation. Hamilton will not shoot them – "they seem more like a parlour trick than anything else." Smith picks up the rate-card for men: "Pro-am blow job, 50-75 dollars, maybe 100. That's for thirty minutes work. Average for a full shoot, 100-200. For a regular movie boy/girl shoot, two to three hundred – and maybe not quite double if a guy drinks a lot of starch as we say and can do two of these scenes in a day."

A hard man is good to find, as Mae West would have it, but finding him for porn movies is difficult. "Of every twenty guys who come in, probably one, two, maybe three can do this work – it's that extreme," says Smith. "Any guy can excite himself with a magazine for the Polaroids, but it's a mental thing being able to perform in front of a crew and those hot lights glaring at you. A guy feels the pressure of getting it up." "I've had a lot of men who were probably wonderful lovers, very good-looking men, big studs in the bedroom, and they couldn't do a thing in front of the cameras,"

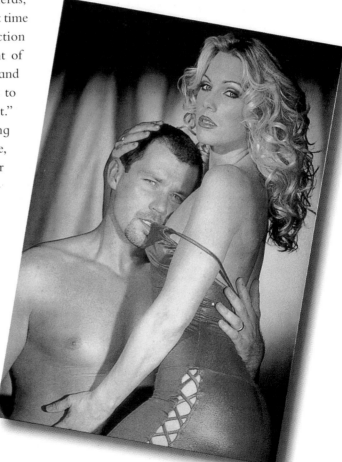

agrees director Paul Thomas. "I love it. First time in their lives they're not getting an erection when there's a gorgeous woman in front of them. They probably left the set and went and banged about five women that night just to prove to themselves that they still had it." Adds Hamilton: "When we say 'getting wood' we're not talking about a fireplace, we're talking about a stiff male member and you need it for your graphic close-ups. I've covered cable stuff with a gentleman who wasn't able to perform, but when it came to my hard-core version I had to go back and do inserts of another gentleman. When I was in the movies, if a man couldn't perform, he couldn't perform – a normal guy has good days and bad days, it happens. Now the production pressures are so great some men inject themselves – there's a lot of

A promotional still from a movie by Candida Royalle, one of the successful female directors of porn.

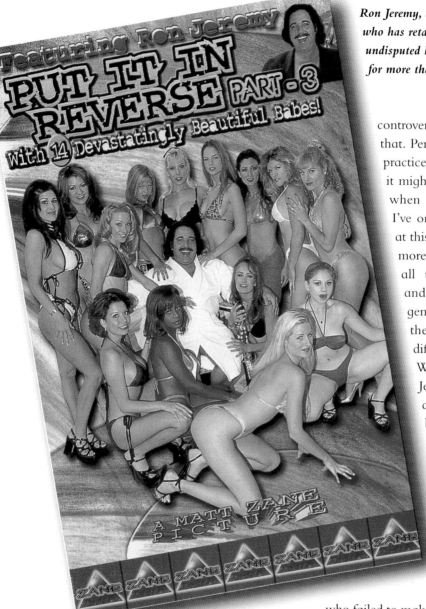

PUT IT IN REVERSE PART - 3
Featuring Ron Jeremy
With 14 Devastatingly Beautiful Babes!

A MATT ZANE PICTURE

Ron Jeremy, the "average looking guy" who has retained his place as the undisputed king of American porn for more than two decades.

controversy in the business about that. Personally I'm against the practice, you don't know where it might go. But as a producer, when time is money, when I've only got two more hours at this location, we've got one more set-up to do and we're all twiddling our thumbs and whistling because a gentleman can't get wood – then maybe I think differently."

When it comes to Ron Jeremy, however, it is almost a case of not being able to see the trees for the wood – his ability to perform virtually on command has made him the most famous person in American porn for twenty years. Indeed, so famous is this former teacher, who failed to make it in New York theatre, that he appears in rock videos, has jokes made about him on prime-time TV and regularly appears on chat-shows. When *Hollywood Men* was seen on British television, he made the cover of *The Guardian Guide* and appeared on *Ruby Wax*. "The main key to my success is I guess I have a big penis, it works, I've always been able to keep an erection," says Jeremy, who is short and tubby and whose long once-curly hair is thinning. He retains his considerable body hair, whereas most male in porn, like body-builders, are shaved. Jeremy also has a considerable sense of humour. "It helps being the average-looking guy I am. When they see a guy like me getting off with beautiful girls, it's like 'Wow! there's hope for us all.'" He adds: "The guys who watch porn aren't interested in my schlong, they're only interested on what's on the other side of my schlong."

Traditionally women are supposed to find visual porn distasteful. But in the Nineties, while the porn movie audience remains predominantly male, some women have developed a taste. The number of American couples who go shopping for video rentals has increased, half the men who bring porn home say their partner watches it with them, and women make up about a fifth of all customers, accounting for a high proportion of gay video rental – "because the men are better looking and they want to know what guys get up to together," says Hamilton. Now, with more women getting to direct porn movies – Hamilton and Candida Royalle from the older school among them, as well as Juli Ashton, currently one of the industry's biggest draws – there is a move to make the genre more woman-friendly. What do women want from porn? "I honestly don't know, there are conflicting messages," Hamilton answers. "What is a fact is that woman watch. One of the largest viewing times for pay-per-view adult material is the afternoons, and who's home in the afternoon, typically? Some women aren't watching the soaps. And more women than you would think admit that they find the cheaper, harder stuff exciting. What women don't like is degradation and some films pretty much treat women like pieces of meat. So as a film-maker, as a mother, as a wife, as a woman, I find this very upsetting." She thinks it is possible to bring some romance into porn and is trying to "veer away from the formula – which is head, head, three positions and a pop; that's your typical porno tradition." In the film she is now making "the first sex you see

is a blow job, but the second sex is soft, has more foreplay, is sensually based." She is no wide-eyed romantic, however. "This is porno, right? I'm not getting rid of the obligatory money shot [the male ejaculation], which is usually an outside money shot because people want to see he's doing it for real. You can't veer too far."

Ron Jeremy thinks Hamilton is wasting her time. "Porn is for guys and the big difference between men and women is that men get off on body parts, women almost never can. For a woman, she's got to like

Ron Jeremy with Divine Brown, the prostitute whose arrest in Hollywood along with that of movie star Hugh Grant made the tabloids worldwide.

the whole gestalt, the face, the ass, the personality. That's not what porn's about. Take that commercial where the women are having a lunch break and the guy down the bottom is drinking his Diet Cola. If the women ran down the stairs and found the guy had a ditsy little voice, they'd got right back up. If the commercial was about a gorgeous girl drinking Diet Cola and a bunch of guys ran down the stair to find out she had braces on her teeth and stuttered and drooled, that she was borderline retarded, they'd go: 'I'm first!'. That the biggest difference between men and women. Women, the whole gestalt: men, could care less. This is not a 100 per cent rule, it's a good 90 per cent rule."

Jeremy is not the greatest fan of men who watch porn, or of porn either. "I'd rather watch Spielberg," he says.

While porn was still in the dark, exploitative Eighties, three young actresses killed themselves – "baby lambs this industry sheared and tossed away," in the words of Bill Margold who created Paws (Protecting Adult Welfare), a foundation which tries to protect the vulnerable. Once a probation officer, then a porn actor himself, Margold became a successful agent and, he says, spent a lot of his time talking people out of getting into porn. "I had maybe 10,000 people who wanted to get into it and I scared about 9,000 out of the office," he says. "This is a rather crude line, but it's one that was very successful. I would ask the woman who came in, 'What are you going to do ten years from now, when your kid brings home a magazine with you laying in the middle of it with a candle shoved up your ass? Tell him you were playing the birthday cake?'" Paws has an 800 number, a twenty-four-hour help line and offers counselling. Its mascot is a teddy bear – Margold's office is overspilling with teddy bears. The message, he says, is that the foundation is there "to sort of hug the kids and make sure no more kill themselves." He adds: "We're in a society that jerks off to them with their left hand and pushes them away with their right. And that can split a person right down the middle. It makes me mad."

In the last few years, the porn industry has been policing itself. Not only has it banned underage performers, but it has reduced the violence to women – verbal as well as physical – that was common. There are still, says Hamilton, "some young punks out there who've got to push it, got to be edgy, making a product which I despise." That market, however, appears to be bottoming out. Even performer/director Rod Fontana, who works for Outlaw Productions and describes himself as "the nastiest guy in the business" ("When I do anal, it's not a pretty slow motion thing, I don't want the girl looking like 'Oh, I'm just doing this to fill up the tape'") is pleased. Some of what his competitors are doing is "just stupid – you've got to stay erotic with the nastiness. I mean, who wants to see fucking on a bed of fish or in a dumpsters filled with trash?". The industry has also introduced monthly HIV tests – no performer is allowed on set without a clearance certificate – and the leading companies have made condoms compulsory. Elsewhere, some performers, female as well as male, refuse to use condoms because they cramp their style. As only four or five people have tested HIV positive in ten years, during which there must been tens of thousands of couplings, they think the risk worthwhile. A problem which an industry that is making money hand over fist has not been willing to address is overcapacity. "The supply has definitely outpaced demand," says

Sarah Jane Hamilton. The hope is that Digital Versatile Disc (DVD), the exciting new technology that allows shooting from multiple camera angles so that, at a click of a button and to quote a salesman at the Las Vegas electronics show, "you get his point of view, her point of view, the creep outside the window's point of view". But DVD is considerably more expensive than video and no-one yet knows whether the punters are prepared to pay around three times more for a machine and up to five times more for the tapes. The attraction of video is its cheapness. "The most expensive video comes in around 200,000 dollars, plus editing and advertising," porn actress Nina Hartley explains. "In our terms that's like *Gone with the Wind* – and it's not even the catering budget for a regular movie." "Video will remain the gravy for years," comments Russ Hampshire.

To protect its interests, the industry has also become politically active through its lobbying group, the Free Speech Coalition, and has tried to convince legislators that porn movies are not just a matter of free speech, but an economic powerhouse in California – the only state other than New York in which shooting pornography is legal – generating thousands of jobs and billions of

The biggest female names in porn can make $300,000 a year, the biggest male names only a fraction of that. In porn, men are just necessary props.

dollars – more than $4.2 billion last year, compared with $10 million twenty-five years ago. In 1997 the Coalition persuaded the California state legislature to abolish a five per cent "sin tax". The industry is also asking what can be done about the hard-core that satellite channels outside the US are beaming in illegally – profits are beginning to be creamed off. But as Britain – which has the strictest controls on video porn in Europe – has found out, such transmissions are almost impossible to bring to heel. The situation could be met with a response which might make hard-core even more widely available. On their own doorstep, the porn barons are looking over their shoulder. From time to time communities across the US try to shut down porn end-distributors through "zoning" laws. According to Russ Hampshire, "their biggest kick now is that a retailer or a theatre has to be 500 feet from anything else. Then it's going to be 1,000 feet. Then it'll be outside town, eighty miles from nowhere." One of the industry's main concerns is who will be the next president; under the Clinton administration, pornography has had an easy ride. "Reagan and Bush got elected because of the religious right-wingers and they owed something," says Hampshire. "Then they had this obscenity unit in Washington to go after us. This administration feels that the FBI's time is better spent on drugs and child pornography on the Internet."

THE NEW FRONTIER

As with other new communications technologies, pornographers have been the first to maximize the Internet's potential to make money; not even the defence industry capitalizes on developments so swiftly. Major porn companies are among the biggest customers for high-end, state-of-the art computer equipment and they use the best Internet services to give ultrafast connections. Millions of porn dollars have pioneered all today's advances. Anyone who has ever clicked on a live chat show or online video or used two-way conferencing has been involved in a porn-backed spin-off. Undoubtedly there is a moral problem here, but it is impossible to wrestle to the ground. *Internet Magazine* put it like this:

> So if you are opposed to porn and everything it touches, and cannot accept the tacky truth that we must continue to thank the porn masters for future red-hot technological development on the Web, what is the solution? Alas, it is all too clear: throw away your modem.

The Internet has turned the world into a porno village and there are sites, big, small and bizarre, for every taste; CyberQueer, Spankers' Paradise and Buttman's All-Butt are examples that require no explanation. Tragically, the World Wide Web has proved to be a world-wide noticeboard for paedophiles, whose sites like Sex and Kids and Welcome to Lolita Paradise require

A third of Internet users admit to accessing sex sites – of which there are an estimated 28,000.

Virtual sex as depicted in **The Lawnmower Man** *– will science fiction become twenty-first century fact?*

no explanation, either. Today, some 28,000 of the Web's hundreds of thousands of sites are identified as purveying sex. A growing number of porn movie stars including Juli Ashton, Annie Sprinkle and Kylie Ireland have their own. Sprinkle's offers "room cervix" – a photographic tour inside her vagina. Ireland's live sex show gets 10,000 hits a day at five dollars a hit. "Do the math," she says succinctly. Former stripper Danni Ashe taught herself HTML (hypertext markup language, used to produce Web pages) in order to set up Hard Drive, a site more explicit and more popular than *Playboy*'s, averaging five million hits a day. Doing the math in her case indicates a gross of 3.5 million dollars in 1998. "Let's face it," says Ashe, "every man in the world masturbates and they're just looking for new source material." Porn has made Web silicone as ubiquitous as silicon.

A third of Internet users admit to accessing sex sites – and the number of Internet users is doubling, unbelievably, every hundred days. Millions accessed the stolen home movie of ex-

2000
1990
1980
1970
1960
1950
1940
1930
1920
1910
1900

*Millions watched ex-**Baywatch** actress Pamela Anderson (opposite) have sex with her rock-star husband, when a stolen home movie was shown on the internet.*

Baywatch actress Pamela Anderson having sex with her husband Tommy Lee and more than 200,000 bought the full video over the Internet – a tale that epitomizes the convergence of lust, technology, entrepreneurship and money which is the American way of life at the end of the century. The company which made the tape available, Seth Warshavsky's Club Love, has since made a three million dollar offer to Monica Lewinsky, in partnership with *Penthouse* magazine, to pose partially nude. "She hasn't responded yet and we don't expect her to in the near future," he says, "but it's on open-ended offer." Warshavsky, who got into commercial sex when he spotted the possibilities of sex phone-lines – he put 7,000 dollars on two credit cards to run newspaper adverts and ended up employing nearly 300 girls to take the calls – now runs Internet Entertainment Group. Club Love is the group's main Web site, but he supplies live videos to over 1,500 other sites. His is the only company offering a second phone-line which

allows a caller to talk to one of his strippers (on one of seven sets which include a shower and a dungeon) and give her instructions about what he would like her to do. In 1997 Warshavsky grossed 20 million dollars; a year later it was closer to 50 million. "It doesn't matter if I'm selling strippers or I'm selling widgets," he says. "I'm a businessman. It's all widgets to me."

Club Love's interactive sex is the closest we have yet come, in human terms, to the 3D virtual reality sex with cyberbabes and cyberstuds that can be found on the Web. But "teledildonics" is coming – which will offer not just visual interactivity but interactivity through touch; soon, expect to find a 3D replica

Hand-in-glove with virtual reality. Within a decade, getting and giving virtual satisfaction will be possible.

of a human model explicitly animated and programmed to do anything it is bidden. Within a decade, it is predicted, when a helmet that gives entrance to a computer-generated world is developed for use with a dataglove, getting and giving virtual satisfaction will be a reality. This is not a question of *if;* just *when.* For the moment, the closest thing to the real thing is the Real Doll, the most advanced sex toy in existence. Matt and Kimberley, her creators, borrowed technology from the best of Hollywood's special effects artists to design her. Available only on the Internet, the Real Doll is custom-built – height, colour of eyes, hairstyle, breast size – a full-sized woman in perfect detail, right down to her fingerprints and her orifices. At the design stage, Matt checked these out "to make sure they were pleasant

2000

1990

1980

1970

1960

1950

1940

1930

1920

1910

1900

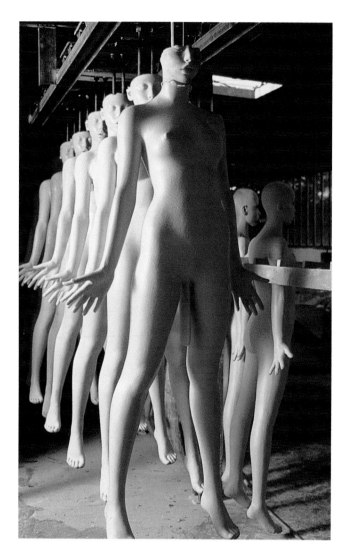

Almost real and ever ready: sex dolls sell, and not only to the lonely.

and the softness of the silicone could accommodate any size of men." Price? A dollar under 5,000, or 5,249 for a model "with the third orifice". Matt and Kimberley average an order a day from "married couples who want to try a little *menage a trois,* divorced guys who don't yet feel able to get back into dating, guys in places like Alaska where basically there are no women."

"Adult novelties" – equipment for enhancing, or replacing, the sex act – are illegal in many American states. Texas, Georgia, Louisiana, Mississippi and Kansas all outlaw the sale of any device designed or sold to stimulate the genitals. Yet, in recent years, the sex toy business has rocketed: vibrators, dildoes with realistic veins painted on them, fake vaginas complete with pubic hair, bandage and discipline paraphernalia, strings of anus love beads (small, medium, large and extra, soft or hard), "pervertible" furniture. "Realistics" are big, moulded from the genitals of the porno-famous. You can purchase a usable replica of Ron Jeremy's formidable not-so-private parts or Juli Ashton's vagina and anus (as it states on the box cover). Moulds of her breasts are available, too. Ashton is serious about the other products she endorses: "I try to keep it to things that I like," she says. "I go in with the designer and we talk about the toys and I'll have a box of them home and try them in my private life and say, 'Well, this handle needs to be a little bit longer, or that hurt or that was really great.'" Both she and Jeremy are represented by Doc Johnson, one of the biggest manufacturers of sex toys in the US which has a turnover of 8 million dollars, . Most of Doc Johnson's customers are couples who want to play together. Its lines sell particularly well in the "women-centric" or "women-positive" sex shops that have sprung up across America and Canada.

One of the biggest is Good Vibrations in San Francisco. "We founded this store," says Carol Queen, "because we saw that sexual products were only being sold in seedy sex shops that sold pornography for men." Another is Good For Her in Toronto, where there are pot-plants

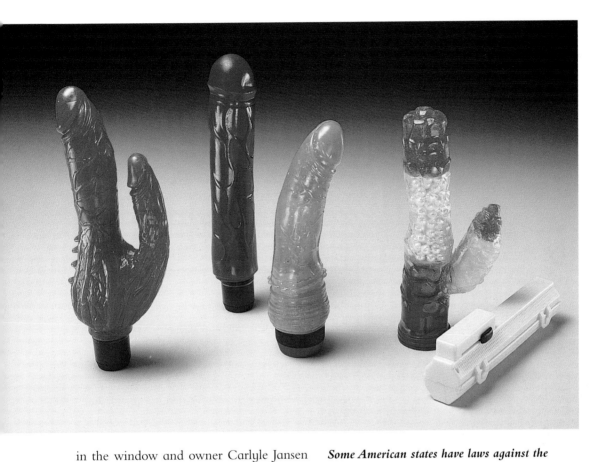

in the window and owner Carlyle Jansen will get you a herbal tea before giving you a tour of the sex toys, which include plastic corn-cob vibrators for vegans. Jansen holds seminars on how to use what she sells. She has a vulva puppet to show women the location of their G-spots. Good For Her carries a large stock of books, including a selection of erotica and has "women-only" hours for browsing. Ten years ago she would not have been able to carry a tenth of the titles, but pornography for women, cloaked in the prettier label of "erotica", is a booming market. Once, rather like sexual satisfaction, women were not supposed to have fantasies, but they do – and the reason they are not ashamed about it is largely due to Nancy

Some American states have laws against the sale and use of sex toys – but they are available everywhere over the internet. "Realistics" – moulded body parts of male and female porn stars– are popular lines.

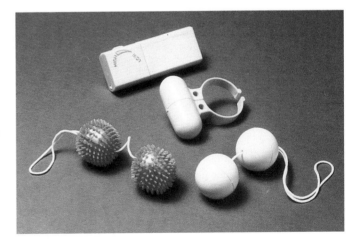

Friday. In the early Seventies she put an advert in newspapers and magazines: "Female Sexual Fantasies wanted by serious female researcher. Anonymity guaranteed". The result was *My Secret Garden,* a book that has sold millions and is now in its twenty-ninth reprint. In it she explained what made her decide to compile it. Her lover, at the crucial point in their love-making, asked her what she was thinking about. She told him that she was fantasizing, imagining herself in a crowd at a football game:

Men tend to assume only they have erotic fantasies. Nancy Friday presented a truer picture

Someone, a man – I don't know who, and in my excitement I can't look – has got himself more closely behind me. I keep cheering, my voice an echo of his, hot on my neck. I can feel his erection through his trousers as he signals me with a touch to turn my hips more directly towards him … He's got his cock out now and somehow it's between my legs; he's torn a hole in my tights under my short skirt … We are all leaping about, thumping one another on the back, and he puts his arm around my shoulders to keep us in rhythm. He's inside me now, shot straight up through me like a ramrod; my God, it's like he's in my throat! … I can feel whoever he is growing harder and harder, pushing deeper and higher into me with each jump … A player has the ball and is racing towards the goal. My excitement gets wilder, almost out of control as I scream for him to make it as we do, so that we all go over the line together.

Friday's lover pulled on his pants and went home. In a another book of women's fantasies, *Women on Top,* written in the Nineties, Friday commented:

There has been in the conventional view no such thing as feminist lust. Locker room wisdom – as well as the consultation rooms of many psychiatrists – said that only men were capable of separating sex from emotion; women could enjoy sex only if presented to them within the context of ongoing, emotional relationship. These women, of every age and socio-economic class, say otherwise; their favourite erotic scenario is not about their husbands or lovers but about a man they will never see again, someone with whom there is no relationship.

The mainstream publishers on both sides of the Atlantic are into erotica these days, but Britain's Virgin Publishing has put itself well to the fore with its explicit Black Lace series launched five years ago – all written by women. Canada's Harlequin Enterprises, which totally dominates romantic fiction world-wide, brought out its Blaze range in response. "We're seeing an appetite for something that is more sexy but still romantic," Harlequin editor Birgit David-Todd says in a manner a great deal more discreet than the behaviour of Blaze heroines. "It's pornography, plain and simple," responds sexologist Marilyn Fithian. She treated a number of women who had orgasms without recognizing them as such and she identified the source of their arousal as the erotic fiction they read. "But they didn't see it as porn, you understand, they read *romance*. Yet it was pretty much the pornography men used to read in the old days. It just wasn't identified that way." Comments Black Lace novelist Sylvie Ovellette: "In my mind, pornography has always been something very visual, like *Hustler*. Erotica is very much in the head."

Images of sexual fantasy are not restricted to soft covers: they are the very stuff of advertising and, in the end-years of the century, there is no escaping them. Men have their place as advertising objects but, essentially, they are as much a prop as male performers in porn movies – for advertising is about women's bodies, or body parts, whatever the product

Sex sells everything from ice cream to shampoo and, say feminists, the male-dominated advertising industry still has a sexist attitude towards women.

being sold. And, always, the gestures of intimacy are caricatured: lips are licked in sexual invitation, phallic chocolate bars are sucked, phallic bottles of table water stroked. The feigned ecstasy of orgasm is employed to sell everything from ice-cream and pizza to shampoo. Even the male erection is a tool of the advertisers' trade. A Benetton ad displays genitalia and the boundaries of public acceptability shift ever outwards. In a thousand small ways, advertising makes yesterday's pornography today's "so-what"? Since rock videos are advertisements for recordings, it is hardly surprising that they share the same visual language. Some, however, have moved deliberately into the darker reaches of fantasy – a place which Madonna, with her Jean Paul Gaultier cone-nippled bra and her projection of bondage, rape, lesbianism, sado-masochism and group sex, has made largely her own. Certain elements of fashion, too, have sold themselves on decadent sexuality which wallows in drug culture – a trend that many have found disturbing. Porn director Sarah Jane Hamilton, hardly a woman with a narrow view of life, thinks that the way "Obsession and Calvin Klein used the younger kids in such a sexual way was bad taste and pushed the line."

According to psychiatrist Oliver James, the relentless bombardment of sexual imagery in all media "has played an important role in making men and women dissatisfied with their own bodies and with their real partners." He attacks capitalism which "makes money out of the disappointment … and rage engendered by overheated aspirations and unreal comparisons."

If large sections of the US remain unenthusiastic about the commercialization of sex, it is not the capitalists. Americans spend 10 billion dollars a year on hard-core porn, telephone sex, live sex shows, computer porn and sex magazines – more, in strip clubs alone, than on theatre, opera, ballet and classical music performance combined. As pornography in particular continues to grow, so other massive industries benefit. Almost every major communications or entertainment conglomerate has a finger in the sexual pie. The telephone giant AT&T introduced pay-per-call numbers in 1990 – doubling the phone sex business. AT&T and other long-distance carriers make millions from selling band-width to adult-content providers. Porn on cable puts money in the bank for mainstream companies like Time-Warner and for hotel chains like Sheraton, three-quarters of whose pay-per-view profits come from porn. All the big search engines on the Internet sell adult advertising – at around eighteen cents a click-access, compared with one or two cents for regular ads. There are two bottom lines to the story of adult entertainment in America. The second is that the moral division between the admitted pornographer and the distanced corporate executive has vanished.

The worry for some is that explicitness will keep advancing into everyday life. That is an extreme view and porn actress Juli Ashton replies to it: "You're not going to see an explicit spreadshot on a billboard when you're driving down the street. You're never going to see a hard-core scene on *Friends*. You're just not." Al Goldstein removes his ever-present cigar and, in a Woody Allenesque mode, heads the argument in the opposite direction: "In 2002 I see pornography being two people holding hands."

Madonna constantly reinvents herself – no-one
better understands that sex sells.

2000

1990

1980

1970

1960

1950

1940

1930

1920

1910

1900

WHAT'S LOVE GOT TO DO WITH IT?

ZIPPERGATE. A VAGINAL CIGAR. ORAL SEX IS NOT IN THE BIBLE, SO HOW CAN IT BE CONSTRUED AS ADULTERY? PRESIDENTIAL SCANDAL IS HARDLY NEW. WHEN GEORGE WASHINGTON WAS FIGHTING THE WAR OF INDEPENDENCE AMERICANS WERE AWARE THAT A CONGRESSMAN PROCURED WOMEN FOR HIM. IT WAS PUBLIC KNOWLEDGE THAT THOMAS JEFFERSON HAD A SECOND FAMILY WITH A SLAVE GIRL BEFORE HE WAS ELECTED, THAT JAMES BUCHANAN WAS GAY — HIS LONG-TERM LOVER WAS THE VICE-PRESIDENT IN THE PROCEEDING ADMINISTRATION AND WAS KNOWN AS MRS VICE-PRESIDENT — AND THAT GROVER CLEVELAND HAD AN ILLEGITIMATE CHILD.

The press grew reticent about the White House sitting tenant only during the Second World War: it seemed inappropriate against the scale of events to reveal that Roosevelt lived in one wing with his mistress while his wife lived in the other with her lesbian lover. Press reticence carried over into peacetime, protecting Dwight Eisenhower's sedately sexual relationship with his female wartime military driver. Less worthy of such discretion were John F. Kennedy, who liked to take two girls at a time and said he was never finished with a woman until he had had her three ways, and his gross successor, Lyndon Johnson, who enjoyed showing his penis to people and who celebrated signing civil rights legislation into law by having a black girl in the Oval Office. "I've had more women by accident than Kennedy had on purpose," he boasted.

Hugged by a hands-on President, Monica Lewinsky was not to remain just a figure in the crowd for very long.

Not until after his death did the many affairs of John F. Kennedy – here with Grace Kelly – become public knowledge

As the first incumbent post-war First Citizen to be exposed for sexual shenanigans after years of Teflon-coated philandering, Clinton came unstuck, before the Starr Chamber, in a show of sweating, hair-splitting dissembling, well aware that he was staring down the barrel of impeachment – not for cavorting with plump and eager Monica Lewinsky, but for lying about it to Congress. As its president squirmed so did America, setting angels dancing on the pinhead of where private behaviour ends and public behaviour begins. Meanwhile, the world looked on amused. "Almost no-one in Britain thinks it's very important, politically," says Nigel Cawthorne, author of *Sex Lives of the Presidents*. "America knew what it was getting when they elected Clinton. I think that subliminally people find him charismatic, and charisma is sexual, surely. When it was alleged that previous Prime Minister John Major had been involved with a caterer at 10 Downing Street, suddenly he seemed a more colourful man – he'd always seemed very grey. Now we joke about Tony Blair being a eunuch and you see mentions in the papers that perhaps we should have some interns at Number Ten. The Clinton scandal has been a lot of fun all over the world. The Italians think the president's behaviour should be a source of national pride, not a matter of shame; and President Chirac of France is so jealous that he now boasts about his youthful affair with the actress Claudia Cardinale and instead of going like President Mitterrand to see his mistress very discreetly, he goes with a full motorcade and outriders so everybody knows."

That British-born New York media luvvie and editor, Tina Brown, told the glitterati who attended a White House dinner for Prime Minister Blair to "Forget the dog-in-the-manger, down-in-the-mouth neo-Puritanism of the op-ed tumbrel drivers, and see him [Clinton] as a man with more heat than any star in the room – or, for that matter, at the multiplex," is really neither here nor there. What is interesting, in view of the ruthlessly scurrilous legal strategy that Clinton adopted against Paula Jones' allegation of harassment, is that feminists did not demand his balls in a sling. Then, Barbara Ehrenreich, one of the more thoughtful of feminist writers, declared: "Even a woman with a past has rights ... A president who could allow his lawyer to use such a low-down sexist tactic is guilty of at least one thing: insulting his once-solid feminist constituency"; and Patricia Ireland, head of the National Organization for Women, told Clinton to "grow up." But later, when the Lewinsky affair hit the fan, a gathering of feminists at a luncheon organized by the *New York Observer* was sympathetic to the president. Neo-conservative Kate Roiphe extolled his virility, *Fear of Flying* novelist Erica Jong sounded as if she would have liked to split the Oval Office detail with the intern, and Nancy Friday seemed thrilled that Clinton's sexual prospects might be heightened by added risk ("His next blow job is going to be the most exciting he ever had," she said). Gloria Steinem, who wanted to know what all the fuss was about, was censured by The *New York Times* – the authentic voice of right-wing liberals – which in turn received a blast from Susan Faludi, rebutting the paper's view that Steinem "was suggesting that the nation's workplace declared open season on office virgins." Senior editor of feminist *Ms.* magazine, Marcia Ann Gillespie, throws up her hands when asked why feminists are not hanging Clinton out to dry. Is it because, as a pro-abortionist, a promoter of women, he is their boy, regardless? As far as she is concerned, consent is the issue, and as Lewinsky's is not in doubt, then Clinton's behaviour "is something he and Hillary need to talk about, but it's not our business." As for the Jones' harassment allegation, she dismisses it: "Clinton backs off when he is told 'No'. I think he could have asked first and heard the 'No' rather than show the exhibit. What he did was lewd, no two ways about it, but that's not the same thing as harassment."

Cristy Zercher, one of the long line of woman who claim that Clinton has hit on them, has no doubt that what he did to her was harassment. A flight attendant on a private charter plane

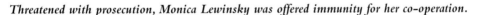

Threatened with prosecution, Monica Lewinsky was offered immunity for her co-operation.

Paula Jones:
her case against Bill Clinton
was settled privately.

that Clinton used for eight or nine months when he was campaigning for the presidency in 1992, he moved, she alleges, from paying her compliments about her blue eyes to groping her breast. "He was always touching when he spoke, whispering in the ear, something like 'That camera guy is checking you out'", she says. "He was touching, inviting you into the bathroom, sticking his finger in his mouth, caressing a deformed orange. And there were so many other comments and remarks, and things that he did that I can't even remember." Then an incident Zercher does remember – Clinton catching her and the other two attendants reading Gennifer Flower in *Penthouse:* "Deborah just blurted out, 'Gennifer complimented you on your oral abilities,' and he said, 'I guess that would be pretty accurate, that's one of my favourite things to do.' He never really admitted the affair, but by the way he was talking never denied it either." The groping incident, she claims, happened when they were flying from New York to LA. She had served the meal, everyone was sleeping and she went up front to sit down. Clinton joined her, claiming he was very tired and laid his head on her shoulder. "My biggest fear was 'Hillary's going to wake up and say something,'" Zercher says. "He got closer, snugger and snugger, and then kind of crossed his arms and snuggled up. And I started talking, and I really thought he was asleep. And then he started stroking my breast. I remember I couldn't even talk any more and I swallowed and I just sat there. I kept thinking, 'Is he really doing what I think he's doing?'" When Zercher told her colleagues what happened, "they joked about it, blew it off – you know, 'That's just him, that's his personality, it's a good thing he's so nice.'" But Zercher felt bad about it – "he'd crossed the line." It was a relief to her when Michael Isikoff, a journalist on *The Washington Post,* contacted her two years later to check out a rumour that was circulating. Isikoff, now with *Newsweek,* thinks he understands Clinton's appeal: "People like Bill Clinton, they voted for him, they feel comfortable with him. And they're willing to forgive his faults that in others they might not forgive. Certainly, if a corporate executive was found these days to be fooling around with an intern in his office, that would be considered a serious matter."

Sexual harassment law was drafted on the back of feminist pressure in the Eighties, but did not really seep into public awareness until Anita Hill made allegations against Supreme Court judge Clarence Thomas. The legislation was well-intentioned, its aim to protect women from sexually demeaning behaviour at work. No-one envisaged where it would lead. There was a rush to legislation, with cases being won on little more than a suggestive remark or come-on e-mail; in defiance of any kind of logic, some woman who had had a failed affair with a colleague successfully sued their employers for "allowing" such a relationship in the first place.

And men also brought suits: sexual harassment can be a two-way street.

In order to protect themselves, companies instituted policies of behaviour. Many adopted a sensible approach, others were less rational – for them, the more usual "no unwelcome physical contact" clause became "no physical touching". Some companies made staff known to be having a relationship sign consensual contracts while others introduced "no dating" clauses, on the assumption that if they drew the line far enough back, no-one could claim that they did not knew when they stepped over it. There are now companies that operate "zero tolerance" (one wrong move and out the door) or employ "cupid police" – human resources specialists who hold training workshops and help enforce policy.

The Equal Employment Opportunity Commission, the federal government agency in charge of discrimination issues, presided over 6,127 cases in 1991, with awards for damages totalling $7.7 million. By 1997, that figure had risen to 15,889 cases, with awards of $49.4 million. And that is the tip of the iceberg: innumerable other cases have been brought under individual state laws. In the eighteen months to the middle of 1998, sales of insurance covering sexual harassment settlements more than doubled to over $200 million.

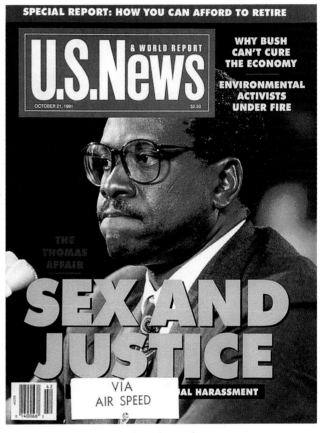

Clarence Thomas: the judge who set harassment law bandwagon rolling – unintentionally.

In the eyes of British employers who have their own low-key policies, the rules that govern the interaction of men and women in the American workplace are so harsh they almost rival Islamic fundamentalism; Britain may have had its share of harassment cases that have turned common sense inside out, but nothing that touches the American experience. There, men and women who are involved are forced to be as furtive as *1984*'s Winston Smith in the Ministry of Truth. Those who are not are still nervous about smiling at each other – particularly if they are on different salary grades – much less paying each other a compliment. "Men are afraid to say 'Boo'," says Cristy Zercher who, despite her Clinton experience, thinks the whole thing has gone too far. "They're afraid to say 'That's a nice suit' or 'You're having a great hair day'. They're afraid to say anything because women in some circumstances are taking advantage." Absurdities abound: a man sacked for telling a female co-worker a mildly dirty joke in the office – not that she was offended but another woman who overheard him was; a man sacked after refusing to remove from his desk a holiday snapshot of his wife; a gay man sued

*Not only men commit sexual harassment as the movie and the
novel of* **Disclosure** *intimated.*

(unsuccessfully) by a female colleague because he talked about his sex life. A high-profile case involved an episode of the *Seinfield* television series in which, to ensure he remembered her name, a woman with whom he had just had a one-night stand, joked that it rhymed with a part of the female body. The following morning, in a brewery company in Wisconsin, a man named Jerry Mackenzie related this to a colleague, Patty Best. Because Mackenzie was embarrassed to say the word "clitoris" – which Seinfield had rhymed with "Dolores" – he photocopied a dictionary definition and showed her. Best was shocked, reported Mackenzie to her superior, he was brought to court on a charge of sexual harassment, and subsequently fired. Still out of work two years later because his record made him unemployable, Mackenzie successfully sued his former company for wrongful dismissal.

"There's been a lot of focus on cases that seem quote/unquote 'trivial'," observes Marcia Ann Gillespie, "and as a result many people forget that most of the cases that are coming into courts are not about 'Did he look at me askance?' They are about outright rape in the office; they are about fondling and physical assaults." And they are also about the abuse of power "as a way to gain sexual pleasure." But, Gillespie concedes, there is a problem: a lot of companies have "nitpicked the issue to the point that it has made people feel, this is really ridiculous." She adds: "We cannot just say to people, 'Thou shalt not date your co-worker, thou shalt not smile with co-workers,' especially since we're asking people to work longer hours and the workplace is often going to be where you have your social interaction – your love affairs. There has to be some reality here." It would be hard to find anyone, except those making money from the $10 billion a year "harassment-awareness" business, to disagree. For the moment, however, most employees are being told that the issue really comes down to one thing, respect – which leaves no-one any the wiser. New York columnist Candace Bushnell, a critic of "victim mentality", thinks the solution lies in women's hands. "I'm not saying harassment doesn't take place, it certainly does," she says, "but I think there are a lot of situations where a quick remark can take care of the situation. I also think that women should have the confidence to say, 'You wanna fuck with me? Go ahead. I'll take a certain amount of abuse. But then I'm gonna fuck with you.' You need to have a little attitude."

A NEW VOCABULARY?

Thirty years ago when the sexual revolution began, the agenda was bold but simple: to make men and women sexually equal and, in its most positive idealism, as Richard Davenport-Hine wrote in *Sex, Death and Punishment:*

> To de-erotize guilt and to discard the false mystification, sentimentality and manipulative obscenity which ecclesiastics and some writers have propagated about sex, and to establish sexual intercourse …

as a series of imaginative acts to satisfy physical and emotional curiosity, rather than as the chief distinction in an adult life between a chaste and a monogamous existence.

Spice Power. But do Spice Girls dilute the feminist message?

If some of that has been achieved, there has been a price to pay. When the wagon rolled, there was a sexual – and societal – structure to kick against. That has gone, leaving a fragmented world with no clear view of what types of sexual practices and behaviour are appropriate. Even feminism, which blazed the trail and invented the vocabulary, appears to have lost the compass. Erica Jong now renounces "the idea of sexual freedom because it doesn't work." Germaine Greer advocates celibacy and the remaining pioneers bicker with the New Feminists whom they dismiss as being concerned with self-promotion and materialism rather than "traditional" issues. Camille Paglia dismisses old and new alike: "Leaving sex to the feminists," she says, "is like letting your dog vacation at the taxidermist's." In June 1998, *Time* magazine tried to nail feminism in its coffin with a cover story that asked: "Is feminism dead?" Yet half of American women and over a third of their British counterparts claim some kind of allegiance to feminism, even if they do not hear the Big Message to which the Sixties and Seventies

Ally McBeal: post-modernist icon – or "a little animal to put on a leash"?

marched, or see feminism in a political and cultural framework. Perhaps this is because the message has been diluted. "Feminism" for many simply means equal rights to a satisfactory orgasm and, for a minority, the right to behave as badly as some men behave. The message is also trivialized by somehow seeing a Spice Girl goosing Prince Charles as an act of feminist empowerment – what if Liam Gallagher goosed the Princess Royal? Don't tempt him – or in seeing in the insecure *Ally McBeal* a post-modernist feminist icon. Empowered? "Ally McBeal is a mess," says Nancy Friday. "She's like a little animal. You want to put her on a leash." In the British *Guardian,* Linda Grant considered the *McBeal* appeal and queried: "Why should women think that they will be treated with respect while wearing skirts halfway up their arses." She queries "if dressing like a pubescent girl is the smartest move you can make when you're trying to push through into real power."

What *do* women really, really want? And men for that matter? To be single, to be married, to sign up for virginity until the wedding night, to be faithful, to enjoy "hot monogamy", bisexuality, one-night stands, flings, affairs? Tune in to *Jerry Springer* or "Dr Drew" on MTV's *Love Line* and the extent of human sexual yearning and behaviour, its muddle and complexities, leave the mind reeling.

For many women, the greatest change in their lives, and therefore their dealings with men, has come from economic independence. That, says Candace Bushnell, has led to a growing band of women to choose to be single, forsaking other considerations in favour of their careers. "At one time to be a single woman who worked, didn't get married, was basically the equivalent of a witch," she comments. The *New York Observer* column she used to write, observing life among The Big Apple's mostly single high-flyers, led to her novel *Sex and the City,* now turned into a much discussed television series. *Sex and the City* expresses her own experience and her belief that "Here in New York you can lead your own life and it's a wonderful, wonderful freedom. There are so many women who say things like 'Gosh, I thought by the time I was thirty-five I would definitely be married and have kids and now I don't even want to get married.'" As for herself, she does not think she will ever get married, although she leaves the door ajar: "Everyone thinks there's this vast pool of people out there, that the Cinderella fairy tale will come true and Prince Charming will come along. But it isn't so. People are probably more damaged by romantic ideals than they are by the truth. Relationships are very hard to make happen. You sort of have ideas that this fabulous guy is going to come along and it turns out to be a guy who sleeps with three other women – last night. And that, unfortunately, is the truth."

Sex in the city? "My sense is that people are having sex quite often and they're having it pretty easily and freely. I mean, it's not unusual if you go on a date with a guy three times you're probably going to end up having sex with him. One of the problems is that, after you've had so much of this kind of sex, what does sex mean to you any more? What does it mean to anybody?" Bushnell adds: "So much sex stops people from making good relationships." She has sympathy for a lot of men who belong to the career-woman set: "They're under social pressure to go out and get laid and not make a commitment. And they're kind of damaged and saddened by the fact that they have to have all this meaningless sex when they would be better off in a monogamous relationship with a woman who really loved them."

Twenty per cent of women born in both America and Britain since 1960 are expected to choose to remain childless, if not unmarried; this is predicted to rise to thirty per cent by 2010. Many of them believe that a career and a relationship are not compatible. Comments Angela Giveon, managing editor of *Executive Woman* magazine: "A lot of women are making the choice to be single because they realize they can't have it all. They've usually had a failed relationship – not necessarily marriage – when they make this decision. Something is thrown at them like, 'You think of your job more than me,' and they think like a man: 'Sod it, it's not worth the bother.'"

But career thirtysomething women grow older. And then, asks David Anthony, editor of *Notorious* – an American magazine which aims to attract readers of both *Playboy* and *Cosmopolitan* – where do they find themselves? That, he says, is "one of the really big issues in the Western world in the late twentieth century." He adds: "There are a lot of women in their forties, even in their fifties, who want to have a vibrant, rich, sexual life who don't have a husband, so where do they go get it? How do they do that? How do they meet someone to have that? It's very much OK for a man who's in his forties to have a twenty-year-old girlfriend – that's almost cool. But if a woman were to do that, there's something wrong. And I think that's one of the contradictions of all the freedom that we have."

Such considerations do not concern those to whom forty is almost an entire lifetime away, like the "lads" and "ladettes" who, in the Nineties, form a significant segment of young people in

Magazine for the "lads", whose culture involves beer, football and a regressive attitude towards women.

"Ladettes": matching "the lads" excess for excess and living life with "attitude".

Britain and live their lives with "attitude".

"Ladism" was a reaction against female pressure in the late-Eighties to make men into New Man, who was supposed to show his feminine, nurturing side. Ladism became a form of tribalism involving, besides beer and football, a regressive attitude to women – "use 'em and then have a laugh with your mates about it". How much of this is a kind of self-protection is debatable, but Derek Harbison, editor of Britain's *Loaded* magazine, ascribes to the view. Some men, he thinks, feel threatened by women's new sense of empowerment – induced by the simplified version of feminism, but feminism nevertheless – and their willingness to bring sex out into the open and talk about it. As he sees it, such men feel "nervous about the demands being made of them and worried about whether they can meet expectations."

James Few, with his City job and red Ferrari, is a fairly typical lad and hardly seems to be suffering angst. "Yeah, we enjoy fucking," he says brashly. What kind of woman? "Something that's pretty wild in the bedroom. No-one likes sleeping with a bit of wood. Some, even if they're having orgasms, they're just pretty boring." He is very sure of himself. "Even when some women don't want sex they can always be talked into actually having sex. You just tell 'em that you really like 'em and you've liked 'em for a while. They'll always fall for that one." He elaborates: "If they look a bit tarty, they're going to be more easy to sleep with than others. But most women, even classy-looking women, you can sleep with that night." And if a woman wants to be wined and dined and develop a relationship? "Don't bother with them." Few has been so drunk when he has taken some women to bed he has not remembered in the morning and "finding someone in your bed, a naked woman … it's pretty scary." If he has slept at her place, his policy is to "get out early while they're still asleep." He admits "I use 'em for my needs and they normally come off hurt. But what of it? There's just not commitment. You go out, you get self-satisfaction and that's all you intend to get from the night. You're not intending to see that person again, so no point in falling in love."

"Ladettes?" They arose to challenge the "lads", prepared to match excess with excess and to treat the opposite gender in the same predatory fashion. Meet Leah Dowling, proud of her ladette credentials and her ability to drink more than her male friends and "get more smashed than them." But she adds: "I like being girlie … you don't want to lose that." For Dowling, sex "is something there for you to enjoy." She resents the male attitude that if a woman "sleeps about, she's a slag – if a bloke does it, it's like, oh, pat on the back, same old thing. But now more girls are sleeping about it's like, 'What?' We don't care what you think of us." She cannot, she retorts, stay faithful – which is "something they can't really deal with. And they're like 'I can't believe you. I can't believe you went behind my back. And I've been faithful to you' – like I should be privileged."

MTV presenter Sara Cox disdains the "ladette" description but is in favour of women frankly expressing their sexuality. "When I get asked about women's lib and about how women have changed, I don't feel qualified to answer," she says truthfully. "But, yeah, women have definitely changed in the last ten years, they've got more powerful … women are carrying condoms and women are choosing to have one-night stands, to have sex with whoever they want, whoever they fancy. And they can have a one-night stand and they can get up in the morning and deal with it. It's not that tortured sense any more, it's just, yeah, I had a great shag last night, tell your mates about it the next day." Women "can now talk about shagging and not feel obliged to bring in the romance or the commitment or what he actually thinks, or whether there's any love there. You can actually just talk about sex for what it is, just for pure pleasure, for satisfaction, a good bit of exercise, a nice way to wake up or a way to help you go to sleep." And if the sex is not satisfactory, Cox adds, "they won't just lie back and think of England, grit their teeth and pretend, and fake orgasm to please the man. Now women take control much more during sex. I mean, I'm sure it used to be frowned upon for women to want sex. Surely, it was always the man who wanted sex… but actually we *do* want sex, we do *need* sex." About herself, Cox says: "I'm actually quite a good girl when it comes to sex. I'm not the sort of girl to have one-night stands. But sex, I love sex, …" She demands fidelity, as three-quarters of under thirty-fives appear to do – an explanation being that as a third of this age group have grown up with their parents' divorce they understand the consequences of hanging on when a relationship turns turtle. Any woman with an unfaithful man should "just get rid of him and move on, don't waste your energy on getting revenge. Men wouldn't bother to torture themselves and try to get revenge, men would just move on, and I think that's what more and more women are doing now."

Such an approach to life would make New Yorkers Ellen Fein and Sherrie Schneider reach for the smelling salts. They believe in a back-to-basics approach to relationships laid out in *The Rules* (and *Rules II*), which tells women how to winnow Mr Right from the chaff of mankind. Most people would agree with Marie Ann Gillespie that there are no rules, that "life is complicated and messy and there's a random factor – life isn't about rules, but about exercising choices." She dismisses *The Rules* with the comment: "Someone once came up with a gimmick called the Pet Rock, do you remember that? And people bought it. Which proves to me that, in this land of the consumer, you can come up with practically anything and you will find somebody who's going to buy it." In fact, over two million women have bought volume one and "Rules" support groups have sprung up all over the world.

The Rules is prescriptive and simple: don't sleep with him on the first date; don't go out with him more than once a week in the beginning; don't call him back too often; never be the first to say "I love you" – and a great deal more, not least finding other interests that will make him believe there are other things in your life than thinking about him. Tangentially, the last of these "rules" is something advocated by Elizabeth Wurtzel, writer of *Bitch,* a book extolling women who have gained power from their sexuality. Her reason, however, has nothing to do with man-catching but with self-esteem: "The whole point of the sexual revolution was to give women better lives," she wrote in *The Guardian.* "If women had the kinds of consuming passions men seem to, that they will not allow a single fucking thing to get in the way of – be it watching sports or drinking with the boys – women would do more to assert their own rights."

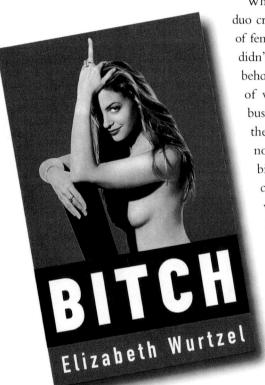

Writer of a book about difficult women, Wurtzel has advice for all women: get a life!

Why did Fein and Schneider feel the need to write *The Rules?* The duo crackle with energy and earnestness. "Because with the advent of feminism, women got a little mixed up," says Schneider. "They didn't realize they were turning men off by their aggressive behaviour," says Fein. Who are their readers? Schneider: "A lot of women in their thirties, especially, they're successful in business, they own their apartments, they're financially secure – they still want to get married, they still want a partner, maybe not a marriage partner, but somebody who remembers their birthday, somebody who doesn't forget them." Fein: "We do consultations, we get thousands of letters from all over the world, these women feel that something is missing in their life when they don't have a husband or a partner. We're not making this up. They say to us, 'I have the job, I have the apartment, I run, I go to the gym, I feel something is missing because I don't have a man who's crazy about me.' And we offer a plan. This isn't fiction, we offer a plan, a methodical way. If you are beautiful and you don't do *The Rules,* you stand less of a chance of getting married than an attractive woman who does *The Rules."*

In Candace Bushnell's *Sex and the City,* the main character meets an old boyfriend and they go to bed in the middle of the afternoon. To Schneider such an action is "disgusting – and I don't think most women out there really want to behave in this fashion. This is upper-class behaviour? I'm sorry, to me that's no more than being a hooker, except you're not even getting paid." She adds: "When you're in a loving relationship with your husband you have real intimacy. But these one-night stands you're talking about, these afternoon meetings? That's not intimacy, that sucks."

The bookstore shelves groan with relationship advice, books dependent for attention on some new angle or insight or, at least, a catchy title. One that rose to the top of the heap in 1998 was *What Men Want.* Written by three male friends – a doctor, a lawyer and an accountant "in the middle of the dating scene" – it claimed to tell women what men think and feel. "What we're doing," says Rich Seldes (the doctor), "is throwing up the white flag, surrendering the game plan. We're telling women: we know there are problems. Please, here, understand us better."

Like *The Rules, What Men Want* has rules, though they do not entirely coincide. There is agreement, however, that a woman is almost certain to get dumped if she tries to change a man, and that having sex on a first date is a no-no. "A man who has sex with a woman on the first date will not ever have her in his mind as wife potential," says Brad Gerstman (the lawyer). "Because a man will say to himself immediately: 'She must be doing this with every other guy.' There is nothing worse than a guy thinking of his tender, loving sweet little girlfriend having slept with fifty or sixty or, god knows, how many men before he got into the picture." Yes, we are talking age-old double standard here: "The feminist revolution has not changed the man's mind and every guy asks that stupid question at some point: 'How many guys have you had sex with?'" If it is a lot, say the authors – lie.

What, in essence, do men want? "We're looking for women who are nice," says Chris Pizzo (the accountant). "Women who are

*There is a lot of **Sex in the City** … but much of it is meaningless and doesn't make people happy.*

proactive. Who understand that it's OK to approach a man. To say hello. To call a guy first. To ask a guy out. We're looking for women who want to progress the relationship at its natural pace. Not play games. Not be somebody they're not. Not expect the guy to be someone that they're not." And women who have an understanding of the power they have over men: "Women don't understand the insecurity that men have. Women don't understand how scared a guy is to go up to a woman and have her say 'What are you doing? I'm a ten and you're a four, get away from me.'" Where the *What Men Want* trio particularly part company with *The Rules* duo is over the matter of playing hard to get. Says Pizzo: "Any man will go after the chase. I mean, most guys are very competitively brought up, they play sports, and then they get into a business world. And they're competitive by nature. They're going to go after a chase because no-one's ever going to tell them 'You can't have this'. But after they get it, that's it. They've conquered the challenge. It's on to the next chase. What we're trying to say to women is 'Forget that playing hard to get. Wouldn't you rather be open, be sincere, be yourself? And if it works out, it works out. If it doesn't, it doesn't, you just know much sooner. You'll save yourself a lot of time and heartache'"

Where commitment is concerned, both parties run on the same rails. "Here," says Pizzo, "we get to one of the ugly truths in our book – the good old 'I'm not ready for commitment'." Gerstman picked up: "'Oh, I just finished a big business deal, just yesterday, and it's not the time. I mean, I'm getting into another project now'. Or, 'I just moved from this state to this state and I'm just not ready for commitment'. 'I just graduated, I'm not ready for commitment'. 'My parents just got a divorce, I'm not ready for commitment'. Guys are shameless in giving these excuses. But what they mean is 'I'm not ready for a commitment – with you'." Adds Seldes: "Men are pigs in a lot of senses. A man will date a woman who he's not interested in, in terms of a long-term relationship, just to have sex with her. He will string her along. He will wine and dine her with the sole purpose of trying to sleep with her. Men can be pigs." "Dogs," agrees Gerstman.

It was in recognition of irresponsible male behaviour that former football coach Bill McCartney eight years ago founded the Promise Keepers, a religious movement of men dedicated to becoming better husbands and fathers by making seven pledges of social and moral conduct that include honouring Christ and practising "spiritual, moral, ethical and sexual purity". In November 1997, an estimated three-quarters of a million Promise Keepers descended

If a woman has a lot of sexual partners she should lie – unlike the character in **Four Weddings and a Funeral.**

on Washington, thronging the mile-long Mall between the Monument and the Capitol Building. The "Stand in the Gap" rally – the gap which sinfulness has breached in the walls of society – was the biggest religious meeting in American history. There have been many other PK rallies held in stadiums all over America, where men wearing T-shirts proclaiming "Real Men Love Jesus" and "Men Behaving Godly" sing hymns, clap, hug, and cry in mass exhibitions of manly emotion.

Public admission of their faults is part of being Promise Keepers. Typically, Pastor Dan Best is a member of the movement who repents his past. As a young man he walked out on his first wife and five children, had affairs from which "other children popped up", got married a second time, and for sixteen years carried on as he had before – "a life of gambling, a life of playboying, a life of money laundering on the Mafia side," he says contritely. All this ended a quarter of a century ago "when Christ came into my life" and he "began to realize it's not money, it's the relationship, first of all with Christ and then that relationship goes with your wife." Yvonne Best, who brought up her husband's illegitimate children with their own remembers those years: "He was a playboy who went out with other women. It was rough, it was hard." Several times she made plans to leave, but each time "the Lord just threw a monkey wrench in it."

The Promise Keepers' emotional bonding with the Lord and each other would probably make most Britons uncomfortable. Many Americans are uncomfortable about the Promise Keepers, too: not for their public displays – an infinitely more God-fearing country than Britain, America is accustomed to touchy-feely religious revivalism – but for their stated intention of making women submit, on biblical interpretation, to masculine authority. A speaker at the "Stand in the Gap" rally put it like this: "The first thing you do is sit down with your wife and say something like this: 'Honey, I've made a terrible mistake. I've given you my role. I gave up leading this family and I forced you to take my place. Now I must reclaim my role.'" Pastor Best elaborates: "We see Christ as the head, with the husband under Christ and then the family under the husband. So if Christ is the saviour or the provider of security for the home, spiritually, then so should the husband be for the wife." Yvonne Best agrees: "God placed the man in the home as the head – and that's his role, because he is the guide, he's the guard, he's the provider, he is the governor … the patriarchal system is what God has instituted.

The message of PK domination has semantic twists – leadership means submission, submission means leadership; a man who takes charge of his family is a man who becomes a servant of his family. These cut little ice with the National Organization for Women. "It's an American version of the Taliban," says Karen Johnson, a vice-president. Others have an even more extreme opinion, encapsulated on a placard held up during "Standing in the Gap": "Promise Keepers want women barefoot, pregnant, battered and in the kitchen". *Ms.* magazine's Marcia Ann Gillespie stands somewhere in the middle of the two viewpoints: "I recognize that the impulse that's driving this sort of group is not all bad, there is what I want to call a real spiritual hunger and that is worldwide now. Unfortunately the other thing that drives them is real old-fashioned patriarchy – and we don't need this idea of man coming back to resume his place as the head of the family, as if women are supposed to be the foot."

Whether the Promise Keepers are a manifestation, as feminism would say, of men on the run from women's empowerment, seeking safety in male fellowship and a demand for a

2000

1990

1980

1970

1960

1950

1940

1930

1920

1910

1900

return of penis power, is open to argument. What is certain is that, three decades of feminism which has asserted that gender differences are principally socially constructed and therefore changeable, have proved to be wrong. Many of the differences between men and women seem to be "hard-wired". At the "Stand in the Gap" rally, a British journalist watched feminists on a National Organization for Women stand talking to Promise Keepers – "baffled interchanges between people who look at each other as though they come from different species." Or planets. Mars and Venus shall we say? Comments John Gray, author of *Men Are from Mars, Women Are from Venus,* the best-selling guide to improving communication between the sexes: "There's a whole range of differences between men and women. We think differently about certain things, we react differently, we feel differently. Most importantly, our emotional needs are different, what we feel good about ourselves. Quite often, men feel good about what they do, they identify the results of their actions with who they are. Not that women don't feel good about who they are, based on their actions, but women particularly build their self-esteem and their sense of self based upon the quality of their relationships."

SHIFTING SANDS

When it comes to sex, men and women probably do believe in the stereotypes: men want sex, women want relationships; believing that sex requires emotional involvement continues to give women a moral superiority. And yet many young women now pay no more than lip service to that belief. In a study of twenty-year-old college students reported in the academic journal *Sex Roles* in 1993, sociologist Ilsa Lottes noted that 92 per cent of women thought love was necessary for sex "most of the time or always", yet almost half admitted having casual sex. "Since they had already had four or more sexual partners," Lottes commented, "they either possessed an extraordinary talent for falling in love, or they were breaking their own rules on a fairly regular basis."

Over the years of sexual revolution, men's sexual behaviour has changed only relatively. Women's behaviour, however, has changed beyond recognition: they start to have sex earlier and have more premarital partners than any previous generation. And by considerable margins. In 1994, the National Health and Social Life Survey (referred to as the "Sex in America" report) showed that women under thirty were twice as likely as women ten years older (and six times more likely than those thirty years older) to have had multiple partners by the age of eighteen – ten per cent having five or more partners. 25 per cent of single under-thirties had had between two and four partners in the previous twelve months and six per cent five or more. "In fact," says Kate Fillion, author of *The Truth About Women's Darker Side in Love, Sex and Friendship,* "the youngest women in the NHSLS behaved more like the 'typical man'." Lottes had already made that same observation. In both initiating relationships and in sexual activity, she wrote, many young women "had begun to assume roles once thought to be appropriate for men."

The first large-scale study to compare sexual behaviour and attitudes in Britain and America – conducted by the University of Chicago over seven years (to help frame effective public health policy and tackle sexually transmitted diseases) and finally published in 1998 –

pointed to considerable variations between the two countries. Where it found that seven in a hundred American women under twenty-four had had sex with five or more men in the previous year, in Britain it was only one in a hundred. Another surprising discovery was that the behaviour of young British women now is not very different from that of their mothers: 89 per cent of those in their late twenties and early thirties had only one sexual partner in the past year – and four in ten of all women had had only one lover, whether or not they were married to him. Whereas 18 per cent of eighteen/twenty-four-year-old American brides walked up the aisle as virgins, only four per cent of British brides did so. When it came to teenage sex, 86 per cent of British girl under nineteen had had intercourse, the highest in the world, with America third (after Liberia) with 75 per cent. Britain also had the world's highest rate of unmarried teenage mothers: 87 per cent, three times that of such countries as Rwanda and Colombia. In the USA, the figure was 62 per cent, although it did have the world's highest rate of pregnancy among twelve- and thirteen-year-olds.

The British statistics are described by Cornelia Oddie of Family and Youth Concern as a "shameful indictment" of British sex education. Dr Jocelyn Elders, former Surgeon General of the United States, could not agree more from an American perspective. "We're doing a very poor job," she says, pointing out that there was more sex education in American schools in the Thirties than there is today. "For the most part what we get now is a 'sex education lecture' in the eighth or ninth grade and that," she says, "is usually too little, too late – a plumbing lesson." Only two or three years ago, a teacher was fired for showing his class a nationally approved film about AIDS which leads Elders to comment: "We don't want children to know anything about sex." She lays the blame for much prostitution, child abuse, teenage pregnancy and abortion on sexual ignorance. "Ignorance and innocence are not the same thing," she says. "Ignorance is not bliss."

Two hundred years ago, the mean age of onset of puberty was seventeen; today it is eleven years and four months. Thirty years ago, the average age at which women got married was nineteen or twenty; today it is twenty-six. Says Elders: "Everything has moved, has shifted. And we've got to shift with that – you can't expect children to wait until they're twenty-six or thirty years old to have their initial involvement in sexuality." The answer, she says, is "to empower children to say 'No' to sex." And to explore their own sexuality through masturbation. This latter view, which she expressed at the United Nations, forced her resignation as Surgeon General. Elders – who when she was health director for the State of Arkansas was thwarted by the religious right in her

Proud to be pregnant: Melanie Blatt of pop group All Saints. But will unmarried teenagers want to follow suit?

America has the world's highest percentage of pregnant twelve- and thirteen-year olds.

bid to provide condoms in schools – becomes very angry about the subject of masturbation. The activity which went from being degenerate and physically harmful to being harmless to being right-on PC, now, it seems, has gone back in the closet; a half century after Kinsey, boys are asking questions about blindness and hair on their palms. "There are probably very few people talking about masturbation, and we should be talking about masturbation," says Elders forcefully. "It is a normal part of human sexuality. 90 per cent of men masturbate; 80 per cent of women masturbate. And the rest lie." John Gray supports her: "There's not a sex therapist in this world who will tell you there's anything wrong with masturbation. That this part of life is made to be ugly, and makes people feel there's something ugly about them … is shameful." And, Gray adds, inhibition about masturbation "also pushes kids into sex too soon."

"We do such horrible things to teenagers?" laments sex educator Susie Landolphi, who is not only in favour of masturbation but promotes "mutual self-masturbation" in a boy-girl relationship as a kind of staging post on the road to full sexuality. "We sell every single product to them – their clothing, make-up, everything – with sexuality. Everything is about sex. We shove it down their throats constantly that the only way to be cool is to be sexual, or sexy, or look that way. And yet we don't want them to have intercourse." She blames parents as much as the education system: "Most of my friends are terrified to talk to their kids about sex for fear that they're going to have to answer the question, 'Well, when did you have intercourse, Mom and Dad?' Or "Did you ever have an affair?' 'Did you ever give someone oral sex on the first date?'"

There is nothing earnest about Landolphi, whose teenage classes in Malibu, California frequently howl with laughter. The part she enjoys most, and which, she says, "probably gets the most attention," is when she discusses the way in which males and females are brought up to view their genitals differently in emotional terms. Most males love what they have; most women feel ashamed – which is why the majority of oral sex "goes from female to male." Landolphi suggests that young women should put a mirror on the floor "to have a jump, and look," because sooner or later "someone will ask to use them." She adds: "Do you really think that young women are going to feel comfortable having a boy's face in their crotch when they haven't even see their own clitoris? I don't think so."

As the twentieth century ends we can look back and say with certainty what the main engines of the sexual revolution were. The development of the cinema gave shape and form to sexual desire. Two world wars gave many women the sexual licence of men, gave many men the opportunity for unrestrained indulgence - and gave homosexuals not only a similar liberty but, more significantly, allowed them to become aware that they were not in such a small minority as they might have supposed. Feminism told women that they were individuals whose individuality did not have to be merged with a man's for completeness, and gave them the confidence to seek equality in and out of the bedroom. And biomedical science, which with the Pill separated intercourse from pregnancy, moved conception into Huxley's world of sperm and embryo storage and fertility treatment – first sex without pregnancy, then pregnancy without men, if required. The wider implication of the revolution was that everyone was invited to enjoy the liberty that had always been enjoyed by that section of society which included artists, intellectuals and the rich. Everyone could now throw off their inhibitions, express their sexuality – even, in an agnostic age, to seek some kind of spirituality through sex. It is a growing trend and for those prepared to learn, says Nik Douglas, author of *Spiritual Sex,* "it can be a path to the soul". Comments John Gray: "I see a beautiful future

Sex and the nymphet: Nabokov's **Lolita** *(Jeremy Irons and Dominique Swain here in the second cinema version) still causes controversy more than 40 years on.*

for the alignment of sexuality and spirituality".

In the beginning, the revolution was for the young. In time, the middle-aged became beneficiaries with the realization that people in mid-life remained sexual beings and their children's age of sexual activity did not have to signal the cut-off point of theirs. "I enjoy sex now 800-squillion times more than when I was young," British columnist and agony aunt Virginia Ironside (aged fifty-four) wrote recently with joyous exaggeration. The old have benefited as well. As Honor Blackman, the original leather-clad sex symbol of *The Avengers* television series – and now a vigorously attractive seventy-two – says: "Sex isn't just for young people. I believe we can enjoy some of the best sex of our lives when we're older and know exactly what we want from intimate relationships." Indeed, with people living longer and in good health, some of those "on the shady side of seventy" as *Ms.* magazine's Marcia Ann Gillespie puts it, have delighted in shocking their (middle-aged) children by moving in together. All you need, as Masters and John said, is an interested and interesting partner.

There is, of course, no gain without pain and the revolution has brought that as part of its baggage. Exposure to the all-pervasive imagery of sex, to talk of sex, to the casualness of sex itself, has led to a coarsening and desensitizing of society in general. At the start of the century, it took only the sight of a woman's ankle to make a man's heart pound; in the middle it required a hand on a breast; at the end, nothing less than intercourse is enough and perhaps not even that suffices. Sadly, when in Germaine Greer's words "shagging has become a substitute for conversation" and New York children barely in their teens refer to having sex as "hitting skin", the most intimate of human acts can sometimes now be no more elevated a bodily expression than blowing one's nose. Sex has also been so commercialized and trivialized that in many of its aspects it is nothing more than a consumer product, a mere element of fashion and rave culture. A growing worry is that the rountinization of sex has created a need for violence in intimacy. Sex therapist Mark Schwartz was once asked to be a judge at an erotic film festival. He found that watching ten films in a row dramatically changed his ability to be aroused. "Once you start exposing people over and over and over again, that which turns them on, no longer turns them on," he says. "What we're finding today is that satiation levels keeps going up – and once you get violence coming into sexuality something is lost." The debate continues as to whether hard-core pornography, to

which many men are addicted, prevents them from forming relationships. Some people are addicted to sex: An estimated 8 per cent of adult men and 3 per cent of adult women are addicts, according to Dr Patrick Carnes, a psychologist at the Sexual Recovery Institute in Los Angeles. In Britain there are now twenty centres treating a condition unheard of a decade ago and many times more in America, which also has four national helplines offering counselling. Thousands of men are in therapy and on "sexual sobriety plans".

While there has been a male crisis during the sexual revolution (caused to greater degree by the computer chip and the loss of traditional masculine jobs than by ousting by females in the workplace and female sexual empowerment), there

Sex has become so routine that some films go beyond the normal for their kicks – as in the film **Crash.**

have been problems for women, too. It is not only men who now need to worry about their sexual performance: woman have had "passivity" taken from them and they, too, must deliver in the bedroom – while worrying whether they measure up on the orgasmic scale of self-fulfilment that is endlessly sold to them. The commercialization of sex also sells body-image to both sexes with sometimes devastating results. Clinical psychologist Oliver James blames the relentless bombardment of sexual imagery in all media for "overheated aspirations and unreal comparisons" which not only make "men and women dissatisfied with their own bodies, but with their real partners". The many pressures of the revolution have brought about casualties in relationships, again because of unrealistic expectations, but more especially because of selfishness and a lack of willingness to compromise. Schwartz is now seeing people who complain "'We're only having sex once a week, I demand to have sex more frequently than that. Or 'My husband won't have oral sex with me, I'm not going to stand a marriage without cunnilingus'".

Once it was said that sex was 10 per cent of a happy relationship and 100 per cent of an unhappy one; now sex appears to be 100 per cent of almost any relationship, the only measure of it; and, if it does not measure up, you get another. We live, after all, in the throwaway society. Marriage is in meltdown: half of US marriages end in divorce, 40% of British (the highest in Europe). The vows talk about death being the only intervening agent, but increasingly marriage is being seen as one bookend with divorce as the other. Marriage

rates are plummeting in any case. According to the British Government's Office for National Statistics, the number of weddings has fallen by a fifth in a decade.

So great is people's need for constant sexual stimulation that, John Gray says, "they are prepared to destroy relationships, whoever gets hurt, even children." Today, over a third of births are to unmarried mothers and a fifth of children are being brought up in single-parent

Adultery may be exciting – but may be a **Fatal Attraction.**

homes. Gray describes the situation as a "crisis". The paradox is that, according to Schwartz, the biggest sexual problem of the modern age is lack of desire - "inhibited-desire syndrome" —an intractable problem with many roots, including stress, the fast pace of modern life, fear of sexually transmitted diseases, an upswing in conservative values and the longevity of the ageing baby-boom population's (more or less) monogamous relationships. And then there are Prozac and other mood-elevating drugs with desire-suppressing side effects – in the US a third of adult Americans are on one of these medications at any one time; in Britain four million. Women who juggle home and work are frequently too exhausted to think of making love.

While recognizing that love can die and some marriages and long-term relationships will not respond to mouth-to-mouth resuscitation, others can be saved – if those in them want to save them, like Laura and Harris Schiller, who in the early Eighties found their long-term marriage falling apart. "We were sweeping everything under the rug and we weren't talking about it," she says. "He was angry at me, I was angry at him, the passion was dying and we were giving up." Only when she told him that she was interested in somebody else, he says, "did we finally hit the wall and, all of a sudden, big pain". Not wanting to lose his wife, Schiller attended a seminar of John Gray's, then both he and Laura received counselling from him. The Schillers are still together. "John Gray helped us find different ways of approaching each other," Schiller says. Comments Gray: "What was wrong with their marriage is what's wrong with almost every marriage. We love someone but we don't really understand the way they're thinking or how they're looking at something, or we misinterpret their behaviour, and we get our feelings hurt. When we listen the love can flow again."

Ken and Ines Goldstein knew what their problem was – the onset of his impotence two years ago – but, again, an unwillingness to discuss the issue began to drive them apart. "He didn't realize how badly I felt, but I didn't want to hurt him," she says. For twenty years she and her husband had had "a very sensual, sexual life." When it stopped, she felt "abandoned". On his wife's suggestion Goldstein resorted to Viagra when it came on the market in 1998. Now, Ines Goldstein says, "he's back, he's touching me and feeling me and grabbing me like he used to – and I don't care if I never have an orgasm again the rest of my life, it has brought us together again." Viagra has also brought a dimension to the relationship of Doctor Marilyn Volker and her husband David Yoblick. They have been married for only eight of the twenty years they have been together because she is a sexologist and "I wanted to show people that a piece of paper did not make a commitment." Yoblick has suffered from erectile dysfunction for some years, without it affecting their sexual life together. He and his wife practice "outercourse" – making love without intercourse – which she teaches. Her husband, says Volker, is "a wonderful lover". When he took Viagra, she adds, "seeing an erection on him the first time was like 'Wow! It was exciting and sparky and let's take a picture.'" Adds Yoblick: "Tie a ribbon round it." "Tie ribbons," agrees Volker. Both admit they cried with happiness.

It is estimated that one in ten men suffers from impotency. Viagra holds out to a high proportion of such men the hope of renewed sexual activity. Although there are side-effects and in certain circumstances the risk of death, most sufferers are not dissuaded from taking it. All of this has received saturation media coverage. What has not is that some women, who

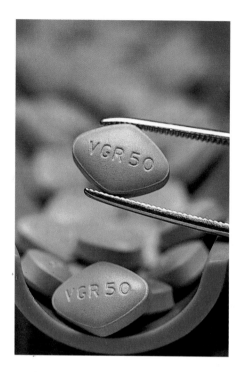

Viagra: the diamond-shaped blue pill has brought sex back into the life of many men

have come to terms with their partner's condition, have found it difficult if not impossible to relate to chemically induced tumescence. "You can't turn the light switch on and off," observes Mark Schwartz, who is already "having women coming in saying that they have sex with their husbands but it feels almost like they're being raped. We forget that erection is a sign for a woman that a man finds her attractive. When you have a purely physiologic erection from a Viagra pill, it's hardly romantic."

In the Twenties, anthropologist Margaret Mead believed that she had found in Samoa an island paradise of total sexual freedom, which led her to conclude that the differences between men and women were shaped by cultural conditioning and could therefore be changed. Some of those who brought about the sexual revolution in the late Sixties argued from the same premise and sought the same utopia. What three decades have taught, however, is that human feelings – jealousy, betrayal, the need for trust and monogamous stability (even if it becomes serial monogamy) – are remarkably resistant to permissiveness. But, then, as research in the Eighties found, Mead was wrong about Samoa. She drew her conclusions about Samoan sexual mores by interviewing adolescent girls – who amused themselves by lying to her.

According to the film-maker Kenneth Anger, the sexologist Alfred Kinsey eliminated love from his studies. "Love was a taboo subject with Kinsey," he says. "Because he was interested in sexual behaviour he steered away from love. He said love is an area of philosophy and metaphysical inquiry. It is not a scientific thing that can be studied." But love refuses to be dismissed and today, in an age so quick to kill relationships, it appears to have attained a greater significance than ever before. According to John Gray, "never in history has love been so important to people". Another paradox? Perhaps. And perhaps not. What is wrong with trying to write ourselves into a story that promises to have a happy ending?

In the course of making *The Sexual Century,* the producers asked its many interviewees to define love. It is not an easy thing to do without being trite. Most of us circle the question, as Francois Mauriac said of Henry James' prose, "like an elephant circling a pea trying to pick it up with his trunk." Here are two responses.

Marcia Ann Gillespie, senior editor, *Ms.* magazine:

One can have great sex and it doesn't necessarily have anything to do with love. One can have wonderful love and not necessarily have great sex, but together, seeing the magic in yourself and the magic in somebody else – that is what people want, a joining not just of bodies but spirits and hearts. Love is about pleasure, but it's also about connecting. We reach out to each other for comfort. We reach out in hope. We sometimes reach out in frustration and sometimes even in anger, but we are still reaching.

Candace Bushnell, author of *Sex and the City:*

I always think of love as some kind of ideal state that you could achieve with someone. I don't think it's an instant thing, although there has to be an instant thing in the beginning to get it off the ground. For both sexes, when you make moral decisions that sort of supersede your immediate desires, in the long run you are happier. Love is a really good sex life if you have this trust with one person and you probably only have sex with them and for the two of you it's your own secret space … a form of communication. I actually think most people are not emotionally and intellectually equipped to deal with having a lot of sex partners. It starts to eat away at your soul.

In 1929, James Thurber and E.B. White wrote in *Is Sex Necessary?*

During the past year, two factors in our civilisation have been greatly overemphasized. One is aviation, the other is sex. Looked at calmly, neither diversion is entitled to the space it has been accorded. Each has been deliberately promoted. In the case of aviation, persons interested in the sport saw that the problem was to simplify it and make it seem safer. With sex, the opposite is true.

Towards the end of his life in 1950, the English novelist, essayist and observer of the human condition, George Orwell, noted the first stirrings of the modern world's obsession with sexuality, judged that it would escalate but thought that, as and when it abated, future generations would look back on it "as we do things like the death of Little Nell." For now, the tarantella whirls, unabated. Can it go yet faster? Must it slow down? Who knows? For now, leave it to this *Playboy* cartoon. A man sits in a restaurant with a female companion. He is saying: "We're born. We die. Enjoy the interval."

The man who still fulfils most men's sexual fantasies – James Bond here in the shape of Sean Connery in Goldfinger.

INDEX

PICTURE ACKNOWLEDGEMENTS

The publishers would like to thank the following sources for their kind permission to reproduce the pictures in this book:

AKG London 5br
All Action 225
Ann Summers 221
Associated Press 180
Bridgeman Art Library, London/Musee des Beaux-Arts, Nantes, France *Happy Games (1869-1937)* 25
Canal +/Image UK 247
Corbis/ AFP 229, 230/Bettmann 15, 17, 35, 36, 41, 42t, 44, 48, 64, 76, 78, 110, 126, 131, 134, 140, 153, 169, 172, 176, 228, 251/Bettmann UPI 18, 42b, 58, 82, 88, 91, 96, 97, 98, 111, 112, 121, 129, 165tl, 171, 179, 183, 184, 185, 193/UPI 19, 43, 82/Henry Diltz 139/Everett Collection 104, 116, 142, 143, 148tl, 151tl, 160, 207, 234, 239, 240/Eye Ubiquitous 199/Owen Franken 198, 202/Richard Glover 181br/Robert Holmes 165br/Hulton-Deutsch Collection

8, 21, 70, 169, 170/Kurt Krieger 201, 204/Library of Congress 75, 107, 164/The National Archives 65t, 65bl, 72, 81, 87/Gianni Dagli Orti 166/Pacha 243/Neal Preston 5bl, 196/Roger Ressmeyer 178
et archive 10, 11, 32, 54
Mary Evans Picture Library 5tl, 12, 24, 29, 71tr, 74br, 167
Ronald Grant Archive 173, 174tl, 175
Hulton Getty 3, 4, 31, 38, 39, 40, 45, 50b, 50t, 52, 60b, 62, 66, 68tl, 68b, 69tr, 77, 92, 113, 124, 128, 152, 156, 157, 188, 194
Image Bank/Archive Photos/Lass 109t
Imperial War Museum 60tl
Ron Jeremy 212
Kobal Collection 34, 46, 49, 56, 80, 85, 86, 90, 103, 105, 108, 109b, 114, 115b, 158, 162, 174b, 177, 186, 192, 200, 205, 206, 208, 215, 217, 226, 232, 246, 248
Magnum/JC Sauer 1
Lewis Morley/Akehurst Bureau 6
PA News 227
Pictorial Press Ltd 138, 203, 218

Paul Raymond Publishing 211
Rex Features 216, 220, 233/Eric Pendzich 213
Science & Society Picture Library 13, 14, 20
Science Photo Library 219, 250
SIN/Antony Medley 236
Tony Stone Images/Steve Taylor 132
Marie Stopes International 22, 23, 27, 130tr, 130bl
Topham 93, 94, 122
Vin Mag Archive Ltd 53, 55, 61, 73, 74tl, 83, 99, 100, 101, 102, 115t, 117, 118, 136, 144, 145, 146, 147, 148br, 149, 150, 151bl, 155, 189, 197, 231, 244
Roger Viollet 166

Every effort has been made to acknowledge correctly and contact the source and/copyright holder of each picture, and Carlton Books Limited apologises for any unintentional errors or omissions which will be corrected in future editions of this book.